D0105319

DATE DUE

APR 2 8 2011

BRODART, CO.

Cat. No. 23-221-003

PLAYING BACH
ON THE KEYBOARD

Title page from the original edition of J. S. Bach's *Goldberg Variations* (1741).
Editions Jean-Marc Fuzeau

PLAYING BACH
ON THE KEYBOARD

A Practical Guide

Richard Troeger

AMADEUS PRESS, LLC
Pompton Plains • Cambridge

The quotation from Putnam Aldrich is reprinted from *Notes: Quarterly Journal of the Music Library Association*, Vol. 27, No. 3 (March 1971) by permission of the Music Library Association.

Passages from Johann Philipp Kirnberger's *The Art of Strict Musical Composition*, translated by David Beach and Jurgen Thym, are reprinted by permission of Yale University Press.

For quotation of passages from *The New Bach Reader*, edited by Hans T. David and Arthur Mendel, and revised and enlarged by Christoph Wolff, gratitude is expessed to W. W. Norton.

J. S. Bach's Table of Ornaments, from the *Clavierbüchlein vor Wilhelm Friedemann Bach*, is transcribed here by permission of the Yale University Music Library.

Published in 2003 by
Amadeus Press, LLC
512 Newark Pompton Turnpike
Pompton Plains, New Jersey 07444
U.S.A.

Amadeus Press
2 Station Road
Swavesey
Cambridge CB4 5QJ, U.K.

For sales, please contact
NORTH AMERICA

AMADEUS PRESS, LLC
c/o Hal Leonard Corp.
7777 West Bluemound Road
Milwaukee, Wisconsin 53213 U.S.A.
Fax 1-414-774-3259

UNITED KINGDOM AND EUROPE

AMADEUS PRESS
2 Station Road
Swavesey, Cambridge, CB4 5QJ, U.K.
Tel. 01954-232959
Fax 01954-206040

E-mail: orders@amadeuspress.com
Web site: www.amadeuspress.com

Printed in China

Library of Congress Cataloging-in-Publication Data

Troeger, Richard.
  Playing Bach on the keyboard : a practical guide / Richard Troeger.
      p.   cm.
Includes bibliographical references (p.) and index.
ISBN 1-57467-084-0
1. Keyboard instruments--Performance. 2. Bach, Johann Sebastian,
1685-1750. Keyboard music. 3. Bach, Johann Sebastian,
1685-1750--Criticism and interpretation. 4. Keyboard instrument
music--18th century--Interpretation (Phrasing, dynamics, etc.)
I. Title.

MT179.T76 2003
786'.092--dc21

                                                    2003012791

A catalog record for this book is also available from the British Library.

Visit our Web site at www.amadeuspress.com

I dedicate this book to two people of fundamental importance in my life:

To Ron Haas,
maker of keyboard instruments,
whose work and friendship
have inspired me for many years

and

To Elaine Fuller,
Muse, colleague, inspired singer, and beloved wife

CONTENTS

Contents

Contents

PART III. SPECULATIVE MATTERS

"Teachers should instill precepts, not pieces."

—Arnold Dolmetsch
(1858–1940)

PREFACE

This work is intended as a practical guide to the nonspecialist: students, teachers, amateurs, and players of all keyboard instruments, as well as the interested listener. My goal is to provide a grounding in the historical, musical, instrumental, and technical matters that confront anyone who plays J. S. Bach's keyboard music. The clavier music is my focus, but the discussion relates to, and draws upon, the organ repertory as well. The subject areas include instrumental sonorities, notational and performance practices, issues of musical genre and style, and other pragmatic aspects of interpretation and performance. Historical facts are presented for practical use. Above all, I try to convey the importance of considering musical context when making musical decisions and implementing historical information.

In this book I present:

1. Concise descriptions of many style features in Bach's keyboard music.
2. Condensed explanations of relevant notational idioms and performance practices (regarding rhythm, phrasing, tempo, articulation, dynamics, ornaments, and keyboard technique) in usages from Bach's time that are not self-evident today.
3. Consideration of the practical aspects of the relationships of early keyboard instruments and nonkeyboard idioms to Bach's writing and to the modern piano, and of what this information offers the pianist.
4. Concise essays on keyboard temperament (especially relevant to *The Well-Tempered Clavier*), rhetorical analysis (looking at the essentials of musical analysis as understood in Bach's time), continuo playing for the pianist (using either the piano or harpsichord), practical informa-

tion on baroque dance styles, fingering and technique, editions, and the role of research for the pragmatic, nonspecialist performer.

Many of the points presented here have clarified matters for students when I have taught master classes and seminars in baroque performance practice, as well as in my private teaching of harpsichord, clavichord, and piano. The areas where musical, notational, and playing styles of the era before 1800 differ from the subsequent common practice have not really entered the mainstream of keyboard teaching except in special university and conservatory classes. They tend to be cultivated well apart from the norms of piano and organ teaching. The gap is in the process of being bridged, and this book is offered as another brick in that bridge.

Although I have necessarily tried to be comprehensive, in some ways this study complements the Bach guides written by Paul Badura-Skoda and Anthony Newman (I contributed the dance chapter to the latter effort) and Ralph Kirkpatrick's book on performing *The Well-Tempered Clavier*. Kirkpatrick's work is an invaluable, if sometimes quite personal, study of elements that form an interpretation; however, it deals very little with specifics of historical performance practice. David Schulenberg's catalog of Bach's keyboard music (a comprehensive survey of the repertory and main sources, with commentary on each work) is a very useful adjunct to all of these. A very significant core addition to the literature is the study on dance in Bach's music by Meredith Little and Natalie Jenne. Inevitably there is much overlap and some disagreement among all of these works. On the whole, this book addresses several issues not before treated in print for the nonscholar and looks at some other matters with new or different emphasis or from a different perspective.

Topics and approaches included here that have not been brought into mainstream (or sometimes even specialist) consideration include (1) much commentary on practical aspects of playing Bach's keyboard music on the modern piano; (2) serious discussion of the role of the clavichord in Bach's milieu; (3) an outline of the rhetorical model in musical analysis and its relationship to musical characterization and performance needs; (4) a summary for the general student of the genres and styles used by Bach; (5) certain points regarding Bach's phrasing structures and their local-level contrasts; and (6) several performance practice topics, notably certain aspects of dynamics and phrasing, and continuo playing for pianists. Perhaps also new is the discussion of piano playing in terms of what the harpsichord and clavichord, as well as nonkeyboard media, have to tell the pianist about performance choices. This book complements my previous book, *Technique and Interpretation on the Harpsichord and Clavichord*. Although written without reference to the piano, *Tech-*

nique and Interpretation offers further consideration of several topics presented here. However, in that book performance practice issues are not explained for the newcomer, but only discussed in terms of musical implementation; in this as in other respects, the focus and coverage are quite different from those of the present volume.

In regard to several particularly knotty subjects of performance practice and notation, I have tried to summarize the essentials and to provide a practical starting point, rather than overwhelm the novice with a host of complex arguments. (This is especially true concerning the subject of ornamentation, which I have tried to keep accessible.) Other works are cited for further reading at the end of each chapter.

Musical examples are provided for the reader's convenience, but I also assume that the interested reader will possess or have ready access to the relevant scores. BWV numbers are supplied in the examples, in the list of Bach's major keyboard works (chapter 2), and when a title (for example, Fantasia in A Minor) could apply to more than one composition. *The Well-Tempered Clavier* is abbreviated *WTC* throughout the text.

Where no attribution of a translation is made, it is my own.

Musical notes are referred to by the standard octave register scheme:

I hope that this book will encourage the reader to delve further into topics of interest. The bibliography and the readings suggested at the end of each chapter are provided as first steps in that direction.

I am indebted to Donna Curry, Karen Epp, Elaine Fuller, Paulette Grundeen, Charles Gunn, and Frank Koonce for reading my manuscript and suggesting points raised in their own experience of teaching, playing, and research. The late Igor Kipnis made some very helpful suggestions. Elaine Fuller's copious assistance with both substance and presentation has been invaluable. I owe especial gratitude to my friend Paul Wachowicz for his expert, understanding, and unfailingly patient work in preparing the musical examples.

Introduction

HISTORY AND PERFORMANCE

Speaking of his teacher, Josef Hofmann, the late Abram Chasins wrote:

> He played very little Bach outside of the splendid organ works in stylistically absurd transcriptions by Liszt and Tausig. Hofmann realized that this was not Bach's language, that performances of the harpsichord and clavichord works on a comparable level with those works which fully belonged to him [e.g., music by Chopin] would take a special scholarship, one that had not been available to him in his youth. Attaining it would mean scrapping lifelong habits, starting afresh. (Chasins, 56)

This arch-romantic pianist, who was of a strongly analytical turn of mind, did not see his approach as all-embracing and had the wisdom to accept the fact that research and rethinking were necessary to play eighteenth-century music.

However, one does not need to be a specialist or a musicologist to play Bach stylishly. A great deal of information that would have been erudition in the early or even mid-twentieth century is now well established and generally available. The goal of this volume is to point out how various facets of notation, instrumental sonorities, and knowledge of a few seventeenth- and eighteenth-century conventions can dramatically shape or refocus one's performance. This is not to say that such knowledge is all that is required. But it provides a scaffolding to support, guide, and sometimes redirect instinctive musical reactions.

Without a knowledge of certain style features, Bach's seemingly blank note picture can lead to some off-the-rails interpretations. Thus, one could think from simply looking at the score that the famous Prelude in C Major (*WTC* 1) might be played largely staccato, whereas a knowledge of the style and of eighteenth-century conventions suggests that this solution is unlikely. I well recall once hearing a university graduate-level piano student play the Fugue in G Major from Book 2 of the *WTC* as it had been taught to him. The piece was rendered slowly, with no notice taken of the cross-rhythms or indeed of any accentual characteristics, let alone the tempo suggested by the 3/8 time signature. An "objective performance" indeed, since the composer "had not specified otherwise." Even the cadenzalike interruption of a rapid run near the end was delivered "straight," in a way that such a flourish would never be treated if written by a later composer. In fact, this fugue shows a clear relation to the style of the corrente; its time signature alone suggests a tempo on the fast side; it frequently employs hemiolas that need to be heard; and its lines are reminiscent of Bach's solo flute writing. None of these historical or musical aspects had been considered in forming the rendition. Not even the notion that the eruption of thirty-second notes might be treated as a real, dramatic interruption had been entertained. Such a pseudo-objective approach is even more off-base than one frankly grounded in a nineteenth-century manner of playing; at least the latter might express some energy!

One encounters many such stylistic anomalies, demonstrably foreign to what we know of Bach's style, both on records and in the concert hall and conservatory. What needs to be understood in mainstream teaching is that certain performance directions are contained in notational habits and style-related conventions that are no longer part of current practice. This sort of knowledge is not esoteric—it is entirely practical and does not interfere with personal creativity or the inspiration of the moment. The same pianist who cites such knowledge as irrelevant would not dream of ignoring similar information that happens to be conveyed differently (in a notational language still generally understood) by Beethoven. Even a performer who frankly is not concerned with recreating anything of the original approach but who takes an entirely "postmodern" view ought to know what he or she is departing from. In any case, one has to be aware of how some notational signals have changed. However, if the composer's intentions are deemed the best point of departure for the music, then the musical-historical approach is inescapable. The "authenticity" movement certainly has its fads and irrelevancies, but it also embraces important, timeless aspects of music: knowledge of musical styles and idiom, not to mention notational details, which are as much to be heeded in eighteenth-century music as dynamic indications in Puccini or Wagner. It is important to remember that there is no such thing as a baroque rule book; these practices concern living music and cannot be applied indiscriminately. But the absence of hard-and-fast rules does not mean that anything goes. A large quantity of evidence for performance practice is consistently presented in many original sources. In the end, it not only respects the composer's intentions but also expands your own aesthetic horizons to extend your imagination and assimilate into your performance instincts whatever you can gather of the original approach to this music.

However hard one tries to find an authentic rendering (and "authentic" is a much-abused word), "it don't mean a thing if it ain't got that swing." Every player, whatever his or her manner of playing, must find an organic, holistic approach that both proceeds from and produces a sense of conviction. Never should one perform as an experiment or to resurrect an artifact. Bach's music is living art first, last, and all the time. On the other hand, a player should be ready, able, and curious to experiment constantly, whether with performance practices or with any other facet that might produce a more vivid, integrated rendition. It takes imagination to assimilate new habits into your range of performer's instincts, and the interlocking of research, imagination, and gut-level musical feeling is a stimulating and creative endeavor. None of this information limits the performer's interpretive possibilities; indeed, it can broaden them. Despite the diversity of possible interpretations, they all need to be founded on what we know about musical styles, notational practices, and performance conventions.

Why am I, who perform Bach on the harpsichord and clavichord, presenting a book of this nature? Because I feel strongly that there is no reason not to use the modern piano for playing Bach's music. However, it requires certain inputs that are not generally part of mainstream teaching. Certainly, one will be closest to Bach's experience, in one sense, through playing on the instruments with which he was familiar; but surely Bach himself would say that it is the music, more than the instrument, that is of primary importance. What is necessary is to have some knowledge of the effects and resources of Bach's instruments so that informed choices can be made in playing his music on the modern piano. Even more important is having a sense of the music's context in style and performance conventions: without some background knowledge, the player may find Bach's keyboard scores forbiddingly uninformative. They often show a complete lack of mood words, tempo indications, slurs, dots, dynamic markings, and other details that a modern-day pianist takes for granted in later music. (Bach's orchestral and vocal music contain much more in the way of performance directions, but again, the notational habits are different from those of later centuries.)

For many decades of the twentieth century, baroque notation was treated almost as a code, to be deciphered by the erudite performer. Something might be notated one way, yet mean something entirely different. This approach seems to be dying out, and we are now seeing notation from a more human, practical standpoint. We realize that, given the musical conventions and performance circumstances (an enormous amount of music had to be composed, copied, rehearsed, and performed on very short notice), certain habits of notation and performance arose, but the notation is far from being an esoteric code. Its interpretation merely requires that certain stylistic traits and notational signals be understood as conveying information that they no longer convey in nineteenth- and twentieth-century music.

In fact, I would suggest that we need to speak less of "performance practices" and more of notational habits and aspects of style that are no longer part of current practice. Compared to these, actual performance practices whereby the existing note picture is rendered differently from what is before the player (as with French *notes inégales* or, of course, continuo realization) are rather in the minority.

What is different? The orientation to the metric frame of the music; certain relationships among phrases, subphrases, and periods; a number of small notational conventions that have since changed or disappeared (for instance, the close correlation between tempo and time signatures); certain conventions in both notation and performance regarding dynamics, rhythm, and articulation; the tempos, accentuation and rhythmic freedom appropriate to certain styles (especially dance traits and the free styles); a wide range of instrumental sonorities, and with them certain correlations between texture and dynamics; accompanimental styles; the role of improvisation in both solo and accompanimental playing; and aspects of ornamentation and embellishment. Another difference is the sense of freedom in playing. Despite the last century's breakthroughs in the realm of early music, far too many students are still taught that early repertory, generally, is strict and "classical" in its unbending observance of time, and I have often been astonished by conventional wisdom to the effect that early music must inevitably be less expressive than later works. Less expressive if we are not accustomed to its language, or if it is stiffly played, yes—but not otherwise. Music in all eras was regarded as expressive. This volume is intended as a guide to stylish and above all expressive playing of Bach's incomparable keyboard music.

PART I

SOUNDS AND STYLES

Chapter 1

INSTRUMENTS

M uch ink has been spilled on the subject of which instrument Bach desired for particular works or collections of works. In fact, most of Bach's clavier works appear to be intended for any stringed keyboard instrument. The organ is a viable option in some instances, just as some organ literature is eligible for performance on the harpsichord or clavichord. Only in special cases, such as Parts 2 and 4 of the *Clavierübung*, is a work specifically created for one instrument only. There are many things to learn and many joys to be found in exploring a work from a variety of different sonorities, whether on the harpsichord, clavichord, lute-harpsichord, fortepiano, organ, piano, or synthesizer. This is not to say that the works are not composed with keyboard idioms in mind. Indeed, some textures are better suited to one instrument than another. But interchangeability should remain as a point of departure, instead of the anachronistic nineteenth- and twentieth-century urge to assign one, and only one, instrument.

Long ago, Wanda Landowska, indefatigable crusader for the harpsichord, remarked that pianists often exclaimed, "What difference does it make whether Bach wrote for the harpsichord or the clavichord, if we play the music anyway on the piano?" Although Landowska's basic message included playing music on the instruments for which it was originally intended, she was not in principle opposed to performing Bach on the piano. The essential point was and remains that the music must be played with knowledge of the musical style as well as of the original instruments. Even in the heyday of romanticism, one of the most revered of pianists, Anton Rubinstein, observed (with complete common sense and practicality) that the instruments of an earlier time "had tone-coloring and effects that we cannot produce on the pianoforte of today; that the compositions were always intended for the character of the instrument in use, and only upon such [instruments] could be fully heard as intended—and so played upon the pianoforte of today would perhaps be heard to disadvantage" (Rubinstein, 91–92). Rubinstein was not alone in this outlook. His point of view gathered force in the late nineteenth century and led to what we today call the early music revival. Another romantic pianist actually involved himself with early instruments: Franz Liszt's brilliant pupil Bernhard Stavenhagen, who in Munich directed an orchestra, founded in 1905, of early instruments (Haskell, 55). In short: to give a well-grounded performance, the pianist has as much responsibility to learn the characteristics of the harpsichord and clavichord, as to learn about musical styles.

To the pianist who is first approaching early keyboard instruments, the lack of standardization, in addition to the new sounds, new touches, and even new tuning systems, can seem almost willfully annoying. For instance, sampling the instruments displayed by builders at early music festivals and conferences and finding the differences in keyboard range, key size, depth of key descent, action "feel," disposition of harpsichord registers, and so on—to say nothing of different sound qualities—can sometimes send the fainthearted scurrying back to the familiar eighty-eight standard-size keys of the modern piano. A very fine pianist who plays a great deal of Bach once tried one of my clavichords and, appalled by how demanding it was, remarked, "I'm glad that you have to deal with this, and not I." Fortunately, many pianists are more exploratory in their approach and have found the harpsichord and clavichord to be stimulating new resources. Among the famous pianists who have found the harpsichord and clavichord rewarding and stimulating are Claudio Arrau, Ferruccio Busoni, Paul Jacobs, Keith Jarrett (who has recorded on both instruments), Oscar Peterson, Donald Francis Tovey, and Rosalyn Tureck.

Variety should be taken as a source of delight. Even the standardization of the modern piano is relatively new in the keyboard world. (The differences between modern pianos are altogether slighter and subtler than the kinds and number of variations to be found among the early keyboard instruments.) The piano had become essentially the modern instrument by around 1860, but strong national and even regional differences persisted through the early years of the twentieth century. (For example, the Bösendorfer firm offered the Viennese action—a mechanism having a simple, direct contact with the hammer—as an alternative to the now-standard action until circa 1910.) The piano had evolved with astonishing speed from the early eighteenth century to the middle of the nineteenth, and the great romantic players preferred one or another style of piano building according to their individual styles of playing and composition. Liszt even rewrote some of his earlier works to accommodate changes made in piano design since their composition. Still greater variety is to be found among keyboard instruments of the seventeenth and eighteenth centuries. Certainly, each nation and period used, for example, a few standard types of harpsichord. For a particular time and place, the choice would not have been so varied as a builders' display at an instrument exhibition might suggest to the novice. Nonetheless, the choice of instrument (let alone the particular style of harpsichord, clavichord, or other keyboard) was rarely specified in the baroque and classical eras.

Thoughtful, informed performance requires the player to develop at least some acquaintance with sounds known to Bach. Newcomers to the early keyboard instruments should seek out a fine instrument and spend some time experimenting with it. One should also listen to a variety of recordings in order to become acquainted with the instruments' characteristics and resources. It is equally important to hear orchestras, choruses, and small ensembles using original instruments and balances of forces in order to experience more than the keyboard side of Bach's sound world.

Some especially celebrated performers of the past, whose artistry can greatly inspire us today, recorded on modern reconstructions of harpsichords that have nothing whatever to do with historical styles of instruments. The much-circulated recordings of such superb artists as Wanda Landowska, on her piano-derived Pleyel harpsichords, and Ralph Kirkpatrick, on a variety of non-historical harpsichords and clavichords, are prime examples. Awareness of issues stemming from choice of instrument is not pedantry. The revival period reconstructions of early keyboard instruments depart so far from baroque instruments as sometimes to seem entirely reinvented, and the musical responses take on the aspects of a different dialect, if not a different language altogether.

Authenticity is concerned with many other aspects besides instruments. But even if instruments are only tools, we should not ignore Bach's tools. Much can be learned from the ways they and the music interact. An instrument with a strong character can and will hold a stimulating dialogue with the player, and the player who is open to such dialogue will discover that certain seeming limitations of the earlier instruments in fact are unexpected advantages. For example, the harpsichord's comparative lack of sustaining power assists the clear articulation of the instrument. The clavichord's curmudgeonly action is demanding in direct correlation to its unrivalled immediacy and sensitivity.

Chapter 1

THE HARPSICHORD

As mentioned already, various types of harpsichord were used in Bach's time, to say nothing of the variety that came before and after. The differences were in outward size, range, number of keyboards (one, two, or occasionally three), quantity of stops, and acoustic design. Most importantly, different schools of building had different tonal characteristics. For example, the instruments made by the Hass family in Hamburg are different structurally and tonally from the Berlin-built instruments of Michael Mietke.

A larger, more complex harpsichord or clavichord, incidentally, is not necessarily a better instrument than a smaller one. Only with the development of the piano did smaller instruments become compromises of larger ones. A small harpsichord can have virtues lacking in a larger design. Indeed, harpsichords with fewer registers, and with fewer strings loading the soundboard, can function better both mechanically and acoustically than more elaborate instruments.

To understand the musical responses of the harpsichord, some knowledge of its mechanism is required. The harpsichord's strings are plucked. At the far end of the key lever rests a vertical slip of wood called a jack. Mounted in the jack on a pivoted tongue of wood is a plectrum. When the key is pressed down, the jack rises and carries the plectrum past the string to pluck it. On the way down, once the key is released, the pivoted tongue allows the plectrum to slip lightly over and past the string, and a damper (a piece of fabric mounted on the jack) silences the string. A spring at the back of the tongue immediately restores the tongue and plectrum to the initial position. In the eighteenth century, the plectrum was normally cut from birdquill, very occasionally from leather. Today, a special plastic is typically used. A good harpsichord action repeats with great rapidity and is very sensitive to subtleties of touch and articulation. However, the plucking action is not dynamically touch-sensitive. Striking the keys hard or gently produces essentially the same dynamic level (although minute attack-related subtleties are possible on some instruments).

A harpsichord may have only one row of jacks and one set of strings and be an expressive instrument. This is the case with spinets, virginals, and some early harpsichords. Most harpsichords, though, have two or more rows of jacks, each with its corresponding set of strings. Each set of jacks and strings is called a stop or register, as are an organ's different sets of pipes. A stop is turned on or off by a slight lateral movement of the register. When on, the plectra pluck the strings; when off, they pass by their strings without plucking, because they have been moved out of the plucking position. This makes different register combinations possible. Again, as with an organ, different stops may be pitched in different octaves. Usually a harpsichord with two stops has two 8′ (normal-

Harpsichord by Walter and Berta Burr (1999) after Ioannes Couchet (c. 1650).
Photo courtesy Charles Metz

pitch) stops or one 8' and one 4' stop, the 4' sounding an octave above normal. A harpsichord with three stops usually has two 8' stops and one 4'. With three or more stops, the instrument is likely to have two keyboards, with one slightly softer 8' on the upper keyboard and the other, stronger 8' and the 4' on the lower. A coupler allows the upper manual to be activated from the lower, so that a registration of 8' + 8' or 8' + 8' + 4' can be produced and sometimes contrasted with the single stop on the upper manual. This is the mechanical background to Bach's *forte* and *piano* indications in the Italian Concerto and the Overture in the French Manner (*Clavierübung* 2).

Pedals to change the stops were invented in the seventeenth century and again in the eighteenth, but were never generally adopted. The stops were almost universally controlled by hand-operated levers. The use of pedals to produce rapid shifts of registrational effects is a phenomenon dating back only to the revival instruments of the late nineteenth and early twentieth centuries.

An eighteenth-century two-manual harpsichord most often had the 2 × 8', 1 × 4' disposition with coupler just described. It would also likely have a buff stop, which presses leather pads against the ends of the strings for a special pizzicato effect. This and other registrational effects were scarcely ever notated; even the dynamics shown in *Clavierübung* 2 are a rare case. Sometimes a particularly opulent harpsichord would also have a 16' stop, sounding an octave below normal. The importance of this stop was overemphasized in many harpsichords of the first half of the twentieth century—instruments whose design was not historical, in any case. It is not known whether Bach owned or often played a harpsichord with a 16' stop, but it is absurd to assume that he would have ignored it had it been present on an instrument he was using on a given occasion. Rather, the contrary could be expected, given his interest in organ stops and instrument construction generally. Recent research by Christian Ahrens and Hubert Henkel has shown that the 16' stop seems to have appeared on a fair number of German harpsichords—it was not quite the rarity it has long been thought to be (Christian Ahrens, private discussion; Henkel, "Remarks on the Use of the Sixteen-Foot"). However, the most commonly found two-manual harpsichords were probably those with two 8' stops and one 4'.

Sometimes a fourth register would be a third stop of 8' strings, as appears on antique harpsichords by Hass from the 1720s. This provision adds variety to the sound and a wider range of stop combinations.

A 2' stop was the most unusual extra of all, and it had to leave off in the treble where the strings would become too short to span the area occupied by the jacks. Its purpose seems to have been that of reinforcing certain overtones in the lower range when using several stops together in order to brighten the ensemble without drawing specific attention to itself. The 2' occurs on two or more of the largest surviving German harpsichords by the Hass family: instruments that have a 16' register as well.

A good harpsichord has a clear but colorful sound that varies slightly in timbre from treble to bass. This characteristic aids contrapuntal clarity and colors the opposition between high- and low-register writing. The tone colors of varied registration can be attractive, but color is not the main issue. Musically, a good harpsichordist is most often concerned with expressive use of the tone to bring out the dynamic effects that are written into the musical texture. Timing and articulation are the primary means of expression. Therefore, a strong rhythmic shaping is essential to playing the harpsichord.

The relationships between musical textures and the harpsichord's ways of suggesting and realizing dynamics are discussed in chapter 4.

THE LUTE-HARPSICHORD

Bach was deeply interested in the construction of musical instruments and was involved in the invention or modification of more than one. He was acknowledged as one of the greatest experts on organ construction of his day. His interest in both the lute and keyboard resources led him to commission two small harpsichords with gut strings. Such an instrument was called the *Lautenwerck,* because it could imitate the lute. One of these is described by Bach's pupil Johann Friedrich Agricola, who saw it around 1740: it was

> of smaller size than the ordinary harpsichord, but in all other respects was like any other harpsichord. It had two sets of gut strings, and a so-called little octave of brass strings. It is true that in its regular setting (that is, when only one stop was drawn) it sounded more like the theorbo [a large variety of lute] than like the lute. But when the stop which on harpsichords is called the Lute stop . . . was drawn with the Cornet stop [probably the more forward-plucking, and hence more nasal-sounding, of the two 8' stops], it was almost possible to deceive even professional lute players. (*New Bach Reader,* 366)

This instrument is of limited overall importance, but it obviously meant something to Bach and it is probably the instrument for which several works were primarily intended. The few modern reconstructions (there are no surviving examples from Bach's time) have a fascinating sonority: softly ringing, with something of the intimate quality of an actual lute.

Chapter 1

THE CLAVICHORD

Unlike the harpsichord, the clavichord has only one keyboard and no variation of stops. (Some sound-moderating mechanics were introduced to the clavichord in the later eighteenth century, but they never became standard features and have nothing to do with Bach's experience of the instrument.) The clavichord's action is the simplest of any of the keyboard instruments'. When the key is depressed, the far end rises and a metal blade (tangent) that is firmly affixed near the end, perpendicular to the keylever, strikes a pair (course) of strings and remains on them until the key is released. The tangent's impact sets the strings to vibrating, from the tangent to the bridge on the right. The string segments to the left of the tangent are muted by a piece of cloth, which damps the strings entirely once the tangent is released from the strings. The action is extremely sensitive to touch dynamics. Since the tangent is in direct contact with its strings as long as the key is held down, vibrato (called *Bebung*, "trembling") is possible. (It is really a half-vibrato, since the pitch is raised but not lowered from the basic pitch.) The same capacities that allow *Bebung* also allow subtler inflections of touch and pitch that can be used to create a variety of colors and shimmerings. These include a suggestion of vocal portato, known in the eighteenth century as *Tragen der Töne*, whereby the pitch is raised in the process of stepwise, legato linking of notes.

The action is difficult to control and in most sensitive instruments is prone to blocking. That is, without a carefully managed touch, the tangents can readily ricochet on and off the strings rather than maintaining a steady contact. The result is a hoarse tone or, sometimes, no tone at all. The touch and resonance are so sensitive that if several players are heard on the same clavichord, each one tends to create a slightly different sound.

Since the tangent's position establishes one end of the sounding length of a string, it is possible to produce more than one note from the same course. Two, three, and occasionally four adjacent keys can operate on a single pair of strings. Clavichords of this kind are called fretted, by analogy with lutes and guitars, which produce many notes on a single string from different frets. In Bach's time, fretted clavichords most often used pairwise fretting: only two adjacent notes (a natural and an accidental) would share a course of strings. Clavichords with a separate course of strings for every individual key are called unfretted or fretfree (from the German *bundfrei*). Some of Bach's music can be played with great success on fretted clavichords, but much of it requires an unfretted instrument. There are as many varieties of clavichord (fretted and unfretted) as of harpsichord, perhaps even more. Fretted clavichords of Bach's period most often have a range of four octaves from low C (with or without an

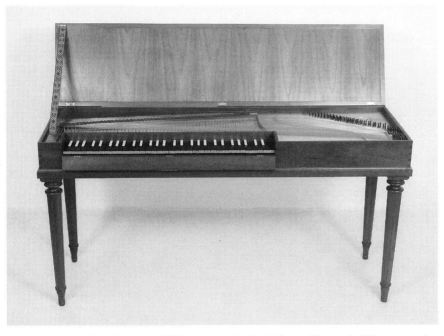

Unfretted clavichord by Ronald Haas (1979) after Johann Heinrich Silbermann (c. 1775).

abbreviated bass octave, called a short octave). Sometimes they rise to d''' or f'''. Unfretted clavichords of the same era have a range of four to five full octaves.

Fully unfretted clavichords are mentioned in the 1690s, and the earliest known extant specimen, by Johann Michael Heinitz, is dated 1716. Its range, appropriate to most of Bach's music, is C–d'''. From 1723 there survives a large, unfretted clavichord of almost five octaves, FF–d''', by an important builder, Johann Christoph Fleischer. This instrument is the first known of many similar clavichords by the Hamburg school of builders: Fleischer, Gerlach, Hass, and others. The old argument that unfretted clavichords would not generally have been available to Bach is groundless. This is an important point, because many dissonances involving semitones in his music cannot be sounded on fretted instruments, where two (or more) adjacent keys share strings. A twentieth-century myth has it that clavichords with pairwise fretting can accommodate almost everything in the *WTC*, but Book 1 alone has more than two dozen passages whose dissonances cannot be sounded by the usual pattern of pairwise fretting.

Fretted clavichord by Ronald Haas (1986) after anonymous instruments (c. 1700).

The clavichord's voice is small, although exaggeratedly tiny in many twentieth-century builders' reinterpretations of it. Eighteenth-century clavichords and good modern copies have a much fuller voice than is generally realized. Nonetheless, it is a solo instrument and not for normal concert use, although it can carry amazingly well in favorable acoustics.

The harpsichord and the clavichord were cultivated side by side for centuries. Both are of primary importance to eighteenth-century keyboard music. A remark from one of Bach's sons, Carl Philipp Emanuel, suggests that the clavichord was the preferred solo keyboard instrument and that the harpsichord's primary role was in ensemble music (see below). Perhaps this is one reason Johann Sebastian specified the harpsichord so particularly for *Clavierübung* 2 and 4, quite apart from the need for two manuals. In the eighteenth century it was recognized that the public and private functions of the two instruments, like their (very different) techniques and interpretive requirements, complement one another. The clavichord was the preferred home instrument for organists in northern Europe, who would perhaps have been the majority of professional keyboard players. It would also have been the most usual instrument for good amateur players, and it was eligible for some public use, such as at court. Its musical capabilities, tuning stability, smaller size, and lower price relative to the harpsichord were all to the clavichord's advantage. The harpsichord would be found more frequently in the homes of princes and nobles and in public performance venues generally (court, church, and theater). Its price and the cost of maintenance were high.

The clavichord is treated with a sense of distance and negativity in many modern commentaries, whose authors relegate it to small-scale, thin-textured works or to that supposedly most abysmal of functions, a "practice instrument." Modern descriptions of the clavichord's tone are usually limited to adjectives of sweetness and weakness. The instrument is supposedly "fascinating," but the implication is clearly made that it is nothing on which anyone wants to waste any time. This reluctance to accept one of the most frequently used and beloved keyboard instruments of the baroque and classical eras, whose praises were sung by many musicians of the time, is hard to understand. It is equally strange to have to defend the performance of Bach's music on one of the primary keyboard instruments of his time. Probably the difficulty of the clavichord's technique and the limitations of its public use have created a generally dismissive climate. However, far from being a limited weakling, within its own dynamic levels the clavichord ranges from sweet and lyrical to very gutsy and aggressive, capable of greater contrasts than the harpsichord. It is important, however, to find a good specimen (a point made also in the eighteenth century). The *Bebung*, although colorful and expressive, is not the instrument's most important feature. Clarity of tone and attack, an articulatory range surpassing that of the harpsichord, and dynamic sensitivity are the main characteristics. They combine to produce an unusually expressive instrument of widely ranging effects.

The clavichord, by the way, is second to none for clearly delineating contrapuntal lines. It is astonishing to read assertions to the contrary in a few twentieth-century commentaries, remarks that can stem only from lack of real experience with the instrument. It is perhaps the keyboard player's nearest equivalent to the experience of playing the lute or violin, for sensitivity, dynamic control, tone production—and sheer cussedness, for the clavichord is as demanding as it is responsive.

The piano is not the modern equivalent of the clavichord (except as a maid-of-all-work), as anyone with reasonable experience of both instruments will readily confirm. The clarity, articulation, and some of the dynamic subtleties of the clavichord, to say nothing of its timbral effects, are quite unlike those of the piano, and the clavichord's range of effective tempos is more limited. The clavichord can guide the player to the outlines, and often the refinements, of an interpretation. The piano is far too open-ended (an attractive trait, of course) to lead the player to definite conclusions in the early repertory. Nonetheless, the clavichord and the piano share the capacity for dynamic shading and the clarity this feature can bring to textures. This is an important parallel. Pianists with experience of the clavichord do, indeed, learn the nature of dynamic flexibility on a keyboard instrument known to Bach and can transfer much of what they learn to the piano.

We have no specific information on Bach's use of the clavichord, nor do we know what kinds of clavichords he liked. No clavichords are mentioned in the estate inventory prepared just after his death, but a note appended to it mentions that he had given a set of pedal claviers (presumably two manuals and pedal) to Johann Christian Bach. As is generally agreed, these would almost undoubtedly have been clavichords, the most frequent practice instrument for organists. It is possible that in the noisy quarters at the Thomaskirche, Bach found the clavichord could not hold its own. Forkel states unequivocally that the clavichord was Bach's favorite instrument. This may reflect Forkel's aesthetic more than Bach's, but it is hardly to be imagined that Bach ignored the clavichord or could have failed to appreciate its merits. It is, by the way, notable that Forkel's biography is treated as a reliable reference in virtually every respect by modern scholarship with the exception of the remark about Bach's preference for the clavichord, which is almost universally discounted. It is also notable that Bach's father-in-law, his sons Wilhelm Friedemann and Carl Philipp Emanuel, and his pupils Johann Philipp Kirnberger and Heinrich Nicolas Gerber all were strongly partial to the clavichord. Such an array of support would be unlikely, to say the least, if Bach had been dismissive of the instrument.

It has been argued that the absence from Bach's music of the *Bebung* sign (⌒) means that he did not use the clavichord. But in fact, the sign seems to have been invented only after his death. Nor would Bach necessarily have written music solely for the clavichord; indeed, the works solely for the harpsichord seem to be altogether exceptional. Part 1 of the *Clavierübung*, like the *WTC*, is simply for the "clavier"—that is, any stringed keyboard instrument. Parts 2 and 4 are quite unusual. Because they employ special registrational effects, their title pages specify a harpsichord with two manuals. These works also show aspects of musical texture that subtly differentiate them from most of Bach's solo keyboard output. However, all of the *WTC, The Art of Fugue,* the inventions and sinfonias, the toccatas, the fantasias, the sonatas, the suites, and the partitas, as well as most of the miscellaneous other works, are as well suited to the clavichord as to the harpsichord; and I am not alone in preferring many of them on the former.

Kirnberger, who was quite conservative and not representative of the aesthetic of the later eighteenth century, assessed the clavichord in a rarely quoted passage:

> The clavichord is the mother of all musical instruments, as much for melody and harmony, which on this instrument can be rendered together, as for the speaking tones, through which true expression, by means of the right handling, is awakened and allows delineation of musical character. The harpsichord, organ, pianoforte, [and] pantaleon do not share this capability equally with the clavichord, and each of these similar instruments has its own characteristics. Only true composers and orchestral leaders, only true singers and understanding amateurs of musical delights know how to assign between the clavichord and harpsichord their esteemed worth, and to make indispensable companions of these instruments. (Kirnberger, in Carl Friedrich Cramer's *Magazin der Musik* [Hamburg, 1783]: 512; quoted in Brauchli, 326. The twisted syntax is carried over from the original German.)

It is sometimes mentioned that Bach's manuscript copies of suites, toccatas, and other works specify the keyboard as "Clavessin" or "Cembalo," supposedly meaning the harpsichord specifically and by implication excluding the clavichord. In fact, research in the late twentieth century revealed that the terms were used quite generically, as loosely as Mozart used "Cembalo" (nominally "harpsichord") to indicate the piano part in the scores of his piano concertos. When Bach unequivocally specifies a two-manual harpsichord for Parts 2 and 4 of the *Clavierübung*, he uses the very specific word "Clavicymbel," not the generic "Clavessin" or "Cembalo." As an example of the generic use of "clavecin," Johann Caspar Ferdinand Fischer entitled his Op. 2 collection *Pieces de clavessin* in French; but in the German preface to the volume he mentions that the music is for the "Clavicordium, oder Instrument" (clavichord, or harpsichord).

Expected use of the clavichord can also be related to keyboard range. Early-eighteenth-century clavichords often had a narrower compass than the harpsichords. The majority of Bach's solo keyboard music is limited to a range that could reliably be found on most clavichords: four octaves, C–c''', occasionally C–d'''. His solo music written specifically for the harpsichord, like most of his harpsichord writing in ensemble music, tends to exceed this range.

The clavichord has something to offer to players of every kind of keyboard instrument. Its technical and musical requirements are stringent but highly rewarding. In the right environment, an audience will perceive a very full range of dynamics; the clavichord can not only murmur, but roar as well. Working out an interpretation on the harpsichord and clavichord (and/or piano) in tandem is an ear-opening experience. C. P. E. Bach advocated just this practice as a standard procedure. The late Ralph Kirkpatrick commented that

> the differences in medium, the difference in sound, the difference in devices that have to be used to accomplish the same fundamental musical ends can be very revealing, not only to the player but also to the listener. This is why, when the time came to record the WTC, I insisted on playing it complete on both clavichord and harpsichord. I felt that neither instrument alone presented an adequate picture. (Kirkpatrick, 44)

One reason that I have recorded all Bach's major solo works on the clavichord (except the harpsichord-specific *Clavierübung* 2 and 4) was to show that the clavichord is more than adequate to deal with the full range of textures presented in this wide-ranging repertory, and that it will handle not only the lyrical movements but also the grandeur of Bach's orchestrally derived passages (such as the Overture of Partita No. 4) and such unabashed virtuosity as the Capriccio of Partita No. 2 or the Toccata in D Major. Works such as these are often unjustly assigned exclusively to the harpsichord without a second thought.

THE PEDAL HARPSICHORD
AND CLAVICHORD

Pedal harpsichords and clavichords were instruments for home use by organists. They consisted of either a separate pedal instrument below the manual instrument or a manual instrument above a pedalboard whose pedals were connected with pull-downs to the bass keys of the manual instrument. Bach seems to have owned a set of pedal clavichords. This would probably have been a pair of manual clavichords, positioned one atop the other, over a separate pedal instrument. It would seem also that he must have had contact with a particularly elaborate pedal harpsichord during his time at Weimar (1708–1717). This instrument belonged to the Weimar court organist Johann Caspar Vogler, who studied with Bach both at Arnstadt and after Bach came to Weimar. Vogler's two-manual harpsichord proper had two 8' stops and a 4'; his pedal instrument had two 8′ stops, a 16′, and a 32′ stop as well. This would have been an instrument of massive sonority (Henkel, 17.)

THE FORTEPIANO

The piano was referred to by a variety of terms in the eighteenth century, including both "fortepiano" and "pianoforte"; the former term has been adopted in modern times as a convenient way to distinguish the earlier forms of the instrument from its modern descendant.

The piano was invented around 1700 by Bartolomeo Cristofori and subsequently adopted, with many structural changes, by German builders. In Bach's time, the most notable maker was the celebrated Gottfried Silbermann, already famous for his organs, clavichords, and harpsichords. His surviving pianos from the 1740s have a range of five octaves or so (FF–d‴ on one, FF–f‴ on another). The action (closely derived from Cristofori's) repeats well and is very responsive dynamically, and the tone is clear and bright. Silbermann's pianos were provided with handstops (not pedals) for raising the dampers, and another device, called a mutation stop, that produces a harder, brighter sound.

As both players and builders of replica instruments have recently discovered, these were not crude first attempts at a piano, but refined and elegant instruments. The fortepiano was described by C. P. E. Bach as too weak in tone for anything but a small ensemble. Stewart Pollens has played the 1746 Silbermann fortepiano that is preserved at Sans Souci, the palace of Frederick the Great:

> While the sound was quite lovely, the piano did not produce much volume and the soft attack and mellow timbre lacked clarity in the live acoustical environment of the Sans Souci concert room. The mutation stop gave the instrument more brilliance, but diminished the sweetness created by the thick, woolly leather hammer coverings. Silbermann's pianofortes would have provided discreet accompaniment for the baroque flute or the human voice. (Pollens, 183–184; see also Badura-Skoda, 165–167)

We do not know to what extent Bach utilized the new instrument. Bach's student Johann Friedrich Agricola tells us that Bach disapproved of Gottfried Silbermann's first fortepianos, saying that the treble was weak and the touch too heavy. The story goes on to say that Silbermann, at first annoyed by these criticisms, later accepted their accuracy and labored to improve his pianos, with

Fortepiano by Thomas and Barbara Wolf (1998) after instruments by Gottfried
Silbermann (1746, c. 1747, 1749). Photo by Ken Garrett, courtesy Jacques Ogg

Bach's subsequent approval. A receipt signed by the composer and dated 1749 proves that Bach acted (at least once) as a sales agent for Silbermann's pianos in his last years, so we may presume that he indeed approved of Silbermann's later efforts, which most scholars agree belong to the 1740s. We do not know how familiar Bach was with the instrument before his extemporary performance in 1747 on the Silbermann fortepianos belonging to Frederick the Great (which led to the composition of *A Musical Offering*). Certainly, we have no evidence that Bach used fortepianos with any regularity, and none are specified among the instruments in his estate (although, again, the word *clavesin*, which appears in the estate account, could have been used generically to include pianos and clavichords). Had J. S. Bach been a fervent enthusiast of the new instrument, it is likely that Johann Nikolaus Forkel would have stressed this point in the first biography of the composer (1802), in his efforts to present Bach in a modern context. Forkel has, in fact, been accused of trying to modernize the composer by emphasizing Bach's love for the clavichord. But if the emphasis on the clavichord was intended to make Bach appear up to date, Forkel could have gone much further by stressing or even distorting Bach's genuine involvement with the early piano. Instead, far from even stretching the truth, Forkel quite honestly remarks that the piano was "too much in its infancy and still much too coarse to satisfy him" (*New Bach Reader*, 436). Perhaps we should take Forkel at his word here, as with so much else. The "coarseness" to which he refers probably represents Bach's first reactions to the new instrument, modified in his last years but too late for it to have achieved a significant place in his keyboard world. The fortepiano was still so far from general usage in 1753 that C. P. E. Bach, in his treatise of that year, discusses the clavichord and harpsichord as the two main keyboard instruments and describes the fortepiano as a newcomer:

> There are two [keyboard instruments], namely the harpsichord and the clavichord, which have had the most acclaim. The former is used in ensemble music [*starcken Musicken*, "strong music"], the latter for solo playing [*allein spielen*]. The new fortepiano, when it is durably and well built, has many good qualities, although its touch particularly must be worked out, which is not without difficulties. It does well by itself and with a not too strong ensemble, but I believe that a good clavichord, except for having a weaker tone, has all the beauties of the other instrument and additionally has the *Bebung* [vibrato] and *Tragen der Töne* [*portato*], which I can produce by extra pressure after the beginning of each note. (C. P. E. Bach, *Versuch*, 8–9)

None of this commentary makes the piano sound well established in use, even by so progressive a composer as C. P. E. Bach, who in addition states his preference for the clavichord. Even less, therefore, might we expect his conservative father to have preferred the newer instrument. The attack of notes on fortepianos of the Silbermann design, both originals and replicas, has nothing of the clarity that characterizes the initiation of a note on both the harpsichord and the clavichord. Although beautiful in its own way, it is an altogether blunter sound that cannot compete with the other two instruments in clear delineation of counterpoint.

If the fortepiano was still new in 1753, it was so much newer a few years earlier that Silbermann's own inscription on his piano of 1746 calls it *Dieses Instrument: Piano et Forte genandt* ("This instrument: called Piano and Forte"; the same phrase is used on Bach's 1749 receipt). It seems clear that the instrument was a newcomer in the 1740s.

Certainly most of Bach's keyboard music was conceived before the fortepiano had made any significant inroads. Even such a late work as the *Goldberg Variations* (published in 1742) specifically calls for a two-manual harpsichord. If Bach had been an early enthusiast of the fortepiano, he might have composed a new unit of the *Clavierübung* designated perhaps "for the new instrument: called Piano and Forte" instead of, like the *Goldberg Variations*, "for a harpsichord with two manuals." No such indication for the fortepiano exists for any of Bach's keyboard works. However, it is hard to imagine him opposing use of the fortepiano, and it is certainly a candidate for the instrumentation of *A Musical Offering*. Whatever Bach's use of the fortepiano may have been, it is likely that the clavichord and harpsichord were and remained his primary stringed keyboard instruments.

THE MODERN PIANO

Today's piano usually makes its best effects in Bach's music when played on its own terms, with its own resources, but informed by what Bach's own world of instruments (nonkeyboard as well as keyboard) has to tell us. (It can be nothing but beneficial for piano students to study the playing of early keyboard instruments. More than one school of music requires that piano students have a semester or two of harpsichord lessons. It is to be hoped that this precedent will be followed elsewhere.) The clavichord can inspire and instruct the pianist by its combination of clarity with an expressive, infinitely varied use of dynamics. Similarly, the harpsichord can imbue the pianist with sensitivity to the music's built-in textural dynamics, which must be reinforced rather than undermined. Both instruments can inspire the pianist to seek clarity of sound and texture and to awareness of fine-spun articulation, and both can enliven one's finger technique in a way that aids clarity on the modern piano. Again, familiarity with Bach's ensemble writing for instruments and voices is essential for the pianist, harpsichordist, or clavichordist, giving a basis for realizing what is largely nonkeyboard music on any keyboard. Bach's keyboard writing more often than not imitates or at least suggests another medium.

In some ways, the clavichord's language is much closer to the piano's than the harpsichord's, although far more immediate and clear. The clavichord is an instrument that every keyboardist ought to cultivate for the technical and musical gains it provides. The pianist can emulate the clavichord's dynamics. Particularly in view of the thinner textures of eighteenth-century music, sensitivity to relative dynamics, so important to the clavichordist, is something the pianist must also cultivate. For Bach's music at least, a gut-level *fortissimo* is far less effective than the energy achieved by carefully balanced parts and refined grading of dynamic levels. By the way, the clavichord's *Bebung* cannot be imitated by note repetition, pedaled effects, or any other device, although this notion has some modern currency. Both the clavichord and the harpsichord indicate to the player the workable ranges of tempo, an area in which the modern piano is more tolerant of divergency, to the point of leading players inadvertently to stylistically invalid approaches.

The harpsichord and the clavichord will often help the player to find a viable range of tempo, because the tonal duration, the sharpness of the attack, and the harpsichord's basically flat dynamic are more limiting than the piano's longer-lasting and dynamically variable tone.

One cannot emulate the harpsichord on the piano by playing at a uniform dynamic level or in a detached style, any more than the clavichord should be imitated by playing at very low dynamics. Again, the harpsichord has its own way of inflecting for dynamic effects, whether or not actual variation in volume results. Occasionally, one hears that harpsichord technique should be transferred to the piano to produce the "right articulation." This notion is false, not least in cementing a (non-)relationship between touch and articulation. Any instrument has to be played with its own technique. The harpsichord can at least teach the pianist more independent use of the fingers (rather than relying on wrist rotation, arm weight, and so forth) and very discriminating use of the pedal. A shallow touch or one based in staccato is not going to suggest the harpsichord. A detached or staccato basis on the piano will highlight the background material in some textures quite disproportionately. This is even more the case on the harpsichord.

Trying to emulate the harpsichord by leaving out natural dynamic grada-tions produces a motoric effect that became popular in some schools of twen-tieth-century pianism but has nothing to do with eighteenth-century musical perceptions. Baroque musicality was intensely concerned with musical shaping and nuance. A deliberately machinelike evenness, shorn of inflections of time or small-scale dynamics, is simply not in accord with the capabilities of either the harpsichord or the clavichord, let alone with anything eighteenth-century sources tell us of the contemporary musical style—which, for variety of inflec-tion, was probably more "romantic" than twentieth-century playing. An unin-flected brilliance is appropriate to some movements or passages that may be intended for such an effect, but such choices as rendering an appoggiatura and its resolution with no diminuendo or reducing pieces with obvious dynamic hierarchies to a uniform flatness are altogether out of place. Any harpsichordist worth hearing strives for all possible variations of stress and dynamic effect, building these against the surface uniformity of the instrument. The dynamic effects implied by the harpsichord and realized by the clavichord can be accom-plished very well on the piano, sometimes with similar means, sometimes with a different approach to a similar end. In any case, Bach is specifically writing less often for any keyboard's natural effects than for imagined other media. The pianist should try to imitate, or at least come from imaginative imitation of, orchestral, ensemble, or vocal qualities as much as from the harpsichord or clavichord. Any player, whether using piano, harpsichord, or clavichord, must voice homophonic textures so as to distinguish the bass from filler parts and these from melodic lines. Counterpoint must be rendered as clearly as possible. Thinking in terms of other media is closely related to such voicing.

What harpsichord-related qualities can the pianist emulate? Any number of effects of brilliance, for one, although the player should guard against per-cussive playing. That aspect of piano sound has nothing in common with the harpsichord's sharp plucking, for the latter evokes resonance, whereas percus-sive piano sound is fundamentally dry. Many a pianist attempts to imitate the harpsichord by playing in a detached or even staccato manner, often in the very passages where a harpsichordist would likely be striving for a legato wash of sound. In fact, if both a harpsichordist and a pianist are trying to express the same musical idea, the harpsichordist will sometimes have to work against the natural dryness of the instrument, while the pianist will have to combat the bluntness and massiveness of the piano's basic sound. The harpsichord's fun-damentally uniform touch response is especially appropriate for brilliant trills and other ornaments, driving textures (as in the Presto of the Italian Concerto), and any movements in which rhythmic propulsion is important. (The flat dynamic basis and clear attack also give dry articulations great rhythmic impetus on the harpsichord.) In fact, any ongoing rhythm tends to produce a crescendo effect on the harpsichord: the effect of relentless accumulation of energy. A movement such as the Corrente from Partita No. 3 is a good example. This is a wildly energetic movement on the harpsichord, so dynamics which reduce that kind of cumulative energy on the piano are generally inappropriate. Any barrage of even notes in a brisk tempo, with no marked textural changes, makes a fundamentally brilliant effect on the harpsichord; a gentle rendition on the piano would be contrary to the composer's probable expectation. Rhythmic profile in general is very important to the harpsichordist, since it is one of the main facets open to shaping on the instrument. The pianist who has no access to a harpsichord should experiment with a movement by playing with no dynamic variations in order to focus on shaping through rhythm and tempo exclusively; pianists quite naturally tend to mingle dynamics with other interpretive elements without thinking twice about it. Note durations, too, can register with the listener as dynamic elements. When notes and rests alternate, as in the bass of Prelude No. 5, *WTC* 1, minutely prolonging some notes and abbreviating others can respectively stress and deemphasize them, while they all remain recognizably of the same basic value. Such durational stress is part of the harpsichordist's palette.

The clarity of the harpsichord's sustained sound is more difficult to emulate on the piano than the bright attack. The fact that the harpsichord's tone decays more rapidly than the piano's is often cited as a fault, but in fact it has its advantages. After a rapid initial decay, the tone settles into a plateau at a lower volume that lasts quite an appreciable length of time on a good instrument. This level of sustain is just right for varied degrees of blurring. On the piano (and on some revival harpsichords, such as Landowska's Pleyel), the long sustain of the initial volume and its far more uniform, gradual decay allows little or none of this delicate legatissimo (or overlegato, as harpsichordists tend to call it). The pianist has to find the clearest kinds of detached and legato touch—factors intimately tied to dynamic levels, dynamic variation, and range. (The lower the range, the less clear the tone is likely to be.) The romantic, "wet" sound with which a melody by Rachmaninoff might be rendered is not as appropriate for Bach.

The harpsichord's articulatory palette is very broad. Because the tone is transparent and the attack very marked, everything from sharp staccato to extreme overlapping of tones is effective. The harpsichordist uses these shadings partly for color, but mainly to create effects of dynamic variety. Silence before a note will give it emphasis; covering it by varying degrees of overlapping legato will deemphasize it. Such articulations and a varied scheme of agogic accents, working in conjunction with the dynamics of texture and relative harmonic and linear stresses, form the harpsichordist's primary expressive means. Experience of these techniques can subtly color the pianist's response to eighteenth-century music on the piano. They teach the pianist to cultivate a light and highly differentiated sound, based on the harpsichordist's reliance on what can be found in textural contrasts.

Of course, the pianist can manage some things that the harpsichordist can only suggest. Especially useful for Bach's music is the piano's ability to differentiate contrapuntal voices dynamically. The clavichord can also do this, with the further advantage of its natural clarity of tone. The pianist can in many cases think of the piano in terms of a very powerful clavichord and strive to emulate the clavichord's tonal clarity. Certain notes that the harpsichordist has to articulate, in order to bring them out at all, the pianist can accent dynamically. The harpsichordist has to gear the rendition to the main line of energy to avoid betraying the actually flat dynamic response of the instrument. Following the same trend, the pianist and clavichordist can further enliven or intensify by use of subtle dynamic gradations along the way.

Chords should rarely if ever be played as blocks. Rather, the individual chord tones should be voiced according to the harmonic and contrapuntal context. This point applies even to closely voiced textures. Whether in chords or in real counterpoint, it is important to find the dynamic range that allows the greatest clarity, so that the attacks of notes are neither muffled nor too strident.

Arpeggiation is a technique frequently used by the harpsichordist, either to sustain the sound at a high volume, as an embellishment, or as an element of timing, and often to absorb gracefully the time used to make an agogic accent. However, a good harpsichord can sound a full chord with all the notes played simultaneously and create a resonant gust of sound. (It was primarily on poorly designed revival harpsichords that arpeggiation had to become almost a way of life.) Therefore, arpeggiation should be applied with discrimination. Whereas the harpsichord's plucking action guarantees a certain snap and strength to a quickly broken (strummed) chord, a quick break on the piano can easily do the opposite, making the chord sound trivial.

A standard technique on the harpsichord and clavichord is that of sustaining harmonic tones beyond their written length. Sometimes called (in modern times) finger pedal, this technique is frequently as useful on the piano as on the harpsichord. It can fill in the sonority selectively, whereas the sustaining pedal is non-discriminating. The pedal can also create a slight haze, similar to the blur a harpsichordist creates with overlapping notes. However, the pedal can quickly muddy the textures, whereas the harpsichord makes only a light, rather transparently resonant haze, thanks to its shorter duration of tone. Properly used, the sustaining pedal can color and sweeten the tone without blurring the textures; the half-pedaling technique is often useful for this kind of coloring.

I have always relished the common sense shown by Wanda Landowska during a piano student's first lesson with her. As the student later told the story, she had decided at the last minute not to use the damper pedal, since the harpsichord has none and the lesson was to be on the *Goldberg Variations*. She played for a minute or two, and then Landowska interrupted to ask gently, "Why aren't you using the pedal?" The student replied with, as she put it, "the classic response of students through the ages: 'I don't know.'" Landowska then explained that the pedal is fundamental to the piano tone and should certainly be used discreetly.

It is important for the pianist to work out the fingering for eighteenth-century repertoire as if for an instrument without a sustaining pedal. Thus, the pedal can be used selectively and discreetly. Finger crossings (see chapter 10) can be as useful on the piano as on the earlier instruments. However, some players will find them clumsy because they are new and because the action of the piano has a much deeper keydip than is normal on the harpsichord or clavichord.

The harpsichord's registers, pitched at 8′, 4′, and occasionally 16′, cannot be imitated by the piano, except insofar as terrace dynamics (alternations between distinct dynamic levels) are relevant to movements imitating tutti versus soli in orchestral style. (This is relevant for the pieces in *Clavierübung* 2, which specifies such manual changes, and in similarly styled movements such as the preludes to most of the English Suites.) The 4′ and 16′ stops are intended to reinforce overtones or fundamental. Playing in octaves on the piano to imitate the 4′ or 16′ can never have the same effect. Even an occasional low note replicated at 16′ pitch tends to throw the rest of the texture out of proportion. In addition, it conjures up an image of Busoni-style transcriptions, which will jar on the ear if a more stylish approach is otherwise being presented. On occasion it can be effective, especially if one thinks in terms of left-hand octave doubling, mentioned by C. P. E. Bach as often appropriate to continuo accompaniment. The effect of bass octave doubling is most natural in actual continuo playing or in continuo-style textures, such as often occur in Bach's harpsichord concertos.

The piano can sustain bass notes in a few passages where Bach either wrote an "ideal" version or used an instrument with a pedalier, such as the organ. The central pedal of a grand piano, which sustains only the notes held when the pedal is pressed, can be used to advantage with, for instance, the famous low A at the conclusion of Fugue No. 20, *WTC* 1.

The response to variations in texture is a significant factor in finding an appropriate dynamic range for Bach on the piano. The piano does not respond to fine-spun shifts in voicing and density to the same degree as the earlier keyboard instruments. Nor do voicings that are strong on the harpsichord or clavichord necessarily come across that way on the modern instrument. Remember that, whereas a four-note chord can set the harpsichord ablaze (as at the openings of the Italian Concerto, Variation XVI of the *Goldberg Variations*, and like moments), it is a relatively small sound in terms of the mighty piano. The piano makes a comparable "combustion" only with denser textures such as those of Liszt and Rachmaninoff. Busoni and other romantics adjusted Bach's textures because they were thinking in terms of the piano's usual orientation. However, pianistic rewriting of Bach's textures is not advisable. The denser components of the original textures should be assisted by judicious pedaling, timing, and dynamics to create the maximum warmth and bloom of sound. Generally, it is most effective to play the original textures so as to make, on the modern piano, the best and clearest balance within the original note scheme. Strong dynamic relief among the parts can awaken the textures on the piano: accompanying parts played lightly, melodies sculpted in strong relief, and polyphony voiced for maximum diversity. Clarity will always produce a more energizing effect than any attempt to graft superficial loud-and-fast brilliance on this music, or unrelated effects of pianistic color. How loudly can an aggressive but thin texture be played on the piano before it starts sounding percussive or otherwise strained? What dynamic nuances and contrasts will lend life to the texture? How can an accent made through time help a line to sing and flow, or to fly forward? How do these effects relate to the natural stresses of harmony, texture, ornaments, and so forth? Do all these criteria mean that the pianist has to think somewhat like a harpsichordist? Certainly. Does this mean that the piano's natural resources of dynamics and color must be ignored? Not at all. In any piano playing, the secret of a beautiful tone lies in the sensitive balancing of textural elements through dynamics and in rhythmic molding. This is also true of managing Bach's textures on the harpsichord and clavichord, and these instruments and textures can expand the pianist's vocabulary with fine dynamic balances and new colors.

Perhaps the ideal for performing Bach on the piano is that the instrument be used on its own terms, played with as much clarity and variety of color as possible, scaling the dynamics according to the inherent flux of the musical textures, and basing the performance generally on all that can be gleaned from the idioms of the instruments and performance styles known to Bach.

THE ORGAN

Particular remarks on the organ and Bach's music for it are beyond the range of this study, although of course much of the commentary on styles, performance, and performance practices is as relevant to the organ literature as to that for stringed keyboard instruments. Two points should be made, however. Firstly, at the organ as at the harpsichord, musical expression is conveyed primarily through articulation, timing, and coordination of these factors with the dynamics that are implicit in the musical textures. The organ, of course, makes far more use of registrational contrasts than can the harpsichord. Secondly, the harpsichordist, clavichordist, and pianist should remember that there is a great deal of manuals-only repertory that, though primarily for the organ, is nonetheless perfectly effective on the stringed keyboard instruments and would certainly have been rendered on them by eighteenth-century players without a second thought about the primacy of one instrument over another. These works include many chorale settings, the early chorale partitas (which rarely if ever require a pedal note), and numerous other pieces. In turn, many works associated with the "clavier" are quite effective on the organ, although the latter is not generally first preference. This repertory includes the seven toccatas, some movements from the *WTC*, and *The Art of Fugue*.

ORCHESTRAL INSTRUMENTS

Apart from the sounds of early keyboards, the player should become familiar with the sounds (and literature) of baroque stringed instruments, woodwinds, and brass, and of their effects in large and small ensembles. The tone of these instruments is generally brighter, more freely resonant, more articulate, and somewhat less loud than their modern, more highly mechanized counterparts. The balance among the different instrument bodies—strings, winds, and brass —was more equable than in a standard modern orchestra, with its heavy bias toward strings. (This held well into the nineteenth century. When Beethoven gave a solo to a lone oboe against the orchestral ensemble, he did so with the expectation of a certain balance of forces, which is not today's standard. Hence the many doublings and sometimes reorchestrations perpetrated in the twentieth century by conductors who cited Beethoven's deafness as the excuse for his "mistakes.") Contrary to modern myth, eighteenth-century ensembles were not inevitably out of tune, certainly no more so than modern orchestras, in which the different instruments are built, tuned, or played to different temperaments. The superbly intoned performances of a number of ensembles using accurate copies and/or original instruments put the lie to this old assertion.

SUGGESTIONS FOR FURTHER READING

Brauchli, Bernard. *The Clavichord.* Cambridge: Cambridge University Press, 1998.

Hubbard, Frank. *Three Centuries of Harpsichord Making.* Cambridge: Cambridge University Press, 1965. [No longer up to date, but a fine, and beautifully written, general survey of the history of harpsichord making.]

Pollens, Stewart. *The Early Pianoforte.* Cambridge: Cambridge University Press, 1995. [A fine account of the early history of the piano.]

Terry, Charles Sanford. *Bach's Orchestra.* London: Oxford University Press, 1932.

Troeger, Richard. "The Clavichord and Keyboard Technique." *American Organist* 30, no. 3 (March 1996): 58–63.

Chapter 2

GENRES AND STYLES IN
BACH'S KEYBOARD MUSIC

Acquaintance with nonkeyboard music gives the keyboard player awareness of the musical context from which the keyboard works sprang. Anyone playing Chopin needs to know (among other nonkeyboard idioms) the vocal writing of Bellini, which greatly influenced Chopin's piano style. Bach's keyboard music is just one facet of his vast outpouring of music for orchestra, small ensembles, chorus, organ, and other solo instruments. These styles are often directly related to the clavier works. The keyboardist should be able to recognize instantly whether a given movement is composed in imitation or evocation of a trio sonata, an accompanied soloist, or a concerto grosso; whether it uses a cellolike continuo bass; and so forth. Compare the response to these matters of an isolated solo keyboard player with that of one who knows from actual ensemble playing, or at least experienced listening, what Bach thought of in terms of trio textures, string idioms, concerto grosso contrasts, and the other media he often imitated in his solo keyboard writing.

It is also important for a player to have some knowledge of a composer's general output for his or her instrument, rather than concentrating exclusively on a very few works. Sight reading is not only an important skill that requires cultivation for its own sake, but a part of practice time that can greatly broaden the student's understanding of styles and repertories. It is enlightening for the player, as he or she learns a particular allemande, or toccata, or fugue, to read through and study other examples of the same genre to gain some perspective on the style.

In this chapter, after outlining the fundamental categories into which Bach's and much other music falls, I will discuss some musical styles frequently employed in Bach's keyboard pieces.

BASIC GENRES

One can get a useful bird's-eye view of musical styles by thinking in terms of five basic categories: free style, dance, variations, art forms, and counterpoint. A work can easily belong to more than one category, although usually it is based more in one than in another. For instance, pieces in the free style usually include contrapuntal sections, and the latter often have dance-derived elements. For example, the final fugues of several of Bach's toccatas relate to the gigue.

Each category in the following presentation lists, first, the primary types of work associated with each, and then the main works of J. S. Bach that fit into that category. All of Bach's major works for solo stringed keyboard instrument are included here, but the list is not exhaustive; it is provided only as an overview.

Free Style (*stylus phantasticus*): Preludes, Toccatas, and Fantasias
    Seven Toccatas, BWV 910–916
    Chromatic Fantasia and Fugue, BWV 903
    Fantasy and Fugue in A Minor, BWV 904
    Fantasy and Fugue in A Minor, BWV 944
    Fantasia and Fugue in C Minor, BWV 906 [fugue incomplete]
    Miscellaneous fantasias, preludes, and fugues

Art Forms: Sonata and Concerto
    Capriccio upon the Departure of his Beloved Brother, BWV 992
    Italian Concerto, BWV 971 [from *Clavierübung* 2]
    Sixteen Concertos for Solo Keyboard, BWV 972–987 [arrangements of ensemble works by Italian and German composers]
    Eight concertos for harpsichord and ensemble, BWV 1052–1059
    Six concertos for two, three, and four harpsichords and ensemble, BWV 1060–1065
    Sonata in D Minor, BWV 964 [arrangement of the Violin Sonata in A Minor]
    Sonatas in C Major and A Minor, BWV 965–966 [arrangements of ensemble works by J. A. Reincken]
    Sonata in A Minor, BWV 967 [arrangement of anonymous ensemble work]

Dance
    Six Partitas, BWV 825–830 [*Clavierübung* 1]
    Six English Suites, BWV 806–811

Six French Suites, BWV 812–817

Overture in the French Manner, BWV 831 [also known as Partita in B Minor; from *Clavierübung* 2]

Suite in A Minor, BWV 818 [early version], 818a [later version]

Suite in E-flat Major, BWV 819

Suite ["Ouverture"] in F Major, BWV 820

Suite in B-flat Major, BWV 821

Suite in F Minor, BWV 823

Suite in G Minor, BWV 995

Suite in E Minor, BWV 996

Partita in C Minor, BWV 997

Partita in E Major, BWV 1006a [arrangement of the Violin Partita in E Major]

Counterpoint: Fugue, Canon, Ricercar, Chorale Prelude, and Fantasia
(In this category, fantasia refers to a strictly polyphonic work, distinct from that in the free style.)

Fifteen Inventions, BWV 772–786

Fifteen Sinfonias, BWV 787–801

Four Duets, BWV 802–805 [*Clavierübung* 3]

The Well-Tempered Clavier, Books 1 and 2, BWV 846–893 [forty-eight preludes and fugues]

Two ricercars from *A Musical Offering*, BWV 1079

The Art of Fugue, BWV 1080

Praeludium, Fugue, and Allegro in E-flat Major, BWV 998

Miscellaneous short preludes and fugues, some of doubtful attribution

Variations

Aria variata alla Maniera Italiana, BWV 989

Aria with Thirty Variations (*Goldberg Variations*), BWV 988 [*Clavierübung* 4]

In addition, Bach's specifically pedagogical works include:

Applicatio, BWV 994 [demonstration of fingering]

Twelve Little Preludes, BWV 924–930, 939–942, 999

Six Little Preludes, BWV 933–938 [not necessarily ordered thus by Bach]

Miscellaneous short preludes

Beyond these fundamental divisions by genre, works can be designated by subgenre (for example, different styles of fugue), instrumental style, national style, and other factors. See also Appendix C.

FRENCH AND ITALIAN NATIONAL STYLES

Bach was an avid student of different styles and composers of his own time and before. The main currents in baroque musical styles were those of France and Italy. Bach wrote in both French and Italian styles, as well as cultivating his German polyphonic heritage. Composers he particularly admired include Johann Jakob Froberger, Johann Caspar Ferdinand Fischer, Georg Böhm, Antonio Vivaldi, Tomasso Albinoni, and François Couperin. (In the modern literature, Domenico Scarlatti is often cited as an influence—as in regard to the hand-crossings in the Gigue of Partita No. 1, which in fact is quite different from Scarlatti's style of hand-crossing—but this is almost certainly inaccurate.)

The differences between the French and Italian styles lie partly in the forms preferred by each and partly in smaller details. The French stressed the dance suite and ensemble writing; the Italians laid more emphasis on the solo sonata, the solo concerto, and the concerto grosso ("orchestral concerto," contrasting large and small groups of instruments). Both schools wrote operas (the one form that Bach did not adopt, although he used elements from it in his sacred music), but the French emphasized orchestral overture, recitative, and chorus rather than solo airs, whereas the Italians developed the large-scale virtuoso aria as the main operatic ingredient.

Bach adopted elements of all of the different national styles in his keyboard writing as in his work at large. A good illustration is provided by Part 2 of the *Clavierübung*. This publication contains the composer's keyboard adaptations of two primary orchestral genres, one French and one Italian. The Italian Concerto is written in the manner of a concerto grosso transcribed for solo harpsichord. The first and third movements imitate the contrasts between the instrumental groups, and the middle movement is like a long solo for flute or violin, with Italianate long lines and embellishments. The other work, the Overture in the French Manner, is again written as if it were a keyboard transcription, this time of an orchestral dance suite. The French overture proper (the first movement) uses the typical slow sections with dotted rhythms flanking a central fugue. The succeeding movements are as French as anything written by any French composer of the time.

Part 3 of the *Clavierübung* illustrates a major German style: the elaborate counterpoint of the Lutheran organ mass.

In keyboard music, the most characteristic Italian genres were variations and the toccata. The elements of the Italian toccata that Bach adopted may have been distilled mainly by Froberger and the German organists. Of his two sets of variations, one is specified as being "in the Italian manner." The other is the *Goldberg Variations*, a work that provides a microcosm of most of the styles Bach studied. These thirty variations provide continual variety and include Italianate melodies, canons, a French overture, dance movements, trios, and duets.

The six "Sonatas a 2 Clav. et Pedal," commonly called the Organ Trio Sonatas (BWV 525–530), are a major tribute by Bach to Italian ensemble and solo idioms. These works are equally effective on organ, pedal harpsichord, and pedal clavichord. Pianists should become acquainted with them, most enjoyably with the assistance of a friend to play the bass part.

The most usual French keyboard genre was the dance suite, a major preoccupation in Bach's clavier writing. Dances are discussed below.

Bach of course absorbed not only the general forms, but also the finest details of the different styles he adopted. His use of Italianate embellishments and French ornaments is, in both cases, entirely in the manner of his models. The same is true of his use of the various French dance patterns, of toccata gestures, and of all other national elements.

In view of these points, the study of Bach's music should include acquaintance with music such as he used for models: suites by Froberger and Couperin, concertos by Vivaldi, and so on. Bach did not write in a vacuum, and his music should not be studied in one. What Bach is getting at in the seeming peculiarities of a courante or a sarabande's *double* (an elaborately embellished or ornamented version, separately written out or improvised by the performer, of an existing movement; see chapter 9), or in his writing in overture style, can often be quickly clarified by a reference to similar music for keyboard or ensemble by the composers whose work he emulated.

HOMOPHONY

Bach does not always write in fully independent voices. In fact, a good proportion of his clavier writing is more progressive than his other, more old-fashioned and strictly contrapuntal compositions. He himself called the music of *Clavierübung* 1 "galanteries." Not surprisingly, his idea of light, *galant* music was more complex than was usual for the new fashion. Nonetheless, far from always composing full-blown counterpoint, Bach writes in a wide gamut between loosely accompanied melody and what might be called near counterpoint. This variety includes:

- *Recitative*: a single line with chordal punctuation at phrase ends. This style is based on the free narrative style used in sacred and secular vocal works. Not often employed by Bach in clavier writing, it appears in the Chromatic Fantasia and certain passages in the toccatas.
- *Melody against a single line in the left hand.* In this style, the lower part has a twofold function: one a purely harmonic foundation, such as a cello-continuo bass line, and the other a contrapuntal-melodic relationship with the upper part. Menuet I of French Suite No. 2 is a good example. (Note that Menuet II is not always included in the surviving manuscripts or in modern editions.)
- *Melody (entirely or predominantly in the right hand) with accompaniment by two fully realized subsidiary lines in the left hand.* This aria style is well exemplified by Variations XIII and XXV of the *Goldberg Variations* and by the Sarabandes of French Suites No. 2 and No. 5.
- Style brisé *(broken style).* In this style the various members of a sustained chordal texture are sounded not simultaneously, but in irregular successions of jagged arpeggiation. This term originated in the twentieth century to describe seventeenth-century lute textures and keyboard textures derived from the lute style. The lute's technique relies on broken chords, since full simultaneous chords are not always feasible. A fine example of Bach's use of the broken style is the Allemande of French Suite No. 1. Sometimes he writes a mainly melodic upper part supported by a quasi-two-part accompaniment with *brisé* characteristics. The texture typically shifts from fuller to thinner without strictly polyphonic treatment. The famous Allemande of French Suite No. 5 is a fine example.
- *Chordal style* ("hymn style"), with varying degrees of polyphonic strictness. The sarabandes of French Suite No. 1 and English Suites Nos. 4 and 6 are good examples.
- *Orchestral style*, with many variations of density from heavy chords to running figures and much two-part writing. Bach, like Liszt, seems to have been greatly interested in orchestrally derived keyboard writing. In addition to original works in this style, he transcribed numerous Italian and Italianate concertos by various composers for clavier and for organ. Orchestral style at the keyboard produces many variations of color and effect. Good examples are found in the openings to Partitas No. 2 and No. 4. The Italianate three-section Sinfonia of Partita No. 2 implies a full orchestra in the grave section, including, at m. 5, a bass trill resembling a drumroll. The next section, Andante, suggests basso continuo with solo flute; and the fugue sketches in only two

parts the tutti and soli of an orchestral fugue, largely through contrasts of range. Tutti is usually suggested by spacious and/or full textures, soli by closer textures and a smaller sound, as in the Overture to Partita No. 4. Perhaps Bach's grandest orchestral imitations are the Italian Concerto and the Overture in the French Manner. In the fugato from the first movement of the latter, and in some of the ensuing dances with trios, one can imagine the full orchestra alternating with woodwind sections.

Beside these suggestions of specific effects, Bach's intention is to give an impression at the keyboard of the different textures and densities of orchestral writing. Both solo concerto and concerto grosso styles appear. The former features "soloist" passages against various types of accompaniment. The concerto grosso style imitates the contrasts between smaller and larger groups of instruments. Other fine examples of orchestral writing are found in the opening of the Overture in the French Manner and the Preludes of English Suites Nos. 2–6. Although some of the sixteen transcriptions of orchestral concertos are pedestrian, several of them (notably the first two movements of the Concerto in D Minor after Benedetto Marcello, BWV 974) are brilliant examples of keyboard styling of orchestral textures.

- *Loose, highly varied homophony*, from thick chords to one or two lines. The first movement of the Sonata in D Minor (an arrangement of the Sonata in A Minor for Solo Violin) is a good example, as are movements from the two sonatas after Reincken. The arrangement of the Sonata in D Minor may stem from another hand than Bach's, but it is entirely within Bach's style.

IMITATION OF OTHER MEDIA

The above list of styles in Bach's compositions for keyboard is not meant to pigeonhole his music, but only to outline the general range of homophonic styles. Bach often mixes various style elements. Each style listed above covers a broad range of its own. Some other aspects of these styles are covered in the present section. Two of fundamental importance are:

- *Imitation of a trio-sonata texture*, with two usually imitative upper parts and a continuo-style bass line. Prelude No. 24, *WTC* 1, perfectly illustrates this. (Note the cello-style "walking bass.") Another beautiful example is Prelude No. 4, *WTC* 2.

- *Imitation of a small ensemble.* The keyboard writing alternates between actual continuolike texture and material that suggests one or more solo instruments or voices. (Similarly, works for obbligato keyboard and solo instrument often include short accompanimental passages notated with figured bass.) The Lamentation from the *Capriccio upon the Departure of a Beloved Brother*, not surprisingly, employs figured-bass notation for the continuo texture in addition to solo lines. Prelude No. 10, *WTC* 1, began life as an example of simple continuo style (cf. the early version in the *Clavierbüchlein vor Wilhelm Friedemann Bach*) and was transformed into a texture suggesting bass line, continuo chords, and solo violin.

Bach's omnivorous interest in different styles leads him to many other elements of variety in his keyboard writing. One gets the impression that the composer is usually thinking, at least to some extent, in terms of something other than the keyboard itself. That he usually thinks (and takes our imagination) beyond the keyboard's real limits is one of the factors that give his keyboard music such appeal. The performer must think in the same way, rather than merely in terms of imitating the historical keyboard instruments, and use the instrument to reflect other musical media.

Sometimes what looks at first like a purely keyboard texture involves other elements. Prelude No. 3, *WTC* 2, is nominally in *style brisé*, with a pattern of arpeggiation. Note, however, the layering of the essentially five-part texture. Over a bass suggestive of resonant notes on a continuo cello, the tenor moves in eighths like a viola pulsing along within an ensemble. Above that moves a pattern of three-note chords reminiscent of orchestral string parts as they might be transcribed for the keyboard. The diverse elements of musical textures are of course important to dynamic layering, articulation, timing, and other aspects of performance.

Continuo-style textures are often implied in Bach's keyboard writing. It is important to listen to, and learn to imitate on the keyboard, the characteristically resonant *detaché* style of a good continuo cellist. To produce an equivalent sound on the keyboard, one has to find a detached style that sustains the notes long enough to suggest the cello's resonance. A blanket staccato is not the solution; the duration must be adapted to the particular instrument. Durational stress is often effective on the more important notes.

Various effects of violin writing are frequently encountered in Bach's keyboard music. The leaps in the Capriccio of Partita No. 2 are violinistic, as are imitations of string crossings. Not surprisingly, the latter turn up in the Sonata in D Minor (transcribed from actual violin writing) and in the Concerto in D

Minor, BWV 1052 (probably based on a lost original version for violin). One can imagine extended melodies, such as that of the Sarabande of Partita No. 4, in terms of the violin. Chords with a sustained soprano note (cf. Prelude No. 11, *WTC* 2, m. 28, beat 3) are suggestive of violin chords and should probably be arpeggiated with that idiom in mind.

Flute and oboe writing is often suggested in the keyboard works. Examples of flute writing include the melody of the second section of the Sinfonia that opens Partita No. 2, and Variation XIII of the *Goldberg Variations*. One can imagine the opening movement of the *Capriccio on the Departure of His Beloved Brother* as an oboe solo with accompaniment.

Prelude No. 7, *WTC* 2, is an example of lute style. This movement's splintered texture, which sketches in elements of treble and bass, is highly evocative of the lute and resembles writing in the Praeludium, Fugue, and Allegro (also in E-flat major, like Prelude No. 7) for lute or lute-harpsichord. The latter work uses several lutenistic textures. Similar flow and texture are found in the Preludes in E Major and B Major, *WTC* 2. These are reminiscent of lute writing by Sylvius Leopold Weiss (1686–1750).

The organ is sometimes suggested in the clavier music, most often in the toccatas. A well-known parallel between clavier and organ works is the opening flourish of the Toccata in D Major for clavier and the analagous passage in the organ Prelude and Fugue in D Major, BWV 532. The opening of the D Minor Toccata for clavier suggests a pedal solo in the organ. It can indeed be so rendered on the organ, although the emulation of organ writing in the clavier works is often more effective as suggestion on the harpsichord, clavichord, or piano than as actuality on the organ. A suggestion of pedal/manual effect toward the end of the F-sharp minor Fugato in the Toccata in D Major is a particularly apt case in point.

Choral polyphony is often implied, as in the texture of Fugue No. 9, *WTC* 2 (a much-cited example of this style). Another example, suggestive of more massive choruses, is the five-part Prelude No. 22, *WTC* 1, which could almost have been lifted directly from one of Bach's Passion settings. This movement also resembles the textures of certain keyboard preludes by J. C. F. Fischer.

STYLUS PHANTASTICUS

Bach's free-style writing derives largely from the Italian toccata, especially as imitated by the Austrian Johann Jakob Froberger (ca. 1616–1667) and north German organists such as Dietrich Buxtehude (1637–1707). As developed by Bach, the toccata includes several opposing styles: fugues; orchestrally styled movements (such as the second main section of the Toccata in G Minor); and the *stylus phantasticus* itself, which embraces flourishes and brilliant passage-work (such as the openings of the Toccatas in D Major and G Minor), recitative-like writing, extravagant harmonic explorations, dramatic contrasts, freely voiced textures, and sometimes long and pensive sequences. A few fantasias by Bach include chordal passages in which the chords are notated as block half or whole notes but are intended to be arpeggiated by the player (see chapter 9). In Bach's day, the word *fantasia* could denote either a very free piece or a work in strict counterpoint. A good illustration of the latter is the first movement of the Fantasia and Fugue in A Minor, BWV 904.

Apart from the suggestions of vocal recitative, the free style itself is a keyboard idiom with few if any of the extra-keyboard associations discussed earlier.

The *stylus phantasticus* was played with considerable freedom in timing, as is of course appropriate to recitative. There are few descriptions to serve as clues; the most famous is Girolamo Frescobaldi's directions of 1615 for performing his toccatas. Frescobaldi's instructions can be read in several editions of his music (though sometimes inaccurately translated) as well as in Apel (*The History of Keyboard Music*, 456–457). The primary point he makes that is relevant to the free style generally, whether as rendered by Frescobaldi, Froberger, Bach, or others, is that the style is subject to great freedom of tempo, including accelerando, and to pauses at appropriate places, even when they are notated in short note values. Frescobaldi explains that this is exactly like the performance of madrigals, where the tempo ebbs and flows according to the sense of the words. In the textless keyboard music, the tempo fluctuations are led by changes of mood and character from one passage to the next.

The toccata, as a genre, derives in large part from keyboard transcriptions of vocal music, such as the madrigals that Frescobaldi mentions. The freedom of inflection and tempo characteristic of the madrigal as he describes it would be preserved in performance of the keyboard arrangements, which often add copious embellishment. The style of these arrangements was adopted for the composition of entirely original keyboard works. The word *toccata* derives from the Italian *toccare*, "to touch," and refers to trying out a keyboard or warming up with some trial flourishes. This is indeed part of the toccata's origin, but the vocal derivation is more significant, and certainly more suggestive for performance style.

Froberger studied with Frescobaldi and adopted the Italian *stylus phantasticus*. His free-style compositions often carry the direction to play with "discretion," by which he seems to mean the kind of flexibility Frescobaldi advocates. The same directive appears when a movement in strict style shifts to free style—for instance, when a gigue dissolves at its conclusion into a free toccata-style passage.

Froberger's *Tombeau pour Monsieur Blancrocher*, an elegy written for a deceased lutenist, is very free in style. Its heading includes the directive (more explicit than usual) "with discretion, without observing precise measure" (*avec discretion, sans observer aucune mesure*). This type of freedom in timing appears to require agogic inflection of strong beats and general exaggeration of the rhythmic profile, to the point where precise measure is lost not through ignoring the rhythmic notation, but through extravagant emphasis of it (Troeger, "Metre in Unmeasured Preludes," 314). The French, writing in the same style, made a logical decision to notate it with no note values at all: hence the famous unmeasured preludes of Louis Couperin and others. (While very free, the French unmeasured style utilized many textural and rhythmic idioms that were understood by the composers and their circles. The notation of the style developed some rhythmic elements when the music was published, although the style remained the same. Its rhythmic characteristics are discussed in Troeger, "The French Unmeasured Prelude." The complete corpus of unmeasured preludes has been published in both facsimile and in a modern edition by Colin Tilney, *The Art of the Unmeasured Prelude for Harpsichord*.)

We find in the Toccata in D Major, BWV 912, the only use in Bach's music of the performance indication "con discrezione," apropos of the free-style section that precedes the final fugue of the piece.

COUNTERPOINT

Bach wrote contrapuntally in many genres. Some of the primary styles are outlined here.

Two-part writing

Two-part writing is fundamental to much keyboard music, whether strict or with added chords and other "filler"—the sonatas of Scarlatti are a fine example of the latter. A large proportion of movements in Bach's suites are strictly in two parts. He can wring endless variety from the possibilities of two lines freely roaming on the keyboard. From a plethora of examples in the partitas alone, I would cite at random the Correntes of Partitas Nos. 1, 3, 5 and 6, and the sarabande and rondeaux from Partita No. 2. Many of the *Goldberg Variations* consist of two-part writing, notably the "duet" variations (Variations V, VIII, XI, XIV, XVII, XX, and XXIII), which exploit both textural effects and the performer's virtuosity in many different ways. Three other variations are also in two parts (Variations I and VII and the last canon, Variation XXVII).

The fifteen inventions, numerous dance movements, many preludes from the *WTC*, the canons from *The Art of Fugue*, and the four duets (from *Clavierübung* 3) all further demonstrate Bach's fundamental interest in two-part writing.

Sinfonia and trio

The fifteen sinfonias ("three-part inventions") are not the only works in which Bach writes in this style of three-part counterpoint. Several preludes in the *WTC* and the Praeludium of Partita No. 1 are further examples of this elegant, small-scale genre. The "sinfonia" in Bach's usage is generally fugal, sometimes according to the most typical features of fugues proper, sometimes more freely. It is as if Bach takes the essential framework of a fugue and shows how it can be modified or interrupted with other effects (for instance, the arpeggio figurations in No. 15). The opening subject statement is always heard over a bass line, rather than unaccompanied, as is usually the case in fugues. Bach's sinfonias sometimes suggest ensemble writing. No. 5 is perhaps the most obvious example, with two imitative upper lines over a repetitive bass line.

The six trio sonatas for organ are a dazzling display of the variety possible with a strict three-part basis. This variety ranges from orchestrally styled movements (e.g., the opening movements of Sonatas Nos. 2 and 6) to movements suggestive of violins or wind instruments in a trio texture. Sometimes the style is old-fashioned and/or fugal, sometimes very *galant* and "up to date," as in the finale of Sonata No. 4. Italianate embellishment is used to glorious effect in a slow movement such as that of Sonata No. 6.

Chorale preludes

Bach's chorale preludes as a group are of course the classic statement on various approaches to setting chorale melodies. These works include fugues, canons, various treatments of a *cantus firmus*, and sometimes homophony.

Fugue

Students are often afraid of fugue, this learned, lean, and forbidding style in which few notes are left to chance or even to a simple accompanimental function. To the newcomer I suggest, for beginning an exploration of this style or of any particular fugue: consider that a fugue dramatizes and plays out the possibilities of the elements presented in its exposition. The form of a fugue is at least partly dictated by the possibilities of the thematic material, and Bach is a master at seeking out the effective and dramatic combination, recombination, and development of his themes. *The Art of Fugue* is the ultimate example of such working out. It is perhaps the richest extended development of music from the fewest thematic ingredients in the history of music.

However, not all fugues are forbidding, and Bach often wears his learning lightly. The *WTC* includes several relatively uncomplicated fugues that are accessible in both style and mood to the newcomer. I recommend Nos. 5, 6, 10, 11, and 21 from *WTC* 1 and Nos. 1, 2, 3, 6, 11, 12, 15, 19, 20, and 21 from *WTC* 2.

Bach's early fugues, like the toccatas, are sometimes more discursive, and perhaps more reflective of actual improvisations, than his later fugues, but they are not to be discounted on these grounds. The listener or player should accept these works on their own terms. The range of modulation and the overall sense of structure may be less important to the composer than various treatments or settings of the subject. Thus, the fugue that makes up the greater part of the Toccata in C Minor offers a wide variety of counterpoints against a nominally unpromising subject. The work feels like an in-depth discussion of the possibilities of the subject and may reflect a manner of improvisation of the early eighteenth century.

I recall running across comments by two very fine Bach players with radically different styles of playing. One referred to Bach's counterpoint as being mainly interesting from the horizontal perspective; he was interested in the interplay of lines, sustained over what I believe he termed "not very interesting chords." The other player felt that the harmonies (the vertical element) were the interesting factor, enlivened by what he saw as a fairly superficial contrapuntal interaction, as opposed to the "real counterpoint" of Renaissance music. In tonal counterpoint, line and harmony both strive for independence, though neither achieves it. It is the tension, the balance between these elements, rather than the dominance of one over the other, that makes Bach's music so compelling.

Fugal analysis pays much attention to appearances of the subject. But performing a fugue involves more than bringing out the entrances of the subject and allowing the other parts merely to accompany. The core of most fugues' material is the interlocking relationship between the subject and countersubject. Much that happens in the course of a fugue is based in this relationship—in exploring (transposing, retexturing, and inverting) this pair of lines.

Bach and his contemporaries wrote fugues in many styles, though the types of keyboard fugue are rarely discussed in books on fugal analysis. The following sections present some of the keyboard styles (an exhaustive list is hardly possible) according to texture and idiom. Naturally, there are various ways of categorizing fugues. The realm of fugue was analyzed with a large range of terms by baroque commentators. Johann Walther's *Lexicon* (1732) devotes several pages to entries on subspecies of fugue, mainly by technical types (for instance, Fuga in Hypodiapente), and a few by mood (such as Fuga pathetica). Other technical categories include double fugue, triple fugue, stretto fugue, augmentation fugue, and so on. (These terms are defined in the glossary.)

Stile antico (antique style)

Baroque composers often wrote in imitation of Renaissance style. The imitation was rarely exact, nor was the intent to make a precise recreation of an earlier manner. Instead, more modern elements were included in an adaptation of the earlier styles. Thus, Bach will use harmonies and dissonances of the high baroque in a pseudo-Renaissance fugue. The *stile antico* includes the genre of the ricercar, an early type of fugue with a slow, solemn opening (for example, Fugue No. 4, *WTC* 1). Bach sometimes entitled such fugues Ricercar, as he did in *A Musical Offering*, even though the first ricercar of that work has many *galant* elements. Bach does not employ the *stile antico* in many of his clavier works.

Strict fugue

In the baroque era, composers differentiated to greater or lesser extent between learned fugues that demonstrated elaborate artifice, and more casual fugues. Strict fugue usually employs elaborate polyphonic devices such as stretto and augmentation, and Bach wrote many such fugues. For him, however, fugue is so natural a language that tendencies sometimes spill over between stricter and freer examples. Thus, although *The Art of Fugue* is one of the pinnacles of learned counterpoint, Bach sometimes relaxes the strictness of the voicing to allow what is more effective at the keyboard, to say nothing of many instances where he adjusts the lines from their fully logical possibilities to accommodate the limitations of ten fingers.

Continuo fugue (or clavier fugue)

The term *continuo fugue* refers to keyboard writing that gives the impression of a fugue but is not always strict in its management of the voices. The texture contains elements of the free and easy voicing of continuo accompaniment, which was improvised over a written bass line. Handel's keyboard fugues often fall into this category: a strong subject entry might be voiced with octaves and/or full chords rather than single tones. Even Bach's loosest fugue textures are more conservative than Handel's. Occasionally Bach relaxes the strictness of his writing, as in the arpeggio passages of the fugue that follows the Chromatic Fantasia.

Near (or mock) polyphony

In his lighter fugues Bach sometimes allows the texture to give the impression of several parts when in fact at least one of the lines is only intermittently sustained. Fugue No. 7, *WTC* 1, is a good illustration of this style. Nominally in three voices, much of the writing is actually in two parts whose notation and deployment suggest three lines.

Orchestral style

Fugues, like other genres, sometimes imitate the textures of orchestral writing, suggesting the opposition of tutti and soli passages and sometimes using the ritornello form associated with the orchestral concerto. Even orchestral *all' unisono* octave doublings may appear, as in Fugue No. 10, *WTC* 1.

Vocal style

Again, a keyboard fugue can emulate, to greater or lesser degree, the textures and style of choral music.

Dance-derived

Many fugues take the rhythmic and metric characteristics of a baroque court dance as a "topic," a point of departure for musical invention. The *WTC* is full of examples (see Appendix C). Thus, the final fugue of *WTC* 2 derives from the passepied. Conversely, Bach's gigues are usually fugal. Canons, like fugues, can use dances as a style basis. Two of the four canons in *The Art of Fugue* derive from gigues.

Motoric

A popular type of virtuoso fugue was that in which the surface rhythm remained absolutely constant throughout, usually in sixteenth notes. The Toccata in E Minor concludes with a motoric fugue.

The types of fugue represented by these informal designations are not mutually exclusive. A continuo fugue may have a motoric rhythm, for instance.

MUSICAL IMAGERY

What we call "program music" has a considerable role in baroque music, as well as in later styles. Programmatic content can range from a brief musical evocation of an extramusical subject (such as the drums and guns represented in the funeral march of Beethoven's Sonata Op. 26, or the funeral bells tolling near the conclusion of Froberger's *Tombeau de Monsieur Blancrocher*) to telling a full story (following a "program"), like Marin Marais's ensemble work depicting a gallbladder operation, or much high-romantic music (see also chapter 12). The habit of putting an irrelevant story to any composition reached the height of lunacy in Hans von Bülow's "analysis" of Chopin's twenty-four preludes, summarized hilariously by Harold C. Schonberg (Schonberg, 136–138). Unfortunately, the idea of making musical images of real-life phenomena became so debased by nineteenth-century sentimentality that today's performers and listeners are often embarrassed by the mere notion. Albert Schweitzer's observations on the use of musical imagery in Bach's cantatas prompted protests from some quarters that are still heard today. However, Schweitzer was right in essence, as can be proven by many citations of baroque musical topics (such as sighs and tears). Composers have long used programmatic topics to one degree or another, although not so pervasively as in some nineteenth-century excesses. Bach's music is no exception. His cantatas and Passions are perhaps best known for their use of extramusical topics and tone painting. These works help the keyboard player to an understanding of the language of the clavier music.

As far as is known, the keyboard works do not use programmatic elements to large extent, but one should be alert to the potential. Thus, grief could be variously represented by dissonances, a descending chromatic bass, a disrupted line, and other devices. The most directly programmatic clavier work of Bach's is surely the *Capriccio upon the Departure of his Beloved Brother*, dated 1704. In this work Bach uses such devices as modulation to remote keys to symbolize possible misfortunes in foreign lands (second movement), a descending chromatic bass and suggestions of weeping in the Lamentation (third movement), and the effect in the fourth movement of musical "crowding" through close imitation (called stretto), representing the gathering together of friends to say farewell. Group pleading and weeping are also suggested by the joining together or two or more parts in the Lamentation. The capriccio's programmatic approach relates closely to the Six Biblical Sonatas of Johann Kuhnau (1700), which often describe the story action in a blow-by-blow fashion: for instance, David's shot with the sling and the fall of Goliath.

More typically, Bach will take a programmatic topic with emotive associations and put it through purely abstract musical paces, the topic supplying a general mood as well as material for strictly musical development. There is no story line to Variation XXV of the *Goldberg Variations*, apart from the grief-laden mood (with descending chromatic bass); but this variation shares mood and bass characteristics with the Crucifixus of the B Minor Mass, whose significance in mood and narrative are beyond question.

It is important to recognize motivic types that are of topical or programmatic significance so as not to miss clues to mood and tempo. If a fugue is based on a dance type (that is, if it uses a dance type as a topic), that topic is important to the tempo, accentuation, and mood of the piece. If a piece is full of "sigh" motives (such as the opening of Prelude No. 12, *WTC* 2), it should not be played briskly and happily.

DANCES

Bach's use of various dance types is fundamental to his music. It is not confined to his dance suites. Many of his compositions, from keyboard pieces to cantata movements, are based on dance styles, although the fact is rarely acknowledged in a title or subtitle (apart from suite movements). The use of dance forms in such movements would have been easily recognizable by contemporary performers, who would have taken the style as a cue for tempo, inflection, and mood. The French organist and composer André Raison takes this point for granted in the preface to his first *Livre d'orgue* (1688):

> It is necessary to observe the [time] signature of the piece that you play and to consider whether it resembles a Sarabande, Gigue, Gavotte, Bourrée, Canaris, Passacaille and Chaconne, smithy tune [*mouvement de Forgeron*], etc. to give it the same spirit [*Air*] that you would give it on the harpsichord, except that one must give the pace a little slower because of the sanctity of the place. (Raison, n.p.)

Just as today a musician would immediately recognize a piece based on the tango and play it with a certain kind of accentuation and verve, so it was for a baroque musician who encountered a movement based on a court dance, even if it did not bear the name of the dance. The modern player, too, can readily learn to recognize the different dance types.

Johann Philipp Kirnberger mourned the passing of this kind of automatic recognition in the later eighteenth century:

> Each of these dance types has its own rhythm, its phrases of equal length, its accents at the same places in each motif. . . . If one neglects to practice the composition of characteristic dances, one will only with difficulty or not at all achieve a good melody. Above all, it is impossible to compose or perform a fugue well if one does not know every type of rhythm; and therefore, because this study is neglected today . . . one can no longer

endure fugues, because through miserable performance which defines neither phrase nor accents, they have become a mere chaos of sounds. (Kirnberger, *Recueil*, 67)

Kirnberger was a conservative who deplored the changes in musical style he had witnessed since the high baroque. His outcry against a changed aesthetic includes one of the strongest outright statements from Bach's circle on the pervasiveness of dance topics in baroque composition and performance.

I will enumerate here a few examples of dance styles that form the basis of movements not designated as dances. (See Appendix C, which identifies the dance styles in Bach's major keyboard repertory.) Prelude No. 12, *WTC* 1, is strongly related to the allemande style, in typical voicing, line, harmonic rhythm, and *brisé* texture; it has no double bar but makes a strong cadence on the dominant in m. 12, as an allemande would (with a full double bar, of course). Similarly, Fugue No. 21, *WTC* 2, has many elements of the menuet: the flowing lines, the harmonic pacing, and the quarter-note pulsing bass in areas of cadential preparation (this is a very *galant* fugue). Prelude No. 8, *WTC* 1, is based on the French chordal style of sarabande. Another sarabande-derived movement is the first adagio section (mm. 5–17) from the Toccata in G Minor. The sarabande elements include the dotted rhythmic figures, varied harmonic rhythm, and full textural style. Bach starts from a sarabande topic but moves into a freer style beginning in m. 14. This section gives a good illustration of the shading from dance style to freer use of dance-related elements—and in this case, fading away from them after m. 14. Invention No. 6 (so often played slowly) is a corrente, complete with double bar and repeat signs, that can in several respects be closely compared with the Corrente of Partita No. 6. Bach is not, of course, the only composer to base movements on dance genres. For example, Mozart's inspiration for the finale of the Sonata in B-flat Major, K. 283, is the gavotte; the finale of his Sonata in D Major, K. 311, is probably based on the gigue. The first movement of Beethoven's song cycle *An die ferne Geliebte* begins in a sarabande style.

Bach's dances are based on courtly dance styles but were not (as far as we know) used for actual dancing. Hence, they are now often called stylized dances, meaning that they use the same styles of phrase and accentuation, rhythmic and metric patterns, mood, and range of tempo as actual ballroom dances. Similarly, Chopin wrote waltzes that were not primarily intended for actual ballroom use. A fine contemporary example of this practice is the superb tangos by Astor Piazzolla, or the concert tango by Igor Stravinsky.

In the three main sets of Bach's suites, the composer seems to be bent on demonstrating the variety that is possible for each type of dance. In the French

Suites, for example, each Allemande is strongly differentiated from the others. That of Suite No. 1 is in a French lutenistic *brisé* texture; it differs in approach from that of Suite No. 4, though the latter is also in a form of *brisé* style. The Allemande of Suite No. 2 derives from trio textures; that of Suite No. 3 is imitative; and the Allemande of Suite No. 5 has a soaring melody with *brisé* accompaniment. The Sarabandes range from the choralelike writing of the example in Suite No. 1 and the French embellishments of the chordal Sarabande of Suite No. 6 to the contrasting approaches to aria style shown in Suites Nos. 2 and 5 and the trio with walking bass in Suite No. 4. Even the Gigues, which are nearly all imitative, are strikingly varied, from the old-fashioned dotted style of the Gigue of Suite No. 1 to the hunting horn motives in that of Suite No. 4 to the perpetual motion in the Gigue from Suite No. 5.

We find in the partitas an extreme, even idiosyncratic extension of dance styles, as in the Tempo di Minuetta of Partita No. 5, which is written in a prevailing 6/8 that changes to 3/4 at the cadences. This is a musical joke based on the menuet's standard 3/4 meter and its usual hemiola effect of 2/4 at cadences, spoofed here with cadences that utilize for brief moments the menuet's normal meter. The master is in very high spirits, saying in effect, "Ha! That's never been done with a menuet before!" Even the title points to its being so highly stylized as to get away from the basic menuet style. Similarly, the Menuet in the early version of Partita No. 3 was in the final version retitled "Burlesca." Bach may have felt that it strayed in too many respects from the normal style boundaries. This sort of writing develops from originality within known parameters, instead of a constant change of the basics. Chopin did the same thing with his "duple meter" Waltz in A-flat Major, Op. 42. Although written nominally in 3/4 time, the 6/8 melody has the effect of duple meter, heard against an accompaniment in 3/4.

For each type of dance (and the subspecies of many), the meter, phrasing style, accent pattern, range of tempo, and rhythmic formulas are all-important. The quickest way to become comfortable with these styles is to play through many examples of each type, by Bach and also by his contemporaries, so that the typical features become familiar. One should make an effort to see such dances performed by dancers who have reconstructed the steps and style from baroque-era choreographies. Try to learn some basic forms yourself, to feel full-body participation in the dance gestures. Such an experience will affect your perception of playing the related music, especially of its natural range of tempo or sense of rhythmic poise. A pupil of Landowska's recounted to me a story of a lesson at which a French courante was being studied. "You play this too fast," said Landowska. "Everyone plays courantes too fast. It is a *slow* dance!" She rose, drew up her voluminous skirts a trifle, and danced a courante with tiny steps and with great precision and elegance. "I never played a courante the same way after that!" the pupil told me.

The baroque court dances did not always use the same step patterns. All drew on a common repertory of steps, but any one dance type could be danced with various specific choreographies. A courante, for instance, could be choreographed in any number of ways, but all courantes would use the standard components, such as the sliding *glissé* step.

In dance, the strong-and-weak beat pattern of each meter must be considered. The accent patterns of the danced steps and musical meter are extremely important. Thus, the two main beats of a 6/8 measure have to sound as the principal accents. The style of what some twentieth-century string players called "Bach bowing," in which all six eighth notes of a 6/8 measure were accented uniformly, is altogether counterproductive.

Each dance had a certain range of mood associated with it. References to period descriptions of the different dances are given at the end of this chapter. There is a danger that such general characterizations may be too prescriptive and rule-bound, but the period authorities are in general agreement. The mood descriptions included in the discussion below of the various dances derive largely from German authorities, who could reasonably be expected to share Bach's perpective on what are generally French court dances. The character associated with each dance type is important not only for dances, but, again, as a clue to the mood of the many movements that use dance styles without the dance designation.

It is impossible to discuss the baroque court dances without reference to the superb work of Meredith Little and Natalie Jenne, whose research on this subject has been groundbreaking. The dancer and dance scholar Wendy Hilton is another authority of major importance. The serious student will want to consult these writers' books and articles. Little and Jenne's discussion of each dance includes illustrative models for each dance type showing the typical basic phrase; metric, beat, and pulse patterns; and the typical rhythmic patterns of these dances. The last are of great importance, as they are a part of the usual vocabulary that has much to do with the shaping of any individual movement.

There are surviving examples of choreographies of specific dance steps for various of the baroque court dances. These sometimes include the music as well. From these cases, it is evident that, while the standard accents and rhythms of each dance type reflect the usual kinds of steps, the particular steps and music do not necessarily make these accents in tandem. Thus, one typical accent pattern may happen at a given point in the music, while the corresponding foot movements in the choreography produce a different (though also typical) accent pattern at the same time. This creates an interesting counterpoint between steps and music. This information may seem somewhat irrelevant to the solo musician, except for two factors. Firstly, it is suggestive about the sometimes ambivalent scansion of these dances (the courante, especially, can suggest more than one meter at the same time). Also, it explains why different choreographies could be used in the ballroom. A dancer's steps did not have to match with the music's sometimes diverse accents.

Diversity of accent is a point to which every player should be sensitive. It is not surprising that composers paid particular attention to variety of accent, since accent patterns have so much to do with the identity of each dance. It is rare for Bach, or any other fine composer, to repeat a pattern from measure to measure. In the discussion below, some examples include markings to show the diversity of groupings. Particularly in the subtler types of dance, it is rare for one and the same accent pattern to be repeated consecutively.

Allemande
The allemande is in duple or quadruple meter (common time or *alla breve*). In the baroque era, the allemande as danced in the ballroom was a rapid dance, using *chassé* steps—a phenomenon quite different from the moderate-to-slow *allemande grave*. The latter was an instrumental form that did not derive from dance steps. Johann Walther (1732) and other authorities described it as serious and dignified.

In my commentary on the allemande in the dance chapter of Anthony Newman's *Bach and the Baroque*, I suggested that the Renaissance alman, with its slow, ceremonial steps, might have been the ancestor of the baroque instrumental allemande (Newman, 136). This slower variety was almost always the style of the independent instrumental allemande and had nothing to do with the ballroom allemande. The instrumental allemande is usually of serious character and musically elaborate. Bach's allemandes offer various idioms: counterpoint, *brisé* style (Partita No. 3, French Suite No. 1); suggestions of trio sonata (French Suite No. 2); aria style (Partitas No. 4 and No. 5, French Suite No. 5); or a mix of *style brisé* and aria (as in the Allemande of Partita No. 6, which is far from the normal allemande in style).

Courante
The word *courante* comes from the French *courir*, "to run." However, the Renaissance coranto was fast and its French descendant is not. The coranto relates to the brisk Italian corrente, discussed below. The French courante is described as "the most solemn of any" (Walther), "majestic" (Quantz), and a dance to be played "gravement" (Masson, 1699). In association with its slow tempo, the courante is usually notated in 3/2 time, with an upbeat and with frequent met-

ric shifts to 6/4, as well as cross-rhythms. The metric variation and even ambivalence produce a subtle kaleidoscope of emphases. Note the variety of metric groupings marked in Example 2-1. Further variety is to be found in the cross-accents that can occur between the actual danced steps and the music. Wendy Hilton has described many features of the courante and points out that the basic rhythmic units made by the steps are o + 𝅗𝅥, 𝅗𝅥 + o, 𝅗𝅥· + 𝅗𝅥, 𝅗𝅥 + 𝅗𝅥 + 𝅗𝅥 (Hilton, "A Dance for Kings," 169). One or another of these fundamental value groupings (with all sorts of surface-level rhythmic embellishment, of course) will be found to underlie any measure in a French or French-style courante, and the musician needs to play in accordance with these stress points.

As a starting rule of thumb: apart from hemiolas and the occasional 𝅗𝅥 + o unit, the player will find stress falling most often on the first and third beats of the 3/2 measure. As Little and Jenne point out (117–118), Georg Muffat, describing French performance styles, indicated that beats 1 and 3 of a courante were played downbow to emphasize the dance rhythm.

The courante was a favorite of French baroque composers. The surviving works of Jacques Champion de Chambonnières, the father of the French baroque keyboard school, include eighty-eight courantes, far ahead of anything else in his output. In his French-style courantes, Bach speaks French with no trace of a foreign accent. Perhaps the most complex example is that of the Overture in the French Manner. In addition to variations on the 3/2 pattern and its shifts between 3/2 and 6/4, the opening measures present the unusual feature of a bass in 4/4 time. Another particularly elegant French courante by Bach is that of Partita No. 2, a movement that is often played too quickly. The Courante of Partita No. 4 is unusual in its forward drive. It gives the impression of starting life as a French courante and then having the rhythmic figure of two sixteenths and an eighth added as a rather Italianate surface embellishment. The result is a movement that can be played with the tempo and movement of a usual French courante but with a highly energizing factor on the rhythmic surface.

Corrente

The corrente is of Italian origin. It is light-textured and rapid ("quick," according to Walther), in triple time—3/4 or 3/8 in Bach's era—and makes a complete contrast to the French courante. As with most dances in triple time, the meter often shifts to a hemiola at the cadences. Little and Jenne show an early baroque example in 12/8, whose steps coordinate little hops with offbeat eighth notes and steps with the quarter notes: a rapid, light, but vigorous sequence (132–133). Bach's correntes are sometimes labeled "courante" in the sources,

Example 2-1. Bach, Courante, French Suite No. 1, BWV 812, mm. 1–8.

but the differences in style from the French courante are obvious. Four of the partitas have correntes rather than courantes. As usual, these show different possibilities for the style, from the triplets opposed to a dotted figure in Partita No. 1 to the almost tempestuous movement in Partita No. 3, the fairly typical if quite elaborate Corrente of Partita No. 5, and the bizarre, very extended movement in Partita No. 6. This last is full of syncopations that seem to try to derail the basic meter; the pent-up energy is released in cascades of thirty-second notes and a wild flourish at the end of each half. Example 2-2 is typical of the light, energetic style of this genre and also shows considerable variety of accent (marked in the example).

Example 2-2. Handel, Corrente, Suite No. 5 in E Major, mm. 1–21.

Sarabande

The baroque sarabande is a proud, noble, stately, sometimes passionate dance. The tempo is slow to very slow. Many baroque movements that are clearly in the style of the sarabande but are not so labeled carry an indication for a slow tempo, such as the Larghetto of Handel's Concerto in B-flat Major, Op. 6, No. 4. The sarabande is described as "dignified" (*gravitätische*) by Walther, and its passionate and majestic qualities are mentioned by many period authorities. In the choreography, the dancer often balances on the toe, a gesture that probably led to the characteristic dotted rhythms ♩. ♪ ♩ and ♩ ♩. ♪ . The The stress often falls on the second beat, sometimes on the first. The very regular phrasing is based on a two- or four-measure phrase. The core of the rhythmic characterization is a two-measure unit containing what Little and Jenne call the "typical sarabande syncopation," which results from second-beat stress: "In this six-beat phrase, the second beat is the high point and is more strongly accented than the first; beat four [the first beat of the second measure] is the thesis, or release from tension, and beat 6 is even more thetic" (97). They discuss the phrase groupings of the sarabande at length (96–102).

In a sarabande such as that of Partita No. 1, Bach creates a metric and rhythmic layering based on the dance's characteristic dotted rhythm. In Example 2-3, it occurs within the quarter-note beats (dotted eighth note plus sixteenth note) as well as on the level of beat groupings (for example, the opening quarter-value figure, itself dotted, moving to a longer dotted note on the second beat). This treatment, in addition to providing a kind of sarabande-related pun, causes the first beat to act even more strongly as an upbeat to the second beat. The effect is enhanced by the octave drop in the bass, creating a heavier texture on the second beat. Note the hemiola grouping in the cadence at the end of the phrase in Example 2-3.

Bach writes sarabandes in various elaborations of chordal style (for instance, those of French Suites Nos. 1 and 6, of English Suites Nos. 1–4 and 6,

Example 2-3. Bach, Sarabande, Partita No. 1, BWV 825, mm. 1–4.

and of Partitas Nos. 1 and 6). Distinctly different is what I term "aria style," with a melody supported by subsidiary lower parts (see the sarabandes of French Suites Nos. 2, 3, and 5). Sometimes he writes a sarabande with a walking bass and elements of both melodic and chordal styles (French Suite No. 4), or in trio style, with two upper parts supported by a much lower range bass (English Suite No. 5, Partita No. 5). The Sarabande of Partita No. 4 combines aria style with a *brisé* realization of orchestral style (in the opening chords). That of Partita No. 5 is much more polyphonic: it recalls a trio sonata, with two high-range parts over a bass line. In Partita No. 6, the Sarabande is highly decorated in a way that suggests a keyboard embellishment of orchestral style. The Sarabande of Partita No. 2 seems to be written in the style of a *double* without the *simple* version (see chapter 9). In this texture of flowing sixteenths, Bach includes considerable figural development.

Gavotte

This is a graceful dance, usually measured in *alla breve* or 2, that can range from "sad to joyful" (Marpurg), but never with extremes of tempo. A famous and typical example by Bach is that of French Suite No. 5. An example by Couperin of the gentle side of the gavotte appears in Example 2-4, a movement marked "tendrement." The gavotte is basically regular in its phrasing, usually with two- and four-measure phrases. These often show musically rhyming question-and-answer patterns. The most characteristic feature is the unusual half-measure upbeat, which lends variety and ambiguity to this dance. Composers sometimes delighted in superimposing irregularities or seeming irregularities onto this basic uniformity. Most often the phrasing and harmonic rhythm remain regular while the melody suggests irregularities, as in Gavotte II of English Suite No. 3 (see Example 6-5). Sometimes, too, the music scans across the bar line, so that the upbeat sounds like a downbeat. At other times the half-measure upbeats really have the quality of upbeats. And sometimes

Example 2-4. F. Couperin, Gavotte, Ordre 8, mm. 1–4.

two different readings are both valid, and the repetitions give the performer the opportunity to recast the performance.

Menuet

This popular dance is often described as "elegant." Mattheson characterized it as being of "moderate gaiety." The time signature is almost invariably 3/4 (sometimes marked simply 3). It is occasionally measured in 6/4, a reflection of the dance's primary two-measure unit. The menuet can range from brisk and lively to moderate in tempo, but it is always graceful. Choice of tempo depends on complexity of line and harmonic rhythm. The simpler examples tend to relate to the brisker tempos.

The dance steps group as 2 + 2 + 2 in quarter notes, whereas the music groups as 3 + 3. Wendy Hilton puts it very well, referring to "the hypnotic cross-rhythm between dance and music. The stressed rise of the second demi-coupé in the step-unit occurs one beat before the downbeat of the second measure of the music" (Hilton, *Dance of Court and Theatre*, 294). The triple feeling can mask a tendency toward a duple feeling. Sometimes the music delicately hints at either scansion, providing considerable subtle tension. Thus, Menuet II from Bach's Partita No. 1 can be heard either in 3/4 throughout or with alternating 2/4 and 3/4 groupings (shown in Example 2-5). As with scansion in the gavotte, the ambiguity allows alternate styling upon the repetitions.

Example 2-5. Bach, Menuet II, Partita No. 1, BWV 825, mm. 1–8.

Passepied

This dance is measured in 3/8 time (occasionally 6/8), with an upbeat, and is rapid in tempo. Walther describes it as "quite fast"; Mattheson calls it "frivolous." The passepied uses menuet steps taken smaller and faster than in the menuet, with the interest moving to the large-scale patterns danced on the ballroom floor (a point made in Little and Jenne, 85). Like the menuet, it is phrased in two-measure units. Although basically light and brisk, many passepieds show high energy and passion—for instance, Passepied I of the Overture in the French Manner. Example 2-6 shows Bach playing with the basic two-measure unit, which contracts to one-measure units without losing evenness in the overall count of measures.

Example 2-6. Bach, Passepied I, English Suite No. 5, BWV 810, mm. 1–8.

Bourrée

The bourrée is a light, rapid, duple-meter dance that employs a number of energetic steps. The mood is sometimes bouncily happy, sometimes brisk in pace but relaxed in mood. Quantz calls it "gay." The two bourrées from Bach's Overture in the French Manner illustrate this diversity of mood very well. The first, and the most typical of the genre, appears in Example 2-7. Normally the time signature is 2 or *alla breve*. The four-measure basic phrase often drives to a point of momentary repose on the third quarter note of the second measure and to a corresponding full cadence in the fourth measure.

Bourrée rhythms often include a short-long from the bar line (♩ ♩ ♩), which characterizes Bourrée II from Bach's English Suite No. 1 as well as an example shown by Little and Jenne (36–37). They also mention the typical cadential formulae ♩ ♩ ♩. ♪ | ♩. ♩ (37). These are often coordinated with octave leaps in the bass, which are frequently found elsewhere in Bach's bourrées.

Example 2-7. Bach, Bourrée I, Overture in the French Manner, BWV 831, mm. 1–10.

Gigue

There are several types of gigue and a wide choice of time signatures, triple and compound, from 3/8, 3/4, 6/4, 6/8, 9/8, and 12/8 to 6/16, 9/16, 12/16, and 24/16. C, *alla breve*, and 2/1 may also be found; they relate to a duple-meter variety discussed below. Whatever the style, gigues are described by many authorities as almost always rapid.

The French gigue is fast and light, in 3/8, 6/8, or 6/4, with consistent dotted rhythms that correspond to leaping and hopping in the dance steps. Little and Jenne say of a representative example that "harmonic changes always occur on the first pulse of a beat and very frequently on the third pulse as well, giving an uneven, skipping quality to the piece. The dance steps underline this rhythm since they move in the same way as the harmonic changes" (146). Examples from Bach's music include the Gigue of French Suite No. 2 and Variation VII of the *Goldberg Variations* (Example 2-8a).

Apart from the French gigue, there are two main categories of gigues, which Jenne and Little term Giga I and Giga II. These have no known relationship to dance steps but seem to be purely instrumental genres. Giga I uses a triple rhythmic division even at the lowest (fastest) level, has a slow harmonic rhythm, features a smooth flow, and rarely shows any strongly articulated inner cadences. This is an Italian genre of sparkling and sometimes powerful and virtuosic forward drive. Examples from Bach include the gigues of English Suites Nos. 2, 3, 4, and 6. The specimen of a Giga I movement illustrated in

Example 2-8b was the inspiration for the opening movement of Bach's English Suite No. 1.

Giga II seems to be of French origin. As employed by Bach, the style is craggier and more complex than that of Giga I, but the dance's main independent feature is duple division at the fastest rhythmic level, usually sixteenth notes. This feature, as opposed to the triple division of the smoother-flowing Giga I style, sets the basis for more rhythmic variety. The harmonic rhythm is often more complex as well, with more variety of pacing. The chord changes are more frequent and sometimes occur on offbeats. Examples include the Gigues of English Suites Nos. 1 and 5 and of Partita No. 5.

Bach's gigues are often fugal or pseudo-fugal and bring a suite to a virtuosic close. Sometimes hunting-horn topics are utilized, as in the Gigues of French Suite No. 4 and English Suite No. 4.

Gigues notated in duple meter are most typical of the seventeenth century, but examples appeared in the eighteenth century, two of them by Bach.

Example 2-8a. Bach, Variation VII, *Goldberg Variations*, BWV 988, mm. 1–5
Example 2-8b. Dieupart, Gigue, Suite in A Major, mm. 1–8.

Scholars remain in disagreement as to whether such gigues were intended to be played as written or were meant to be converted to compound meter by the player. A major issue in this regard is fact that several gigues (not by Bach) appear in different notations in different sources. In one source a gigue will be written in duple meter; another source will have the same piece in a compound-meter arrangement. Little and Jenne discuss this topic objectively (175–184), although they appear to favor the argument that duple-meter gigues must be realized in compound time. As they note, there is no final answer on this issue. My feelings about the seventeenth-century examples are equivocal, but I feel somewhat more certain about Bach's duple-meter gigues. Bach's rhythmic notation is generally so clear that a puzzle aspect seems unlikely. It is my view that his duple-meter gigues were deliberately antiquarian, this being mainly a seventeenth-century type of gigue, and that his notation means what it says. The diverse rhythmic alterations that are required to convert these movements to compound meter are too far-reaching in their complexity to convince me. What could clinch the matter would be the discovery of ensemble gigues by Bach in duple meter, as ensemble members could hardly be expected to produce, in spontaneous uniformity with one another, such complex alterations as Bach's gigues require. It was, however, a common practice for Renaissance ensembles to improvise a triple-meter dance on the basis of a duple-meter example (for instance, a galliard from a pavane), but these alterations are much simpler and more direct than the subtleties of gigue transformation. The two duple-meter gigues in question appear in French Suite No. 1 and Partita No. 6. There is also a *manualiter* chorale prelude, *Wir glauben all an einem Gott*, in common time and in precisely the dotted style and texture of a gigue (see Example 2-9).

Loure

The loure is a slow variety of the French gigue (*gigue lent*), usually notated in 6/4. Brossard (1703) says it is beaten slowly (*lentement*) or gravely (*gravement*). Walther calls it "slow and dignified." It uses the same persistent dotted figure as the French gigue, but is a slow, dignified, even proud movement, with weight on the main beats and varied phrase lengths. Bach's most famous keyboard loure, and the only one so designated, is that of French Suite No. 5. Prelude No. 4 of *WTC* 1 is, by common consent, based on the style of the loure.

In addition to variations in accentual pattern, Bach's dance movements often show a subtle kaleidoscope of contrasting textures and motivic figurations in the lines. The allemande of Partita No. 1 provides a fine example. At the opening we find broken-chord figurations over a bell-like pedal tone, followed by increasing bass motion as the activity between the upper and lower

Example 2-9. Bach, *Wir glauben all an einem Gott*, BWV 681, *Clavierübung* 3, mm. 1–3.

parts crescendos to rhythmic equality as the first cadence approaches. Once the bass becomes more active, a short-long figure is introduced against the flowing sixteenths of the upper line; this gives way in the bass to arpeggio figures in even eighth notes, which is then followed by varied right-hand rhythms against streaming sixteenth notes in the left hand with an implication of three parts. The cadence at the double bar is in four parts. The same variety is created in the second half of the movement with the same elements, and with even one more: the bass eighth notes in mm. 21–24 are evocative of a cello playing basso continuo.

A *double* is an elaborately embellished version, separately written out, of an existing movement. (See chapter 9.) In rare instances, Bach writes a movement in the style of such elaborations. Examples include the Sarabande from Partita No. 2 and the Courante from English Suite No. 3. Both movements feature flowing subbeat values (eighth notes in one, sixteenth notes in the other) in the manner of the continuous-motion style of *double*. However, the possibilities of figural development are more fully worked out than is usual with a normal *double* such as is sometimes provided along with the basic version of a movement.

GALANT STYLE

Galant was the word used for the new, lighter style that was increasingly becoming the norm during Bach's maturity and that became the basis of the styles of C. P. E. Bach, the Viennese school, and the later eighteenth century generally. The *galant* idiom was fundamentally homophonic: melody predominated, and the bass was the only other voice that was reliably maintained. This style was considered to be more "natural" than the older, increasingly archaic style of contrapuntal writing. Bach, in his own time and later, has often been pictured as the stern, conservative contrapuntalist, but that is only half of the picture. He was interested, apparently, in all musical styles and all genres except opera, and the *galant* style was part of his language. The twist that he brought to it was to invest a nominally *galant* movement with as complex a series of developments as any in his most complex "old-fashioned" music. He could almost be seen as perpetrating a conservative revolution from within. Even when cast in the lighter, nominally simpler new mode, Bach's music maintains its usual level of inner diversity and richness. (The inner diversities of varied restatement and irregular phrasings that Bach employed in his *galant* writing are, in essence, the same complications, from a simple beginning, that make Mozart's music so individual.)

Briefly, how does Bach's keyboard output stand in relation to old and new elements? His organ music is, on the whole, more conservative than the clavier music. The preludes and fugues, toccatas, chorale preludes (especially *cantus firmus* movements), fantasias, the Passacaglia and Fugue in C Minor, and so on hark back very strongly to the seventeenth century. This is also true, in many ways, of the seven clavier toccatas. *The Art of Fugue*, too, evokes the high baroque, although with many modern details. *Clavierübung* 2 is a keyboard miniature of the two major orchestral styles (French and Italian) of the high baroque. The *Goldberg Variations*, the inventions and sinfonias, and the *WTC* all present mixtures of elements. For instance, compare the old-fashioned ricercarlike Fugue No. 4, in five parts, from *WTC* 1 to the very *galant* Prelude No. 12 from *WTC* 2, with its sigh motives and variable textures. Among the sinfonias, the first is quite old-fashioned in that it shows tight development of a small germ motive, whereas No. 15 is less obviously developmental and often breaks the three-part texture to make virtuosic arabesques across the keyboard. It is, in fact, quite *galant*.

The three collections of suites have many *galant* elements, and the composer himself referred to them in these terms. On the title page of *Clavierübung* 1, Bach lists "Preludes, Allemandes, Courantes, Sarabandes, Gigues, Menuets, and other Galanteries" to designate what are generally the most complex of all his suites. Bach's suites, of course, contain conservative elements as well as progressive. In the partitas, for example, we find a rather old-fashioned Toccata (free-style sections around a central fugue) opening Partita No. 6; the same work is concluded by a strictly fugal Gigue in duple meter (with the virtually antiquarian time signature of a circle divided by a vertical line, to signify a movement in 4/2 *alla breve*). In Partita No. 5 we find a very light Allemande and a rapid Corrente, a Sarabande in trio style full of *galant* sighing figures, and a Tempo di Minuetta that is a menuet-derived joke. These *galant* movements rub shoulders with a rather old-fashioned fugal Gigue. Even the "frivolous" Passepied is somewhat conservative: it is about as densely packed a *galanterie* as one could expect to find. In the French Suites, we find an old-fashioned Allemande in Suite No. 1, and an up-to-date Allemande with arpeggiated accompaniment, rather in the style of Handel, in No. 5; a dense, mid-baroque French-style Courante in Suite No. 1 and a gossamer-light Corrente in No. 6 that has barely two full parts and often sounds only a single line. As he does so often, Bach moves comfortably through a diversity of styles, mixing old and new approaches. What we never find in his *galanteries* is the relaxed, dinner-music lightness characteristic of much of the newer music of his time. Light-hearted or serious, spare-textured or densely written, Bach always develops his ideas to the limit.

INTERDEPENDENCE OF ELEMENTS

A useful exercise is to try to look at any piece of music (in common-practice style) as an eighteenth-century keyboard musician would: from a continuo player's perspective on harmonic and tonal exploration. Reduce, say, Prelude No. 8 of *WTC* 1 to its basic chords and play those expressively, with careful attention to their relative strengths and poignancy. Next, play it also as a sarabande (the underlying style). Then, on top of these layers, play the full texture as written, letting the prior considerations color your inflections of the melody and refinements of texture. The interdependencies of melody and other textural elements will often become clearer.

Bach sometimes elaborated some of these layers even after first writing out a composition. A famous example is found in the early and final versions of Prelude No. 10, *WTC* 1 (Example 2-10a and b). The early version (found in the *Clavierbüchlein vor Wilhelm Friedemann Bach*) shows merely a bass line and continuo-style chords. When Bach included it in the *WTC*, he added a violin-like melody as well as another section.

The degree to which the surface activity of melodic and textural niceties is subject to varying treatment on the basis of a bass line and harmonies is, of course, demonstrated endlessly in the variation literature. I recommend Paul Badura-Skoda's commentary on the Sarabande from Bach's Partita No. 1 (Badura-Skoda, 512–513), which is similar to the kind of deconstruction just suggested—not his suggested embellishments for the Sarabande itself, but the choral, cello, and keyboard works that Badura-Skoda imagines as possible reworkings of the Sarabande in his examples 20.17 through 20.19.

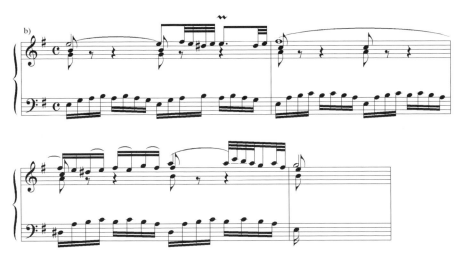

Example 2-10a, b. Bach, Prelude No. 10, *WTC* 1, BWV 855i, mm. 1–4: (a) early version; (b) final version.

SUGGESTIONS FOR FURTHER READING

Regarding dance characterizations, see:

Badura-Skoda, Paul. *Interpreting Bach at the Keyboard*, 85–87. Translated by Alfred Clayton. Oxford: Clarendon Press, 1993. [For quotations from Griepenkerl.]

Donington, Robert. *The Interpretation of Early Music, New Version*, 392–404. New York: St. Martin's Press, 1974. [Provides many quotations on dance characterizations.]

Hilton, Wendy. "A Dance for Kings: The Seventeenth-Century French Courante." *Early Music* 5 (1977): 160–172.

———. *Dance of Court and Theatre: The French Noble Style, 1690–1725.* Princeton, New Jersey: Princeton Books, 1981.

Little, Meredith, and Natalie Jenne. *Dance and the Music of J. S. Bach.* Bloomington: Indiana University Press, 1991. [By far the most complete account of this subject.]

Powell, Newman. "Kirnberger on Dance Rhythms, Fugues, and Characterization." In *Festschrift for Theodore Hoelty-Nickel.* Valparaiso,Indiana: Valparaiso University, 1967.

Quantz, Johann Joachim. *On Playing the Flute,* 289–292. Translated by Edward R. Reilly. London: Faber, 1966.

Regarding other topics:

Krummacher, Friedrich. "Bach's Free Organ Works and the Stylus Phantasticus." In *J. S. Bach as Organist: His Instruments, Music, and Performance Practices,* ed. George Stauffer and Ernest May. Bloomington: Indiana University Press, 1986.

Leonhardt, Gustav. *The Art of Fugue: Bach's Last Harpsichord Work,* 15–34. The Hague: Martinus Nijhoff, 1952. [Provides fine insights into details of keyboard textures.]

Stauffer, George. "Fugue Types in Bach's Free Organ Works." In *J. S. Bach as Organist: His Instruments, Music, and Performance Practices,* edited by George Stauffer and Ernest May. Bloomington: Indiana University Press, 1986.

PART II

PERFORMANCE AND
NOTATIONAL PRACTICES

Part II introduces the main issues of performance practice from a practical viewpoint, defining the basics of each subject and considering how each one relates to Bach's keyboard music. If some of these conventions seem at first strange, remember that a reconstruction of twentieth-century musical performance from its scores and from verbal descriptions made at the time, without recordings, could also produce some perplexity in another two hundred years or more. I hope that the discussion in Part II will further the reader's understanding of why certain notational features appear as they do and how those, together with basic knowledge of musical styles, can help in forming performance decisions that would not surprise the composer.

Johann Sebastian Bach, portrait by Elias Gottlob Haussmann, 1748. Collection of William H. Scheide, Princeton, New Jersey. Courtesy Teri Noel Towe

Chapter 3

ACCOUNTS OF BACH'S
PLAYING STYLE

This chapter provides quotations from Bach's contemporaries and from his first biographer, Johann Nikolaus Forkel, that give informative descriptions of Bach's performance style. I include only those accounts that give musical specifics. There are of course many other surviving descriptions in praise of Bach's playing, but they speak only in very general terms. The accounts given below indicate that Bach's playing was characterized by brisk tempos, deft and efficient technique, strong contrasts, and emotional directness.

BACH'S PLAYING AS DESCRIBED
BY HIS CONTEMPORARIES

On Bach's ornate style of realizing accompaniments from figured bass, Lorenz Mizler wrote in 1738:

> Whoever wishes truly to observe what delicacy in thorough bass and very good accompanying mean need only take the trouble to hear our Capellmeister Bach here, who accompanies every thoroughbass to a solo so that one thinks it is a piece of concerted music and as if the melody he plays in the right hand were written beforehand. I can give living testimony of this since I have heard it myself. (*New Bach Reader*, 328)

Mizler's description is confirmed and expressed more professionally by Johann Friedrich Daube (1756). It would appear that Bach was able, extempore, to create a contrapuntal fabric around a solo part in such a way that it emerged as part of a confluence of polyphonic parts:

> For the complete practical application of thoroughbass it is necessary to know three species: (1) the simple or common [merely playing simple chords]; (2) the natural, or that which comes closest to the character of a melody or a piece; (3) the intricate or compound.

> The excellent Bach possessed this third species in the highest degree; when he played, the upper voice [played or sung by another] had to shine. By his exceedingly adroit accompaniment he gave it life when it had none. He knew how to imitate it so cleverly, with either the right hand or the left, and how to introduce an unexpected countertheme against it, so that the listener would have sworn that everything had been conscientiously written out. At the same time, the regular accompaniment [function] was curtailed very little. In general his accompanying was always like a concertante part most conscientiously worked out and added as a companion to the upper voice so that at the appropriate time the upper voice would shine. This right was even given at times to the bass, without slighting the upper voice. Suffice it to say that anyone who missed hearing him missed a great deal. (*New Bach Reader*, 362)

C. P. E. Bach, writing to Bach's biographer Forkel in 1774, gave further details:

> Thanks to his greatness in harmony [and counterpoint] he accompanied trios on more than one occasion on the spur of the moment and, being in a good humor and knowing that the composer would not take it amiss, and on the basis of sparsely figured continuo part just set before him, converted them into complete quartets, astounding the composer of the trios. (*New Bach Reader*, 397)

On Bach's tendency to lively tempi we have two mentions. The first is from the obituary of Bach by Agricola and C. P. E. Bach:

> In conducting he was very accurate, and of the tempo, which he generally took very lively, he was uncommonly sure. (*New Bach Reader*, 306–307)

Forkel concludes his discussion of Bach's clavier playing:

> In the execution of his own pieces he generally took the time very brisk, but contrived, besides this briskness, to introduce so much variety in his

performance that under his hand every piece was, as it were, like a discourse. When he wished to express strong emotions, he did not do it, as many do, by striking the keys with great force, but by melodical and harmonical figures, that is, by the internal resources of the art. (*New Bach Reader*, 436)

Bach seems, at least in *galant* music, to have played with elegant lightness. Jacob Adlung, a clavichord enthusiast who knew Bach, related an anecdote about his rendition of Louis Marchand's suites:

Only once did they please me; namely, when I spoke with Capellmeister Bach about the contest [scheduled between Bach and Marchand in 1717; Marchand did not appear], during his visit here [in Erfurt] and told him that I had these suites, and he played them for me in his own manner, that is, very fleetly [deftly?] and artistically [*sehr flüchtig und künstlich*]. (Adlung, *Anleitung zu der musikalischen Gelahrtheit*, 858)

Bach's playing, not surprisingly, accommodated the emotional sense of the music. In 1746 his pupil Johann Gotthilf Ziegler wrote, in a letter applying for a position as church organist:

As concerns the playing of chorales, I was instructed by my teacher, Capellmeister Bach, who is still living, not to play the songs merely offhand but according to the sense [Affect] of the words. (*New Bach Reader*, 336)

Bach's playing style seems to have been connected and flowing, as Adlung's and other comments suggest. Ernst Ludwig Gerber, the son of Bach's pupil Heinrich Nikolaus Gerber, let drop an illuminating, if very general, remark when discussing the organist Christoph Gottlieb Schröter:

However, whoever knows the excellent legato style, with which Bach treated the organ, could not possibly be pleased by Schröter's style, for he always played staccato on the organ. (Gerber, 2:455)

The celebrated flutist and composer Johann Joachim Quantz commented on Bach's keyboard technique, starting with what not to do:

Many persons sound as if they were literally stumbling over the notes if they have to produce a run of several step-wise notes. If you accustom yourself at the very beginning to curving all the fingers inwards, each one as far as the others, you are less likely to make this mistake. In the performance of these running passages, however, you must not raise the fingers immediately after striking the key, but rather draw the tips of the fingers back towards yourself to the foremost part of the key, until they glide away from it. Running passages are produced most distinctly in this manner. I appeal here to the example of one of the greatest of all players on the keyboard, who practiced and taught in this way. (Quantz, 259–260)

Quantz's index identifies this player as J. S. Bach.

Forkel seems to have drawn on Quantz for the following account, published in 1802. He was also in touch with C. P. E. Bach for many details of his study. Forkel describes Bach's keyboard technique with specific reference to the clavichord but remarks that the points apply to the other keyboards as well:

According to Sebastian Bach's manner of placing the hand on the keys, the five fingers are bent so that their joints come into a straight line, and so fit the keys, which lie in a plane surface under them, that no single finger has to be drawn nearer when it is wanted, but every one is ready over the key which it may have to press down. What follows from this manner of holding the hand is:

1. That no finger must fall upon its key, or (as also often happens) be thrown on it, but only needs to be placed upon it with a certain consciousness of the internal power and command over the motion.
2. The impulse thus given to the keys, or the quantity of pressure, must be maintained in equal strength, and that in such a manner that the finger be not raised perpendicularly from the key, but that it glides off the forepart of the key, by gradually drawing back the tip of the finger towards the palm of the hand.
3. In the transition from one key to another, this gliding off causes the quantity of force or pressure with which the first tone has been kept up to be transferred with the greatest rapidity to the next finger, so that the two tones are neither disjoined from each other nor blended together.

The touch is, therefore, as C. Ph. Emanuel Bach says, neither too long nor too short, but just what it ought to be. . . .

Seb. Bach is said to have played with so easy and small a motion of the fingers that it was hardly perceptible. Only the first joints of the fingers were in motion; the hand retained even in the most difficult passages its rounded form; the fingers rose very little from the keys, hardly more than in a trill, and when one was employed the other remained quietly in its position. Still less did the other parts of his body take any share in his play, as happens with many whose hand is not light [supple] enough. . . .

He rendered all his fingers, of both hands, equally strong and serviceable, so that he was able to execute not only chords and all running passages, but also single and double trills with equal ease and delicacy. He was perfectly master even of those passages in which, while some fingers perform a trill, the others, on the same hand, have to continue the melody. (*New Bach Reader*, 432–433)

Quantz, in the prior quotation above, seems to be writing in regard to the sliding technique as a way of avoiding unevenness and gaps in scale passages fingered by finger crossing (e.g., 3-4-3-4 ascending in the right hand—irregularities some modern schools of playing have regarded as "authentic"). Forkel does not seem to make the connection on the finger slide's relationship to finger crossing, which was quite outmoded by the later eighteenth century.

It became a modern tradition to believe that finger crossing inevitably produces breaks in the line, the very thing that Quantz says is associated only with incorrect technique. However, experience confirms Quantz's opinion. C. P. E. Bach advocated "modern" scale fingerings but comments, in a rarely quoted passage, that

crossing and turning, the principal means of changing the fingers, must be applied in such a manner that the tones involved in the change flow smoothly. In keys with few or no accidentals the crossing of the third finger over the fourth and the second over the thumb is in certain cases more practicable and better suited for the attainment of unbroken continuity than other crossings or the [thumb] turn. With regard to the latter, when a black key acts as the pivot the thumb is conveniently provided with more room in which to turn than in a succession of white keys. In keys without accidentals crossing should cause no stumbling, but in the others care [as to where the crossings are made] must be exercised because of the black keys. (*Essay*, 58)

Thus, C. P. E. Bach saw the thumb crossings of modern fingerings as prone to the same disruptions that are often, in modern times, mistakenly associated with the older-style finger crossings, and he advocates the latter for smoothness when one is not playing in, say, F-sharp major. He, like Quantz, associated breaks in finger crossing with poor technique, whether involving finger-over or thumb-under motions, and in fact advocates pairwise finger crossings (such as right-hand 3-4-3-4) to promote continuity. Indeed, he specifically states that finger crossing should not cause stumbling. As we shall see in chapter 10, his father seems to have used any and all combinations of fingers, depending on context.

In a frequently quoted passage, C. P. E. Bach wrote of his father's style of fingering:

> My deceased father told me that in his youth he used to hear great men who employed their thumbs only when large stretches made it necessary. Because he lived at a time when a gradual but striking change of musical taste was taking place, he was obliged to devise a far more comprehensive fingering and especially to enlarge the role of the thumbs and use them as nature intended; for, among their other good services, they must be employed chiefly in the difficult tonalities. Hereby, they [the thumbs] rose from their former uselessness to the rank of principal finger. (*Essay*, 42)

The surviving scalar fingerings that are associated with Bach are primarily in the older style of finger crossing, and the pieces in which they appear are in the "natural" keys (see chapter 10). However, playing Bach's music in remote tonalities unquestionably requires the technique described by C. P. E. Bach.

In the famous preface to the inventions and sinfonias (1723), J. S. Bach himself suggests a "singing playing style." This phrase probably refers both to the execution of written works and to the development of a compositional style characterized by melody in all parts. It should be remembered that in the eighteenth century, someone's "playing style" referred as much to the musical idioms that characterized his or her own compositions and improvisations as to the manner of playing the instrument. This preface is the only known written statement on the subject of keyboard style from the composer himself:

> Upright Instruction whereby the lovers of the clavier, and especially those desirous of learning, are shown a clear way not only (1) to learn to play clearly in two voices, but also, after further progress, (2) to deal correctly and well with three obbligato parts; furthermore, at the same time not only to have good ideas [*inventiones*] but to develop the same well, and above all to arrive at a singing style of playing and at the same time to acquire a strong foretaste of composition.

Spitta, in his biography of Bach, points out the relationship between the terminology in this little preface and rhetorical terminology (discussed in chapter 12).

Bach's use of different keyboard instruments has been endlessly argued from various perspectives. As discussed in chapter 1, the clavichord is often unjustly dismissed from consideration, and Forkel's assertion that it was Bach's favorite instrument has been similarly treated. However, there is one statement on the subject that is unequivocal. Agricola, a Bach pupil from 1738 to 1741, tells us, regarding the sonatas and partitas for solo violin, that "their composer often played them himself on the clavichord [*auf der Clavichorde*], adding as much in the way of harmony as he found necessary" (*Bach Dokumente III*, 293).

BACH'S PERFORMANCE DIRECTIONS

Most performance instructions are encoded into details of the notation. The information thus conveyed is far more extensive than appears at a first glance to eyes accustomed to modern notational conventions.

The composer rarely tells us of dynamics or harpsichord registration. In fact, the two are usually indicated in tandem, if at all. The Italian Concerto, the Overture in the French Manner, and the *Goldberg Variations* are the famous exceptions. In these works, *forte* and *piano* markings appear as a means to indicate registrational contrasts on the two keyboards of a double-manual harpsichord. Dynamics are often implicit in the harmony and musical texture.

Articulatory marks are much more frequent in the composer's ensemble music than in his clavier works. Sparse though the markings are, Bach's keyboard music includes more slurs and dots than was usual at the time. This is particularly true of his published keyboard scores. There are of course no metronome marks or mood words and few tempo markings. (Again, the ensemble music is more generous with time words.) Time words sometimes modify the pacing suggested by the time signature alone; again, this relationship is quite different from what modern practice suggests. Every dance-related movement is automatically associated with a certain range of tempo and accentuation. In fact, the tempos and accentual treatment generally are to be understood from the style of various genres, not only from dance-related conventions. For instance, freedom of pacing was understood for freely styled pieces, and imitation of the orchestra or of different instrumental styles can suggest ranges of tempo and articulation. By modern conventions there are no indications of ritardando or *a tempo*, but in fact the words *adagio* and *presto* in the course of a movement can provide these directions, as discussed in chapter 7.

The scores do not specify which movements are to be played as written and which require added ornamentation and embellishment, although answers to these questions emerge with some experience. Bach's written-in ornamentation and embellishment are generally quite complete and rarely require additions by the player.

The instrument is rarely designated with any specificity—even less than has commonly been assumed. It is now known that the word *clavecin*, which often appears in the French-language suite titles, was in fact generic in usage, referring as much to the clavichord as to the harpsichord. Also, the general rule of the period was to play the music interchangeably on different instruments. Nonetheless, the modern literature continues to refer to the clavier works as harpsichord music and troubles itself very little with second thoughts on the matter.

Despite a title such as *The Well-Tempered Clavier*, we have no sure knowledge of the temperament(s) Bach preferred at any time of his life. C. P. E. Bach wrote in his father's obituary that "in the tuning of harpsichords, he achieved so correct and pure a temperament that all the tonalities sounded pure and agreeable. He knew of no tonalities which, because of impure intonation, one must avoid" (David and Mendel, *New Bach Reader*, 307). Temperament is discussed in chapter 13.

Chapter 4

DYNAMICS

Dynamics are primary to musical communication. They allow both emotional expression and clarification of complex textures. Bach's keyboard scores rarely indicate dynamics, but there are many clues in related areas. In this chapter I discuss dynamics in regard to musical texture (especially textural density and range; see also chapter 1); relative strengths among harmonies; harpsichord registration; ensemble style; terrace dynamics (see also chapter 10); phrase shape and agogics; linear contours; and rules for certain standard contexts.

MUSICAL TEXTURES AND THE HARPSICHORD

The musical responses of the early keyboard instruments can yield much valuable information about Bach's keyboard writing. The harpsichord is particularly important for the feedback it gives in respect to the dynamics implied by musical textures.

Since the harpsichord's dynamics are not touch-sensitive, variations in dynamics (actual or implied) are made by bringing out variations in range and texture that are composed into the music. These factors relate to the shape of the phrase in a direct way that piano writing does not have to rely on. For instance, the piano composer can write thick, low-range repeated chords and mark them *pianissimo*. On the harpsichord, the density of that texture would automatically produce a loud effect; a *piano* dynamic level requires a thinner texture and fewer plucks within a short space of time. Therefore, knowledge of the harpsichord's response to musical texture can be of crucial importance in playing Bach's music on the modern piano.

On the harpsichord, then, the vertical and lateral density of musical texture is very much a dynamic factor: heavier textures and/or faster notes increase the energy and volume. In playing the piano it is easy to miss this correlation because of the instrument's flexibility, but it is something that the harpsichordist must reckon with.(The same considerations apply to some degree to the clavichord, although that instrument is dynamically flexible.) Indeed, it is also a reliable tool: the relationship is frequently the basis for musical decisions. Textures that fill the harpsichord or clavichord with resonance can sound relatively thin on the piano, which needs the fuller writing of the nineteenth century to sound "at capacity." Rendering Bach's *fortissimo* on the piano so as to suit the best interests of both music and instrumental effect remains something of an anomaly in all but the most exceptional circumstances. Fortunately, most of his music does not depend on a big sound, but rather on judiciously balanced effects. Again, though, for firsthand comprehension of Bach-style dynamics, the experience of hearing eighteenth-century instruments is essential, as much for Bach's orchestra (with original instruments, in their original balance between strings and winds) as for the keyboard instruments with which he was familiar.

What the pianist can emulate of the harpsichord's sound is not, as early-twentieth-century commentaries sometimes suggest, the variety of registers (primarily the use of upper and lower octaves). The pianist should learn from the harpsichord more general (and musical) aspects of clarity, rhythmic precision and drive, and sensitivity to the dynamic balances implied by variations in the musical texture. The last issue is what concerns us here. While knowledge of the harpsichord and clavichord is important, the primary consideration for the pianist playing Bach is knowledge of the musical and instrumental styles that Bach utilizes in his keyboard music. It is the extra-keyboard sounds and styles that are the most significant elements in Bach's keyboard writing.

Virtually every harpsichordist prior to 1800, whether amateur or professional, had experience playing continuo—that is, accompanying one or more instruments or voices from a figured bass line. The continuo player realizes chords (or improvises more elaborate textures) on the basis of the harmonies indicated by the figures and according to the requirements of the ensemble and personal taste or imagination. (This topic is discussed further in chapter 10.) Five minutes of this will demonstrate to anyone that the continuo harpsichordist's primary resources for dynamic variety are range and fullness of texture. Thicker, faster textures and/or those in a low range produce loud effects; thin textures with slower note movement and/or high range are generally softer, or at least suggest softness by being less intense. Changes of registration can help but are far less effective for subtlety and general flexibility. Every harpsichord composer's continuo experience underlies his or her solo compositions. The often impressionistic, kaleidoscopic textures used by a good continuo harpsichordist are quite directly related to the solo sonatas of Domenico Scarlatti, or to George Frideric Handel's "continuo fugues," in which strict voice-leading yields to impressionistic variations in the fullness of texture. Scarlatti's sonatas oppose crashing eight-voice chords with the thinnest and slowest of two-part writing, a diversity that animates the harpsichord. Indeed, any contrast or gradation of elements may create either the reality or the illusion of actual dynamic change on this instrument. That is, the textural variation sometimes produces actual variations in volume and would register on the levels gauge of a recording device. At other times, if carefully manipulated, the textural flux provides an illusion of dynamic variation. Though it would read as constant on a recording machine's meter, it produces an effect of flexibility on the listener's ear. The clavichord often responds the same way, although it is by no means dependent on textural dynamics. The piano responds to these elements also, but the player accustomed to later styles has to learn the subtler aspects of such dynamic voicing—that is, to become familiar with the details that enliven the earlier instruments.

Bach's preoccupation with strict counterpoint makes the connection with continuo experience often more subtle than, say, the bold contrasts typical of Scarlatti. Nonetheless, Bach's textures contain dynamic cues that any continuo player can recognize. Examples that relate more overtly to continuo playing may be found in Bach's less strictly contrapuntal styles, whether toccatas, suite movements, or orchestral imitations. The first movement of the Italian Concerto, for instance bristles with awareness of the harpsichord's response to textural variation.

Playing in coordination with the textural dynamics (whether consciously or by good musical instinct) can allow wonderful shading and flexibility. It is essential that the pianist understand this far-reaching relationship between musical texture and instrumental response. It is for this reason above all others that pianists should study the harpsichord, to develop a sense of the full nature of this relationship. In most piano writing there is no strong need to rely on the correlation between textures and dynamic effect—which is, incidentally, the main reason piano music sounds so inappropriate on the harpsichord.

To some degree, the clavichordist can work against the dynamic scheme suggested by the textures, but the lightness and delicacy of the sound (not the low volume) limits this independence. Nonetheless, the clavichordist can utilize a host of inflections and colors denied to the harpsichordist. It is hardly surprising that the two instruments were cultivated in tandem throughout the period of their historical use. As Robert Marshall's excellent account of Bach's dynamic markings points out, the composer's dynamic notations in his ensemble music show that graded textures and dynamic differentiation of various lines were as much a part of Bach's ensemble usage as they were in later eras. The harpsichordist works hard to imply these elements; the pianist and clavichordist can feel securely "authentic" in rendering such nuances to the utmost.

The pianist, then, must learn to take cues from the musical textures so that their musical meaning is not lost in translation to the piano. For instance, since thin or higher-range writing often suggests or actually produces *piano*, the pianist should, at the very least, not compensate by playing more loudly. Similarly, when energy accumulates in the lower or middle range, one should not reduce the dynamics. Thus, the apparently thin writing at the opening of Bach's Toccata in E Minor can sound rather grand, set as it is in the low range of the harpsichord or clavichord. The player should begin the dynamic scheme from awareness of such elements and whatever contrasts they suggest. From that basis, the pianist, like the clavichordist, can often make full effects that the harpsichordist can only imply. (These are not grounds for dismissing the harpsichord. Sometimes more can be conveyed by implication than by explicit statement.)

The modern piano requires carefully calibrated dynamics to delineate parts clearly. Dynamics help to make up for the piano's greater density of tone and lack of variation in articulatory attack, in comparison to the earlier instruments. The pianist can learn refinements of articulation, especially as a means of clarity, from the harpsichord and clavichord, the latter being open to both articulatory and dynamic clarification of parts. To produce equivalent clarity, the piano must sometimes make a slight crescendo in the course of an active line so that successive attacks remain distinct. In a real legato, however, the dynamic level at the end of one note must be matched by the dynamic ictus of the next note. This treatment produces a slow diminuendo.

The clavichord can teach the pianist that a crescendo through an intense passage makes the *fortissimo* level, once reached, more effective than if the entire passage were rendered *forte* or *fortissimo* throughout—that dynamic effects are made most dramatic through judicious contrasts rather than through uniformity or, at the louder levels, mere visceral force. But even on the dynamically flexible piano, it is necessary to use refinements of timing as well as dynamics and articulation to convey the nuances of a line, especially when dealing with Bach's onionlike layers of phrase that cohere on both the small and the large scales. As any harpsichordist can confirm, delicate timing can let a line sing and reduce any risk of percussiveness in the note attacks.

Well-judged dynamic contours can of course guide the listener through relatively obscure textures—for instance, the less obvious subject entrances in fugues. Needless to say, the piano's wide dynamic range and sustaining powers can bring out the long notes of an augmented theme very well, whereas on the harpsichord and even sometimes on the clavichord the elongated note values need particular care in handling.

BACH'S KEYBOARD WRITING

I have heard various performers describe Bach's keyboard writing as wonderfully idiomatic to any keyboard. Others comment on how awkward it can be. Perhaps the latter judgment arises from unwillingness to let the textures (and other elements) lead the player to find their intrinsic characteristics. Certainly, Bach's signals are often subtler than Scarlatti's wholesale manipulation of texture and color. However, for the harpsichordist who is attentive to the textural nuances, there is a wealth of dynamic clues and colorful flexibility. As an example, let us focus on aspects of a work that is undisputably for the harpsichord, the *Goldberg Variations*. The textures of this composition are as delicately calibrated as its polyphony.

It is easy to admire the brilliance and inventiveness of the duets for two keyboards and other extroverted effects in the *Goldberg Variations*. But what is extraordinary is that, although the writing is almost without exception very strict contrapuntally, the composer manages to provide subtle nuances in linear and even vertical density. These nuances are beautifully coordinated with the dynamic needs of the flow of phrase and give the player opportunities to elicit great flexibility from the (nominally) resistant harpsichord. Perhaps most startling is the fact that these nuances are especially characteristic of the nine canons (Variations III, VI, and IX, etc.). The canon is a notoriously difficult contrapuntal genre not only from a compositional standpoint, but also in terms of accommodating instrumental considerations. Furthermore, Bach had set himself the task of writing the canons at progressively wider intervals of imitation (at the unison, the second, and so forth), and all on the same harmonic pattern.

Every canon but the last has an independent (noncanonic) bass line. The freedom of this part is naturally of considerable help in creating textural nuance. Thus, even the overall movement through each half of Variation III is made to crescendo by means of the accelerating motion in the bass, from eighth notes to sixteenths. The accumulation of rhythmic energy produces a dynamic effect: helpful on the piano, but crucial on the harpsichord. This is a good example of a broad-ranging contour.

The canonic parts also contribute to nuances, of which a few examples can be given here. In Variation XV (a canon at the fifth, in contrary motion; see Example 4-1), the cadence at m. 8 gives a distinct effect of barrenness owing to the rests in the middle part. Well-placed rests also help the effect of the tapering cadence at the double bar. At the beginning of the second half of the movement, momentum increases gradually when first two, then three parts are heard, and the energy subsides again in mm. 24–25 when the parts are briefly reduced to two and are well separated (creating a thinner sound). In Variation XXIV, the canon breaks (stops the strict imitation) midway through each half of the movement. Then the two upper parts exchange roles: the *dux* becomes the *comes*, and vice versa. Unless Bach had some insoluble problem that forced him to break the canon in both halves, this device would seem to be deliberate—a means of lightening the texture, which then becomes denser again.

Example 4-1. Bach, Variation XV, *Goldberg Variations*, BWV 988, mm. 14–16.

The duet variations (Variations V, VIII, XI, XIV, XVII, XX, and XXIII) use a variety of figurations: large skips against a running line (Variation V) or against arpeggiation (Variation XIV), broken thirds and sixths (Variation XVII), syncopations (Variation XX), and so forth. The lack of change in the density of voicing is compensated for by changes in range and by artful changes of linear density. Bach's favored technique of creating one line from the elements of two (a single line showing distinct upper and lower segments) allows for some subtle but nonetheless telling effects of growing and tapering textures. An example appears in Variation V: Bach takes off with wildly zigzagging lines that are nonetheless so natural and logical that, as Forkel observed, one hardly realizes how bizarre they really are.

Bach does not notate graded dynamics in his clavier works, but crescendos and diminuendos still have their place. However, large-scale crescendos and diminuendos are foreign to Bach's phrasing. For instance, a long diminuendo to the final cadence from halfway through a movement or section is rarely if ever appropriate. This is a nineteenth-century performance habit that, in baroque music, passes over and obscures too much middleground detail and ignores the proportions and relationships among the phrases in favor of an artificial long-term gesture. Bach wrote beautiful long lines, but not in the style of the nineteenth century.

ORCHESTRAL AND TERRACE DYNAMICS

Terrace dynamics involve the structural use of large-scale dynamics, for instance, to articulate the divisions of a concerto grosso movement. The full ensemble (tutti) plays its material, which contrasts with other material played by one or more solo instruments. Of course, smaller-level dynamic nuances will be required within these large-scale divisions of the basic *forte* and *piano*. On a two-manual harpsichord, one set of strings is usually controlled from the upper manual and up to three or four from the lower. Therefore the lower manual is used for the full *forte* and the upper manual for *piano*. In imitating the orchestra, the use of both hands on the lower manual corresponds to tutti, and a soft tutti (occasionally a solo, too) is normally played on the upper manual. Accompanied solos are usually imitated by playing the solo line on the lower manual and the accompanying parts on the upper. In *Clavierübung* 2, Bach indicates the two manuals with the symbols *f* and *p*, and they are deployed for just these orchestral effects.

George Stauffer has pointed out that Bach indicates manual changes, in both his organ and his harpsichord works, by a break in the normal beaming of note groups at the point where the change of keyboard should take place. He cites *Clavierübung* 2, the "Dorian" Toccata for Organ, concerto arrangements for organ by Bach, and a work as early as the pre-1707 *Wie schön leuchtet der Morgenstern* (BWV 739) (Stauffer and May, 203–207). One may also find registration shown by beaming in the arrangements of concerti for clavier (BWV 972–986). However, the lack of such beaming does not necessarily mean that Bach prohibited manual changes, although Stauffer seems to take this view. There are many instances throughout even *Clavierübung* 2 where the beaming is continuous although a change of manual is indicated. Example 4-2a shows, in different parts, both continuous and broken beaming at the manual change. Admittedly, the engraving of *Clavierübung* 2 was problematic, and in at least one instance Bach's separation of beaming appears to have been confused by the printer, who began with a single sixteenth note and then carelessly beamed it through to make a full group of six (the passage shown in Example 4-2b).

Example 4-2a, b. Bach, Grave, Overture in the French Manner, BWV 831; (a) mm. 123–124; (b) mm. 104–105.

Therefore, the lack of such beaming in the preludes to the English Suites, for instance, should not be taken to suggest that these clear imitations of concerto grosso style must be played *forte* thoughout.

Many textbooks on musical history have spoken of terrace dynamics—the alternation between very distinct dynamic levels—as a basic feature of baroque music. This is a vast oversimplification. However, terraced effects do have a role to play. Perhaps the most famous example in Bach's clavier works, and probably the only one that is strictly terraced in the full sense, is the Echo movement that concludes the Overture in the French Manner. In this movement, small subphrases and a few longer units are heard on the harpsichord's soft upper manual, while the rest of the movement is played on the *forte* of the lower keyboard. In the first movement of the same suite, and in the outer movements of the Italian Concerto, the two keyboards are utilized to imitate tutti and soli groups in the orchestra. These suggestions of the dynamic poles of another medium, however, also require nuance within the marked *fortes* and *pianos*. The same is true of other orchestrally derived movements, such as the Preludes to all but the first of the six English Suites. In common with much of the dynamic notation of the later eighteenth century, Bach's *f* and *p* markings are generic rather than literal. A complete scheme of relative dynamics must be realized within each level, both *forte* and *piano*. Rather than restricting the dynamic scheme of a terraced movement to simple contrasts, the pianist must, as always, seek out the dynamics implied by textural contrasts, harmonies, and all other musical elements. The terraced dynamic levels of an orchestra are not altogether static, and neither should they be on the keyboard. This dynamic layering is constantly required in all terraced styles except where a simple echo effect is required.

When Bach is imitating orchestral textures on the keyboard, several styles are found:

1. *A basic contrast between orchestral tutti and soli, leading to many alternations throughout the movement.* Again, the outer movements of the Italian Concerto and of the Overture in the French Manner are the best-known examples of Bach's writing in this style. To them should be added the many concerto transcriptions, the Preludes to English Suites Nos. 2–6, and several movements from other suites.

2. *Accompaniment (usually in two low-range parts) and a solo melody throughout the movement.* This style is evocative of solo playing in an orchestral context and does not include tutti effects. The Andante of the Italian Concerto is the most famous example. Other instances include Variations XIII and XXV of the *Goldberg Variations*, the andante section of the Sinfonia of Partita No. 2, and many sarabandes in the aria style (e.g., in French Suites Nos. 2, 4, and 5).

3. *Overall dynamic contrast between paired movements.* In the Overture in the French Manner, the Gavottes, Passepieds, and Bourrées are all paired movements, and the second ("trio") of each pair is marked *piano* (except in the Passepieds, where *piano* can be presumed). Such contrasts imply orchestral contrasts such as strings or full orchestra (*forte*) opposed to winds (*piano*).

DYNAMICS BASED ON HARMONY

An extremely important consideration for dynamics is described, in greater or lesser detail, in several eighteenth-century treatises: the unstable harmonic elements—chromatic chords, dissonances, deceptive harmonic motions, and unexpected chords generally—are to be played more loudly than the diatonic elements and chords of resolution. C. P. E. Bach puts it succinctly: "In general it can be said that dissonances are played loudly and consonances softly, since the former rouse our emotions and the latter quiet them" (*Essay*, 163). Quantz, who went into much detail on the subject, specified three groups of chords of increasing dissonance and accorded correspondingly louder treatment. He illustrated these points with an Adagio movement, marked with thorough indications of dynamics. His discussion is cited at the end of this chapter and is well worth investigation by the serious player.

Sometimes the realization of the relationship between harmony and dynamics is the opposite of the general tendency, although I offer this suggestion without much historical foundation. That is, the rule of playing the chromatic chords louder can be effectively stood on its head and a contrast of *piano* or *subito piano* used instead. (For example, a Neapolitan chord, normally played louder, can receive its dynamic emphasis by being played more softly than the other chords—a *misterioso* treatment that is effective in some contexts.) Sometimes, too, the textures automatically invert these elements, as in the Fantasia in A Minor (BWV 922). Here, chromatic activity sometimes takes place in a comparatively *piano* texture (high range, two or three parts) contrasted with a more "normal," diatonic cadence in a lower range with denser textures and a contrast of rhythm. In such a case, the louder cadence has the effect of a suddenly assertive, stabilizing influence.

The relationship between dynamics and harmony cannot be subjected to hard and fast rules but depends upon the context. C. P. E. Bach was wise enough to state only the general rule and not to become uselessly prescriptive of details on this subject. However, the general principle provides a very important and useful starting point.

Invariably, the movement from a dissonant note or chord to its resolution is rendered loud–soft. This concept is important for both small- and large-scale contexts. It stems naturally from the fact that dissonance tends to create forward impetus. On the small scale, appoggiaturas and other dissonant notes and chords move *forte–piano*. Appoggiaturas, resolved thus, can suggest a sigh. This diminuendo is not slight. Indeed, later in the century (after Bach's time) it was inflected so strongly that some critics complained that the resolutions could scarcely be heard. The affective power of the appoggiatura, and of dissonance generally, was keenly felt, and this small-scale aspect of inflection is too often overlooked by modern performers.

On the larger scale, the same principle can extend over long areas. Sometimes long-term planning of dynamics can be made on the basis of one or two long-range resolutions, chromatic elements, and similar contexts. An instance appears in Example 4-3. The soprano E-flat of m. 7 resolves to the D in m. 8, suggesting general accommodation of the dynamics to the *forte–piano* motion in the soprano.

On the basis of the chromatic hierarchy, chord patterns can be seen as strong-weak, weak-strong, and so forth. The famous Prelude No. 1 of *WTC* 1 is an apt illustration (Example 4-4). When it is considered on this basis, a large-scale irregularity of measure groupings, originating in the three-measure unit shown in Example 4-4, becomes apparent. It is this element, which places the subsequent paired groups off by one measure from paired uniformity, that helps to propel the piece forward.

Example 4-3. Bach, Sinfonia No. 5, BWV 791, mm. 7–9.

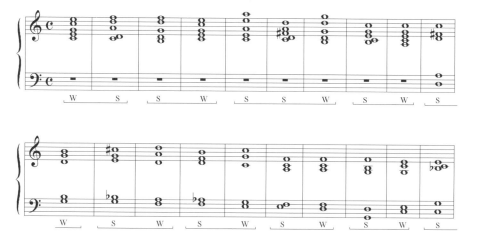

Example 4-4. Bach, Prelude No. 1 (chordal skeleton), *WTC* 1, BWV 846i, mm. 1–20.

DYNAMICS AND MUSICAL CONTEXT

From treatises of the baroque and classical eras, we have a number of rules of thumb that are very specific, highly practical, and often quite revealing of eighteenth-century performance practice. They are also full of musical common sense, regardless of historical considerations. The most important among these can be summed up:

- *The first note of a new phrase or subphrase is accented.* This rule, mentioned by E. W. Wolf in 1785, seems to take a strong-to-weak, trochaic accent pattern for granted (see chapter 5).
- *The first note under a slur receives a slight accent, and the ensuing notes are successively softer.* Thus, a slur implies (indeed, indicates) a slight accent followed by a slight diminuendo to the end of the slurred group, as well as a legato connection. (The diminuendo helps the keyboard player to approximate a real legato, whereby the attack of one note matches the dynamic level reached at the end of the previous note's sounding.) Naturally, the degree of accent must be made relative to the context.
- *The principal notes are always played more strongly than passing tones.* Quantz states this very clearly in two separate passages (Quantz, 123, 241).
- *A change of harmony, made on what is otherwise a weak beat, makes that beat strong.* In other words, the metric frame of accents gives way to harmonic influences, as it does to other factors that create stress.
- *Appoggiaturas are played more loudly than their resolutions.* Performance of this standard dynamic "hairpin" was quite intense in the eighteenth century.
- *Syncopated notes are stressed.* This is common sense.
- *Long notes (notes longer than others in the context) are stressed.* A long note gets an accent so that its effect will be sustained throughout its duration. The accent calls the ear's attention to the note.
- *Notes that stand out from the prevailing range (for instance, an isolated high note) are usually separated out from their context when slurring is marked.* This is the general tendency in baroque violin slurring. It is mirrored in keyboard usage and suggests dynamic emphasis of such notes.
- *Notes that are tied over to principal beats are stressed.* See Example 4-5; the plus sign signifies stress on a note.
- *Notes that are preceded by an accidental are accented.*
- *Dissonances are stressed dynamically, while consonances and resolutions are relaxed and softer.* This idea is a general extension of the rule for appoggiaturas and epitomizes the dynamic-harmonic hierarchy discussed above.
- *Paired notes form a strong-weak pattern.* Usually the paired notes are half the beat value (for example, eighth notes in common time) or less.
- *The final chord of a movement or section is always accented.* This point

is made by Kirnberger. An exception would be the weak-ending cadence characteristic, for instance, of some sarabandes.

Another basic, small-scale dynamic principle is almost certainly invariable for music of any period: a note of anticipation before the bar line is to be played more softly than the reiteration of the note at the bar line. Any lapse of this rule (within common-practice styles) sounds quite graceless.

The dynamic aspect of ornaments is discussed in chapter 9.

Just as slurs have a dynamic significance, so may dots and dashes. Dots sometimes indicate equality of emphasis and evenness of stress (as well as an even rhythmic treatment), rather than detachment per se, although detachment is usually the best way to articulate for this function. In the notation of François Couperin and other French baroque composers, dots signify that the notes are not to be played with the (usually long-short) style of inequality that might otherwise apply (see chapter 8). The equal stress indicated by dots can imply a certain emphasis, along with equality of stress—for instance, in what appear to the modern player to be staccato markings in Variation XVI of the *Goldberg Variations* (see Example 4-6). In fact, the passage probably should be realized with detached or staccato notes; but rhythmic equality may be the markings' primary meaning.

Example 4-5. E. W. Wolf, illustration of tied notes that receive stress.

Example 4-6. Bach, Variation XVI, *Goldberg Variations*, BWV 988, mm. 8–9.

I will end this discussion with two small, pragmatic points for performance.

Long notes can be made to sustain further by giving them a slight dynamic ictus minutely above what they might otherwise be expected to receive. This is as effective in playing Bach on the clavichord or piano as in playing Chopin. Sustained notes, rendered one step louder than the dynamic context, both last longer and sustain at a slightly higher volume level than they would otherwise.

Realization of dynamic markings, whether your own or those of the composer, is akin to trying to recapture the original impetus that produced a poem when giving a reading of that poem. You have to feel your way back to that impetus. Any player can give a technically correct rendition of dynamic markings, but the result can be perfunctory. To find the heart of a composition, one must find what those dynamic markings are getting at. After all, such markings, however detailed, are a notational crudity that attempts to convey the subtleties of musical drive.

SUGGESTIONS FOR FURTHER READING

Marshall, Robert L. "Tempo and Dynamic Indications in the Bach Sources: A Review of the Terminology." In *Bach, Handel, Scarlatti: Tercentenary Essays*, edited by Peter Williams. Cambridge: Cambridge University Press, 1985.

Quantz, Johann Joachim. *On Playing the Flute*, 253–260. Translated by Edward R. Reilly. London: Faber, 1966. [Comments on harmony and dynamics.]

Stauffer, George. "Bach's Organ Registration Reconsidered." In *J. S. Bach as Organist: His Instruments, Music, and Performance Practices*, edited by George Stauffer and Ernest May. Bloomington: Indiana University Press, 1986.

Chapter 5

ARTICULATION

In the broad sense, *articulation* refers to musical enunciation in general: phrasing, legato, staccato, dynamics, and so forth. In the narrower sense, the word is often used to refer to separation of notes. Many subtle gradings are possible along the continuum of connected, barely connected, and detached notes. These shadings, and their effect on musical enunciation, can best be compared to the effects on spoken enunciation of different consonants and ways of projecting.

There is an unfortunate tendency in some modern studies to suggest that articulation in the early eighteenth century and before was rather undifferentiated, and that the delicacy of shading that we associate with later music was just emerging. This attitude seems to derive from the scarcity of performance notations (such as slurs, dots, and dynamics) in the period. However, printed music, including Bach's own, often has more performance directions than do manuscript copies because it is aimed at a wider audience: the manuscript copies were made in the composer's immediate environment, by and for use by initiates. Besides, the composers and performers of any era are just as intrinsically capable of delicate expression than those of later generations. The final word in dismissing this crude notion is to cite the case of Froberger, whose music required such precise nuances that it was said one could not play it properly unless one learned it directly from the composer.

Bach himself suggested a cantabile style of playing in the preface to his inventions. A singing line is as necessary to the performance of Bach's music as to Chopin's, although its musical nature is different and its effects are arrived at often by vastly different means.

Chapter 5

GENERAL ARTICULATORY STYLES

In Bach's day, music written in the slower meters tended to be heavier than that in brisk meters (see chapter 7). Thus, 3/2 signified a slow tempo and a more sedate, and indeed often more connected, style than that appropriate to a "light" meter such as 3/8. In terms of general approaches to articulation, the conservative Kirnberger's suggestions regarding heavy and light meters correspond with the more *galant*-oriented Daniel Gottlob Türk on "heavy" as opposed to "light" style. Türk contrasts the use of heavy style, characterized by firm tone and fully sustained notes and suited to serious sonatas, fugues, and religious pieces, with "light style," less emphatic and characterized by more detached playing, and applicable to playful and lively movements. The systematic but realistic Türk comments that both qualities may be found within a single movement. These remarks reflect musical common sense, whether of the eighteenth century or today—in contrast to many assertions by modern commentators who lay great emphasis on detached articulation as a norm.

"ORDINARY MOVEMENT"

There are various degrees of note connection and separation. Today, legato tends to mean, to the pianist or organist, a smooth connection of notes. In coordination with the very clear articulation of the earlier keyboard instruments, the period descriptions tend to define (and often illustrate) legato as the holding of one note into the next: what we would call overlapping legato, or legatissimo. For notes that are neither slurred nor detached, the baroque and classical treatises specify "ordinary movement"—that is, a simple, clear connection or near-connection of tones, neither detached nor running together. To produce the effect of a simple connection of notes when playing in a resonant room, the keyboard player must sometimes render them with extremely slight detachment, which the room acoustic fills in. The listener perceives an effect of simple linkage. Organists, accustomed to resonant spaces, are well aware of this relationship. Ordinary movement is often today called structured legato, a term that suggests both the overall effect of linkage and the diversity of means required to produce it in differing acoustics. The motion at the keyboard ranges from a scissorlike movement between successive fingers as they move from note to note (in a dry acoustic), to the effect produced by using the same finger on successive notes down the scale, holding each as long as possible and attacking every new note with the same motion with which the previous one is released. One connects the sequence as much as possible, but it is not in fact quite connected. This approach, or one with more note separation, suits resonant rooms.

Note that structured legato can ease the negotiation of a passage that is very difficult to manage in true legato. The effect remains smooth, and indeed clearer in many cases, when this articulation is managed evenly. Such an approach frees the fingers from complicated fingerings. To play everything with a close, gummy legato becomes a technical challenge in some contexts and is generally unnecessary. Structured legato is a very useful, neutral point of departure.

LEGATO

It is a common misconception that legato at the keyboard was unheard of or very unusual in the early eighteenth century and before. However, legato is mentioned in connection with the keyboard at least as far back as the early seventeenth century.

Legato has always been primarily associated with the voice and with bowed instruments. Stringed keyboard instruments, in the past as now, were considered to lack the true legato that characterizes the voice or, for instance, the violin. Stringed keyboards are unable to link successive notes at the same volume, since they die away on the instrument. Even the organist was directed to use overlegato in some baroque sources: despite the organ's uniform sustaining power, one finger was not to be raised until after the succeeding note had begun to sound. So "legato" on the keyboard simply refers to the keyboard's best efforts at imitating string or vocal legato.

Overlegato is sometimes found written out, though it is relatively rare in Bach's notation. An example can be found in the Presto of the Italian Concerto (Example 5-1a). This passage could have been written simply as eighth notes, but Bach groups it in half- and quarter-note units with overlegato in the soprano voice. Badura-Skoda cites similar writing in the cadence before the double bar in the Allemande of Partita No. 1 (Example 5-1b) and suggests that this approach should also apply to the final cadence of the same movement. It has often been pointed out that Menuet I of Partita No. 1 employs a shorthand for this kind of sustaining, comparable to the way Bach copied Couperin's "Les Bergeries" in the 1725 *Clavierbüchlein für Anna Magdalena Bach* (Example 5-1c and d). Couperin's careful two-part accompaniment is merely sketched, in Bach's notation, as a single line, without any indication of the relative sustaining of parts. This approach seems to appear often in Bach's keyboard notation and invites a more sustained realization. However, context remains all-important. David Schulenberg points to an example of written-out sustained nota-

Example 5-1a–d. (a) Bach, Presto, Italian Concerto, BWV 971, mm. 17–19; (b) Bach, Allemande, Partita No. 1, mm. 16–18; (c) F. Couperin, "Les Bergeries," Ordre 6, mm. 1–3; (d) F. Couperin, "Les Bergeries," Ordre 6, mm. 1–3, as notated by Bach.

tion in Prelude No. 12, *WTC* 1, and suggests that therefore other tones in the movement should not be held beyond their written value (Schulenberg, 183).

For the baroque musician, many musical contexts automatically called for legato; it did not have to be indicated by slurs or otherwise. By context, I mean the musical style, instrumental idiom, harmony, texture, relationship of the values of the slurred notes to the beat value, and similar considerations. Conventional applications of unnotated legato and overlegato included:

- Successive notes sung to a single syllable
- Repeated notes, which were to be as smooth as the rest of the line (not virtuosic strings of repetitions, but notes occasionally repeated in the course of a normal line)
- Appoggiaturas and other stepwise melodic ornaments
- Accented passing tones. "Passages in which passing notes or appoggiaturas are struck against a bass are played legato in all tempos even in the absence of a slur" (C. P. E. Bach, *Essay*, 155)
- "Sigh" figures
- Lombardic figures (often)
- Many ornaments
- Most embellishmental gestures
- Arpeggios (It was conventional to hold the tones of broken chords, whether or not a slur is notated. Michel de Saint Lambert mentions that a slur over a written-out arpeggio indicates that all the tones are to be sustained together. Bach uses this notation in, for example, the final [arpeggiated] chord of Fugue No. 10, *WTC* 1.)
- *Style brisé* textures
- Fast scalar runs and flourishes (although legato would not have been the only possibility for their articulation)
- Harpsichord and organ continuo articulation (legato is recommended by many authorities throughout the baroque era; harpsichord continuo often uses *brisé* textures)
- Organ *plein jeu* textures (at least in some French styles)
- Pieces in the "heavy style": fugues, adagios, and serious music generally (all fundamentally legato in style)
- Dotted rhythmic figures (the long note is generally held full length, although an articulatory rest can also be introduced before the short note)

DETACHMENT AND STACCATO

In eighteenth-century notation, articulatory dots have several meanings. These include accentual detachment and staccato as well as a gentle, *piano* release. At times, dots signify accents, with or without separation. At yet other times they have a preventative meaning, already touched on, that is quite outside today's norms: where inequality might otherwise be expected, dots on the notes cancel the inequality. (On this and other aspects of inequality, see chapter 8). Although they appear to the modern eye to signify staccato, their meaning in this context is entirely rhythmic.

A dot or dash, then, can mean accent, detachment, or equality of rhythm; the context is the determining factor. Some cases are by no means clear. Baroque articulation makes many distinctions without a difference in notation.

Pianists often think in terms of a uniform articulation, for instance a passage in even staccato. This kind of approach is hardly ever relevant to baroque music or instruments. The music's enunciation most often requires constant variation in articulation, as in dynamics; and with the harpsichord, these are often one and the same. A uniform touch and articulation are rarely effective on either the harpsichord or the clavichord. Successive notes will usually be shaped by varying durations. A uniform staccato, for example, is scarcely ever in keeping with Bach's or the instrument's requirements, and legato groups, too, are shaded by variations in the degree of overlap. On the piano, one should avoid using hard attacks to make an emphasis. Accents are usually most effective when created by subtle dynamics or with time and duration (agogics).

The early instruments discourage the frequent modern tendency to associate a little accent on each note with detached and staccato playing. Detached releases can vary in effect from sharp to lingering. The player must cultivate the fine line between an accentual detachment and the minutely greater duration that removes the accent when it is not required. Above all, it is important to hear and render slightly detached notes in their logical groupings.

SLUR MEANINGS

Before discussing Bach's use of slurs, I must clarify their general meanings, as baroque usage is quite different from that of modern times.

The eighteenth-century keyboard slur comprises several meanings even at its most basic level: (1) a strong overlegato; (2) a slight accent at the start of the slurred group; (3) a slight diminuendo through the group; and (4) a new ictus following the end of the slurred group. How a slurred group or a succession of them is realized by the performer depends on many contextual factors. Not every slur ending needs to be marked by a gap in sound; often the accent (made dynamically, agogically, or otherwise) beginning the next group is sufficient. Indeed, in some contexts, gaps between successive slurs can often sound excessive or affected. Frequently the main reason for notating slurred groups is to show the distribution of accent. The question for the player is, "What is an appropriate way to render the composer's indications of punctuation?" The realization depends on the particular instrument, musical context, and acoustic. Similarly, someone reading prose or poetry aloud has to make choices among various options in rendering the punctuation and groupings of the author's words. In both cases, a very few multipurpose signs are used to convey a wide range of effects. There are even fewer for music than for words: slurs and dots have to perform many duties, whereas a writer can choose among comma, colon, semicolon, quotation marks, and period, each of which signifies a different kind and degree of pause or accent. Musical context and the player's taste must decide the meaning in every case.

In baroque usage, slurred groups are usually short, from two to perhaps eight notes. Exceptions to this tendency are rare. Long slurs remained unusual throughout the eighteenth century; the change from short to longer slurred groups occurred largely during Beethoven's life. What Beethoven notated as short slurred groups early in his career can often be read as accented groups played as if under a larger slur, and were so notated in later editions. His articulatory notation was adjusted to the latter style during his life and after; and in fact, the newer notational style is often applicable to eighteenth-century slurrings. Again, this is because the slurs generally indicate subphrases, not phrases.

With slurring, context is all-important—the tempo, meter, prevailing harmony, and note values. If the slurs group notes in pairs or in fours, what is the relationship of those note values to the beat value? If the meter is common time and eighth notes are slurred in pairs, the meaning and realization of the slurring may well be different from what they would be for quarter notes slurred in pairs in the same meter. Also important is the suggestion of other media by the keyboard. Slurs may mean one thing when the music is imitating the violin, another in the context of keyboard-idiomatic *style brisé*.

NOTATIONAL HABITS

A vast amount of seventeenth- and eighteenth-century keyboard music is notated with scarcely any articulatory markings, for several reasons:

1. The conventions for applying legato or detachment to certain contexts were well understood.
2. Slurs indicated heavy legato, accents, and other particulars, not generically smooth playing. Therefore, they were sometimes required to show unusual accent patterns and other details of phrasing. They were not used to show undifferentiated smoothness, which is not especially characteristic of the style in any case.

3. Notation of slurs in detail was unreasonable in view of the diversity of instruments that might be used for a given score. At a clavichord, harpsichord, fortepiano, or organ, a player might have to take differing approaches with one and the same composition.
4. The composers produced so much music that often they simply did not go to the trouble, just as Handel often neglected to write in ornaments.

Articulatory notation involves too many contextual considerations, at least in the notation of keyboard music, to allow widespread use of slurs. For a violinist, a slur means, "Play all of the notes under the slur in a single bowstroke." Such direct physicality is not even a partial solution for the multiple meanings of the slur with which the keyboard player is faced. Thus, in keyboard music, slurs had to be used sparingly so that when they did appear, they would be meaningful.

If articulation was notated at all, eighteenth-century notational habits often involved marking slurs, dots, or dashes on the first instances of any figuration requiring them, leaving it to the player to continue to articulate with those patterns even if the markings are omitted from further iterations of that musical figuration. Thus, in the rare instances where Bach marks a fugue subject with slurs or dots, these usually occur only on the first appearance(s) of the subject and thereafter are left for the performer to supply. Similar treatment was expected for ornaments, for instance in fugue subjects. A characteristic trill in a subject might be notated only once or a few times, but it was intended to appear throughout the fugue wherever feasible.

Any effect of accent or articulation that departs from the norms would have to be especially notated. Therefore, something as eccentric as playing the flowing Allemande of Partita No. 1 in pairwise sixteenths would have required Bach to write in a multitude of two-note slurs. An odd slur in a line or composition that is otherwise notable for the absence of articulatory signs probably indicates not a sudden moment of legato, but an accent or other musical function (such as an ornament group) that in the composer's opinion required elucidation.

BACH'S ARTICULATORY NOTATION

Bach's keyboard notation is notably sparing of articulatory signs. A search through the *WTC* yields almost nothing except occasional notation of pairwise slurring, and this situation is generally true of the composer's other keyboard works, for both clavier and organ. Parts 2 and 3 of the *Clavierübung* are exceptional: both volumes are surprisingly full of slurs, dots, and combinations of the two. Possibly this richness of notation in Part 2 reflects the fact that these works evoke the orchestra. In any case, one must turn to Bach's ensemble music to find comparably lavish use of slurs, dots, and dashes.

Bach's notation of slurs is sometimes puzzling to modern musicians, even specialists, because it is not always clear which notes the slurs are intended to cover. For instance, full-measure slurs are sometimes marked high above the notes with small arcs whose meaning was clear to the composer and, one expects, to his circle of students, but has to be learned by those accustomed to modern printed music. Some modern editors appear to make mistakes when they take, so to speak, a microscope to Bach's manuscript and mechanically decide which notes a careless slur is meant to embrace. Some unlikely results can follow. These are uncertain waters, but a useful rule of thumb is to assume that the less clear a slur is, the more generic its meaning, as in two-note or full-measure slurs. Unusual slurring would be shown with more care—or so one hopes. In any case, bizarre slurring patterns in a modern edition should be considered in terms of these factors.

Bach used the slur in his keyboard writing for various purposes, including:

1. To indicate ornament groups. Appoggiaturas are invariably to be played with a heavy legato connection to the resolution, but Bach is often punctilious about including the (rather redundant) slur for this context. (For example, his emendations to the print of *Clavierübung* 1 include many additions of slurs to appoggiatura figures; the slurs had been omitted by the engraver.) The afterbeats to trills are sometimes notated with a slur to clarify that they belong to the trills themselves. Similarly, written-out ornamental groups (such as slides) are often found with slurs that confirm their identity as ornaments.

2. To indicate an accent on the first note of a group. Of course, the ensuing legato and diminuendo in the slurred group reinforce the opening accent by their contrast with it: the accent initiates a smoothly flowing group. The most frequent use of slurs to show accent groups is in connection with subphrases. Such usage accounts for the majority of the small number of slurs found in the *WTC*, with descending (or occasionally ascending) conjunct pairs of notes, generally of half the beat value or less. (See also, for instance, the Largo of Trio Sonata No. 2.) In Example 5-2a, the shift from full-measure figuration (at the opening) to beat-level units is reinforced by the pairwise slurring. Notes slurred in pairs make a strong-weak motion on each pair. Here as else-

where, there are many ways the slur may be rendered: the combination of a slight agogic accent on the first note of each pair with overlegato slurring is as much an option as distinctly separating each pair.

Sometimes in the course of a movement of largely sixteenth notes, only a stray group of three or four sixteenths is slurred. Such slurs indicate either a change of accent or an ornamental function. In Example 5-2b, the first and fourth notes of the soprano in beat 2 of m. 10 are the principal notes, and the two in between are shown by the slur to be ornamental follow-through from the first note of the slurred group.

Example 5-2a, b. (a) Bach, Fugue No. 21, *WTC* 2, BWV 890ii, mm. 1–5; (b) Bach, Allemande, English Suite No. 6, BWV 811, mm. 9–10.

3. To show large phrase units. This notation is comparatively rare in Bach's music, especially in the keyboard works. The most extravagant instance (perhaps in all string writing) appears in Suite No. 4 for Solo Cello. In three of the four principal source manuscripts, it is slurred as in Example 5-3.

   Long flourishes are sometimes slurred to produce a single, arching sweep of energy. Several examples occur in the first canon from *The Art of Fugue*.

4. To show the holding-through of chord tones. This was a notational convention of the time. See Example 5-4a and b. Another example is found in the slurring of the figurated chords in Prelude No. 6, *WTC* 2.

Example 5-3. Bach, Prelude, Suite No. 4 for Solo Cello, BWV 1010, mm. 49–52.

5. To imitate string and orchestral idioms. Many slurs, particularly slurs in combination with dots, suggest string bowings. Some of these appear in Example 5-4c. The opening of English Suite No. 4 (Example 5-4d) appears with dashes on every note in one of the manuscript sources (no autograph copy is known to have survived). In this imitation of an orchestral idiom, the dashes mean not staccatissimo, but a detached and more or less uniformly weighted style in imitation of orchestral string bowing.

Notes that are set apart in the line—that is, that are noticeably higher or lower than the general context—often require dynamic highlighting. This effect is sometimes suggested by slurring in violin music, isolating the accented notes from a slurred context (see Example 5-5a). Many of the slurrings in the Italian Concerto suggest violin slurrings (Example 5-5b).

6. Occasionally to modify the groupings otherwise implied by the time signature and/or the tempo indication. For instance, in the chorale partita *Christ, der du bist der helle Tag*, the second movement, marked largo, is in common time with sixteenth-note motion. As it stands, this notation could readily lead the player to group the sixteenths in terms of an eighth-note beat ("largo" modifying the quarter-note beats of the C signature), but Bach heads off this tendency by slurring the sixteenths in groups of four (see Example 5-6a). Similarly, in Contrapunctus II of *The Art of Fugue*, the quarter-note-value dotted figures are slurred in half-note units, reinforcing the *alla breve* time signature. Full-measure slurs are found occasionally, as in Invention No. 9. In Bach's autograph manuscript of the organ trio sonatas, full-measure slurs are frequently found in both fast and slow movements—for instance, the Largo (in 3/4 time) of Organ Trio Sonata No. 2. Such instances are phrasing slurs: they draw the ear to units larger than the metric units.

7. Slurs are occasionally used to alert the player to a change in pattern. Thus, when the note groupings in Example 5-6b change from six to

Example 5-4a–d. (a) Bach, Fugue No. 10, *WTC* 1, BWV 855ii, m. 42 as notated by Bach; (b) the meaning of the notation; (c) Bach, Bourrée I, English Suite No. 1, BWV 806, mm. 30–33; (d) Bach, Prelude, English Suite No. 4, BWV 809, m. 1.

four and the meter shifts from the notated 12/8 to essentially common time, the new four-note groupings are marked by accentual dots and slurs.

8. The lengthy rapid scales in the first movement of the Concerto for Two Claviers in C Major (BWV 1061) are highly suggestive of glissando treatment.

Bach uses dots or dashes to indicate detached or staccato notes, accented notes, and rhythmic equality. Detached, accented notes that would likely be rendered with some form of heavy staccato are found in the subject of Fugue No. 10, *WTC* 2 (Example 5-7a). These markings appear as dots in the auto-

Example 5-5a, b. (a) Bach, Allegro assai, Violin Sonata No. 3, BWV 1005, mm. 7–9; (b) Bach, Presto, Italian Concerto, BWV 971, mm. 59–62.

Example 5-6a, b. (a) Bach, Partita No. 2, *Christ, der du bist der helle Tag*, BWV 766, mm. 1–2; (b) Bach, Canon alla Decima, *The Art of Fugue*, BWV 1080, mm. 78–80.

graph manuscript, though some editions (such as Bischoff's) render them as dashes. A rather uniform accent and detachment seems to be indicated by the dots assigned to the fugato subject in the Grave of the Overture in the French Manner.

Example 5-7a, b. (a) Bach, Fugue No. 10, *WTC* 2, BWV 879ii, mm. 1–4; (b) Bach, Grave, Overture in the French Manner, BWV 831, mm. 20–22.

A light staccato or detachment is probably signified by the dots in Example 5-8a, notated in the light 6/16 meter.

Accentual dots that do not necessarily mean especial detachment appear in Example 5-8b. This passage is a transcription of an orchestral tutti passage. Since the first chord, and likely the following two, are to be arpeggiated, the dots probably signify equal stress on all three chords, in case the sense of metric stress gets lost in three arpeggiations of the same chord. Whether a detached effect is appropriate would be entirely up to the player's management of the passage in terms of the particular instrument used.

Certainly the dots in Example 5-9a, from the Sarabande of English Suite No. 5, signify rhythmic equality. (The dots appear in late copies of this work.) The eighth notes with which the dots appear are half of the beat value and are eligible for inequality. Whether detachment applies is up to the player; a modern staccato is not applicable.

As mentioned, both the vertical dash and the dot can mean accent, pure and simple, with no implication of detachment. This becomes particularly obvious when the first note under a slur also carries a dot or a dash. Bach's pupil Johann Gottfried Müthel frequently used dashes and dots in this way (see Example 5-9b), and the combination seems to appear in the revised engraving of *Clavierübung* 2 (Example 5-9c).

Example 5-8a, b. (a) Bach, Fugue No. 11, *WTC 2*, BWV 880ii, mm. 1–4; (b) Bach, Largo, Concerto No. 7 in F Major, BWV 978, after Vivaldi, Concerto, Op. 3 No. 3, mm. 1–2.

UPBEAT SLURRING

In the nineteenth century, a tendency developed to slur across the bar line. Certainly this effect often appears clearly in eighteenth-century notation, but it is usually characteristic of melodies over a bass whose rhythm and punctuation keep the meter clear. As a general approach, however, slurring across the bar line can blur the meter and/or create a heavy effect that is sometimes deadening to a lively movement. For instance, an upbeat slurred to the downbeat, when rendered on the harpsichord, can readily suggest that the upbeat *is* the downbeat. This is particularly a risk with fugue subjects and other unaccompanied lines (see Example 5-10).

A slur across the bar line can be effective on the piano because of the dynamic impetus available on the bar-line note. To stress the bar line, the harpsichordist usually has to make an accent through agogics or detachment. A linkage of small-level melodic units moving across the bar can be animated by maintaining a sense of the metric accent. Baroque music often seems to thrive on the tension between the accents of the metric frame and the forward drive of motivic and other phrase units.

Example 5-9a, b, c. (a) Bach, Sarabande, English Suite No. 5, BWV 810, mm. 1–2; (b) Müthel, Adagio mesto e sostenuto, Duetto for 2 Claviers, m. 76; (c) Bach, Gavotte II, Overture in the French Manner, BWV 831, mm. 13–16.

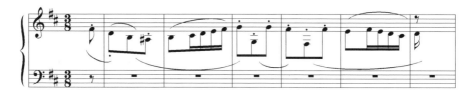

Example 5-10. Bach, Fugue No. 24, *WTC* 2, BWV 893ii, mm. 1–6, slurred variously.

RESTS AND RELEASES

The way rests are observed can provide considerable energy, or reduce it. For instance, at the beginning of the Capriccio of Partita No. 2, the opening third in the left hand is heavy if held too long and lacks weight if held too briefly. If one listens from the continuo player's perspective, it is easier to hit on the right short gust of sound, released so as not to detract from the energy of the ascending perfect fourth in the right hand. Similarly, many notes need efficient or even early release in movements that imitate orchestral sounds, such as the Overture to Partita No. 4 or Variation XVI of the *Goldberg Variations*. If a note has to be released early for technical reasons (in a difficult stretch, for instance), it should be held long enough to allow its release to go unnoticed, rather than released as quickly as a staccato or otherwise accented note.

It is often useful to the overall sonority to release many unimportant notes somewhat early, although this depends entirely upon the context. Holding an unimportant note can put too much stress on it, making it too heavy, even causing it to drag. Again, the careful realization of rests is necessary for the same reason.

ARTICULATION OF THEMES AND MOTIVES

There are two primary modern schools of thought about the articulation of thematic and motivic material. One advocates inflexible consistency: once a fugue subject is stated, the articulation first heard must be replicated every time the subject recurs. The other approach allows some variability, although the basic shape must be maintained. I am of the latter persuasion. Certainly, the outlines of a theme sometimes require more highlighting at their initial presentation(s) than is necessary or even tasteful upon subsequent restatements. The degree of highlighting depends upon the harmonic and tonal drama of subsequent contexts and the contrapuntal context. In some stretti, trying to stress every iteration of a motive might well end up stressing nothing: often the player must consider a larger aspect of phrasing. Changes of articulation, if made, should probably accentuate or soften the initial shaping rather than present a different picture altogether. The effect of a given articulation pattern frequently has to be modified in intensity or for clarity's sake, depending on whether the motive is heard in the treble, middle range, or bass.

Chapter 5

SUGGESTIONS FOR FURTHER READING

Butt, John. *Bach Interpretation: Articulation Marks in Primary Sources of J. S. Bach.* Cambridge: Cambridge University Press, 1990.

Cooper, Kenneth, and Julius Zasko. "Georg Muffat's Observations on the Lully Style of Performance." *Musical Quarterly* 53 (1967): 223–230. [Muffat on string bowings.]

Quantz, Johann Joachim. *On Playing the Flute*, 71–90. Translated by Edward R. Reilly. London: Faber, 1966. [A discussion of flute tonguings.]

Chapter 6

PHRASING AND ACCENT

Baroque music is sometimes spoken of as if it were composed only on a local level, without regard to the larger picture—that is, without large-scale lines or direction. How this idea took root is difficult to understand. Even a casual look at Bach's intricate structures shows that the music is clearly organized from the smallest to the largest levels. An intelligent performance is one that enunciates these elements, or at least allows them to emerge, in their natural hierarchy of balanced emphasis. The music indeed has a long line, although not usually in the urgent sense that characterizes much nineteenth-century music. A work by Bach usually comprises a diversity of motivic units (sometimes of contrasting energy) that can accumulate in a long, arching line. The nineteenth-century line, on the other hand, tends to move forward to one major goal with fewer contrasts than a baroque line. The nineteenth-century line is fairly direct in the requirements it makes for clear rendition. In Bach, one often has to consider a more complex hierarchy. To override the contours and contrasts within a baroque phrase and force them into a nineteenth-century uniformity is to flatten out a garden with a steamroller.

It is foolish to describe playing that acknowledges different phrase levels as "inauthentic" or "nineteenth century." I have heard the comment that a performance had "an almost nineteenth-century sense of phrase—but I liked it!" as if a sense of hierarchy in phrasing were something that required apology, rather than praise.

In this chapter I will discuss musical accents, scansion (strong and weak phrase units), phrase levels (subphrase, phrase, period), contrasts within and between phrases, and some aspects of performance.

Chapter 6

ACCENT

Kirnberger remarks, "But how can the musician ever perform well—that is, how can he make each phrase and motif in the musical period be heard, also indicate each accent, if he does not know all the different kinds of phrases and the accents appropriate to each kind? . . . What sort of movement and what character are appropriate to each kind of measure?" (Kirnberger, *Recueil*, 67).

Fundamentally, any change in continuity can create a musical accent, because that change attracts the ear's attention. What may be called natural or inherent accents in music are those inherent elements that draw the ear: melodic groupings, changes in harmony and texture, sudden shifts of range, and the like. Accents available to the player include dynamics, agogics, detached notes, articulations before notes that are to be stressed, and the underlining of textural nuance. Naturally, performance accents are most successful when they coordinate with the music's natural accents to bring out the its inherent contours. When performance devices call attention to themselves, either because they are exaggerated or because they are not coordinated with the inherent musical structure, the result is a mannered playing style.

In the seventeenth and eighteenth centuries, one point of departure for musical accent was the meter, which had a framework of relative accent strengths associated with it. In modern times, the metric frame is usually seen as organizing a sequence of equal pulses. They are rendered neutrally unless otherwise marked with accents and dynamics. Instead, a diversity of pulse organization was assumed in the baroque and classical eras, and it is further diversified by variations of scansion and stress.

The foregoing must not be taken to mean that a crude emphasis of the bar line and other important beats must be blindly followed. The modern trend one sometimes encounters of strong metric articulation (especially at the bar line) stems in large part from incomplete conclusions based on an equally incomplete assessment of eighteenth-century treatises. The metric hierarchy of strong and weak beats is often described in theoretical and performance treatises, but some players seem to base their performances in it without taking into account the larger aspects of phrasing: strong and weak measures, as described by various authors, and hierarchies that are self-evident in the music. According to Türk, metric accents are overridden by other inherent accents (such as harmonic stresses), and I believe this to be relevant to Bach even though Türk was writing in 1789. Irregular phrase lengths characterize much of the most interesting eighteenth-century music, from Bach to Mozart (see Edward Lowinsky's classic article on this subject in regard to Mozart, cited at the end of this chapter). For example, François Couperin's comma, which he describes in terms of a phrasing mark (and which, he specifies, should be "nearly imperceptible") embraces units of diverse lengths ranging from half a measure to half a dozen measures. This is not regular, "metric" phrasing. Uniformity of bar-line accent is often at odds with the music, and it frequently emerges as a mannerism.

While the sources mainly talk about beats and the bar line, several important authors, including Mattheson and Kirnberger, discuss larger phrasing issues. Both the treatises' commentaries and baroque slur notation often focus on subphrase rather than larger phrase, but the larger-scale organization of phrases, periods, and even larger-scale structures certainly did not happen by chance. Indeed, the series of successively larger levels that make up a musical composition were recognized by baroque theorists, some of whom compared the musical divisions to their parallels in written language: comma, semicolon, colon, period, paragraph, section, and chapter.

Eighteenth-century slurring primarily indicates subphrase levels, unlike the predominant nineteenth-century practice. Apparently it was deemed more important to make the subphrase groups clear than the larger phrases, which are more self-evident. Slurring is a notational device that can either reinforce the natural groupings or indicate groupings that would not otherwise be "normal." The beginning of a slur indicates a slight accent.

Most other stresses can override the metric accent: harmonic change, a strong turn in a melody, some ornaments, textural stresses, and so forth. Naturally, one of the primary sources of inherent musical accent is the harmonic progression. The player must be sensitive to the turning points in tonal direction, the characteristic, colorful shifts and chords, and the main dissonances. Dissonances are always strong, resolutions comparatively weak. It is important to consider the relative weight of the various dissonances and to bring them out appropriately. As an exercise in this way of thinking, one can try playing a movement such as Prelude No. 16, *WTC* 2, without the surface figuration, as chorale-style chords in order to bring out the points of tension and repose. The next step is to orient the surface material to that chordal progression, thinking of the figuration as elaboration of the chords.

Many contexts were understood to require accent (as described in chapter 5), and musicians of the time did not necessarily require articulatory signs to convey the expected accents. Degrees of accent can apply automatically to beats and beat subdivisions, to the measure, to groups of measures, and to various contexts. In general, beats were considered strong and offbeats weak (except in the case of syncopation, when the offbeats are accented). Onbeat, metrically accented notes were sometimes termed "good," "strong," or "long" (in the sense of poetic "long," meaning inwardly stressed; the word has nothing to do with actual duration). Offbeat, unaccented notes were called "bad," "weak," or "short" (again, using the terminology of poetry).

The basis of baroque music in the framework of metric beats extends beyond the boundaries of the measure itself to measure-to-measure relationships. This larger level is not discussed as often in treatises of the period as the smaller levels, because fewer authors go beyond outlining the basics. However, several make very clear statements. The material has been summarized by Anthony Newman in his groundbreaking work on the subject (Newman, 51). Kirnberger mentions that "in duple as well as in triple meter, there are melodies in which it is obvious that whole measures are alternately heavy and light so that one feels an entire measure as only one beat. . . . [In this case,] two measures must necessarily be grouped together to make just one, whose first part is long [strong] and the other short [weak]" (Kirnberger, 398). In the same way, Leopold Mozart, in his violin treatise of 1756, offers bowings for 3/8 measures that make alternate measures strong and weak. Wolfgang Kaspar Printz (1696) mentions that the odd-numbered measures are intrinsically stronger than the even-numbered. These descriptions agree in recognizing the quite natural diversity in strength that will occur in a succession of measures. They all describe the strong-weak-strong-weak sequence Printz suggests as a norm. Indeed, the pattern occurs frequently. Naturally, the possible permutations are extremely diverse. Kirnberger's "grouped-together measures" also allow for such irregularities as phrases cadencing in the middle of the measure rather than at the bar line, as happens frequently in Bach's writing.

METRIC VARIATION

Varied metric groupings are often to be found, especially in triple and compound meters, although they are veiled behind the regularity of the notated meter. Thus, Variation VIII of the *Goldberg Variations* combines 3/4 and 6/8 meters simultaneously (Example 6-1a). The fugato of the Overture in the French Manner shows areas in 3/8, 3/4, and 9/8 as well as the notated 6/8; and the 6/8 scansion itself is often removed from the bar line by a half measure (Example 6-1b). Other examples include Prelude No. 4 and Fugue No. 11, *WTC* 2.

A very standard metrical effect in music generally, and in baroque music in particular, is hemiola. Hemiola is defined as a regrouping of pulses into duple groups from a triple or compound-time pattern. Quarter notes in 3/4 time normally move in groups of three; in hemiola, two measures that are usually grouped as 3 + 3 would be regrouped as 2 + 2 + 2. Note that hemiolas can

Example 6-1a, b. (a) Bach, Variation VIII, *Goldberg Variations*, BWV 988, mm. 1–3; (b) Bach, Grave, Overture in the French Manner, BWV 831, mm. 71–77.

occur with and without a noticeable accent on the second group. Of course, the first group receives whatever degree of accent is natural to it without providing any cue as to the regrouping about to occur.

Sometimes the texture or harmonic rhythm accentuates all three units of the regrouping. In other cases, the accent is left implicit on the second group, so that groups 1 and 3 are the most marked. Since the normal hemiola begins at a written bar line, it is the accent on the second beat of the second measure of the unit that defines the hemiola's presence (see Figure 1). In short, many nuances are possible.

As discussed in chapter 2, Bach's dance movements make the most of the different styles' opportunities for variety of accent. In some movements there are hardly two consecutive measures that show the same pattern of accents.

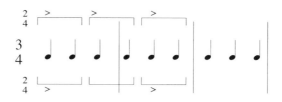

Figure 1. Hemiolas with and without accent on the second group.

MUSICAL SCANSION

In addition to the variety of accent and grouping that is possible under the metric levels just enumerated, much further variation can be found in different patterns of strong-to-weak or weak-to-strong in subphrases, phrases, and larger units. This aspect is more complex and in some ways more important than metric accent, and (like almost any other factor) overrides the metric accent. (For instance, if an accent pattern puts a normally strong bar line in a weak position, it should be played as weak, following the scansion instead of the metric hierarchy.) Borrowing another term from poetic analysis, we refer to this range of accent patterning as "scansion." To make an analogy to gardening, the meter is only a frame; the varieties of scansion are like the infinitely varied leaves and tendrils of the musical vine that grows over the frame.

Fundamentally, musical phrases and subphrases tend to move either from strong to weak or from weak to strong. In poetry, the unit (foot) made up of two syllables that move from strong to weak is called a trochee. An example of such a pattern is the name Henry: the accent on the first syllable makes the name trochaic. In speaking of music, "trochaic" can refer generally to small- or large-scale motion, as in movement from one note to another or in the overall course of a phrase. Similarly, weak-to-strong motion in poetry is iambic, as in the word *stampede*, accented on the second syllable. Weak-to-strong shaping in music can be called generically iambic. (In this discussion, I am using "iambic" and "trochaic" in a general sense as signifying accent at the beginning or ending of a unit, of whatever size, rather than in their narrower poetic sense of a two-syllable or two-note pattern.)

In chapter 6 of his *Der vollkommene Capellmeister* (The Complete Capellmeister; 1739), Johann Mattheson discusses "tone-feet," the smallest rhythmic units. He shows many varieties, of two, three, and four syllables—that is, of two, three, and four note values. These correspond to poetic feet of various accent patterns: the spondee, pyrrhic, dactyl, anapest, tribrach, and others, as well as iamb and trochee.

Many good examples of trochaic and iambic patterns are readily accessible in certain gigues by Bach. The Gigue of Partita No. 1 is trochaic on the level of the measure and iambic on the submeasure level. Each measure starts strong but is approached (except m. 1, of course) by an iambic upbeat (see Example 6-2a). The Gigue of English Suite No. 4 has an iambic "rocket" motive. The opening of the Gigue of French Suite No. 4 is a simple trochaic pattern. The subject of the Gigue of Partita No. 4 is trochaic, but the time signature of 9/16 indicates that the performance style is not to be very accentual. Finally, Invention No. 8 begins with an almost full-measure upbeat to the bar line. This pattern is of course iambic; a contrast to this shape is made by the trochaic groups of sixteenths that follow, which suggest an accent at the beginning of each measure.

In one sense, the language of baroque music tends to be more complex than nineteenth-century writing because of the diversity from subphrase to phrase to period. Each unit, from a two-note motive or rhythmic unit to a subphrase, phrase, or period, can be trochaic or iambic. Thus, for example, a series of trochaic subphrases may build up to make a larger phrase of iambic shape. Any combination is theoretically possible, and with a composer of Bach's caliber, one's expectation of variety is not disappointed. Bach's phrasing can resemble the multiple layers of an onion, each layer having a shape complete in itself and relating diversely to the other units (larger, smaller, or the same size) around it (Example 6-2b). Each layer can also have its own energy. While a series of phrase units may all develop similar energy (as in the motoric fugue, with a surface rhythm of uniform sixteenth notes, that concludes the Toccata in E Minor), it is also possible for each to have its own energy, and the effect of the piece as a whole may depend on the contrasts built in at these local levels. Therefore, the "steamroller" effect mentioned earlier, which flattens out this diversity, must be avoided.

Mattheson remarks that there are only twenty-six poetic tone-feet but that music has more rhythms than poetry. He quite charmingly ends his sixth chapter with the observation that the mathematical permutations of twenty-four tone-feet amount to 62,044,840,173,323,943,936,030—an example of music's incalculable variety.

It should be noted that generations of musicians were trained on Hugo Riemann's theory that, in the final analysis, all musical phrasing is iambic (weak-to-strong). This is a musical straitjacket if ever there was one; the student should beware the dangers of a one-size-fits-all approach to music.

Bach often phrases in two short units followed by a unit twice as long, so that after the two short impulses, their energy flowers in a single impulse of the

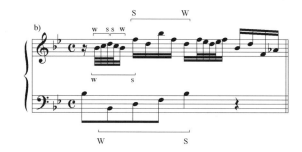

Example 6-2a, b. (a) Bach, Gigue, Partita No. 1, BWV 825, mm. 1–4; (b) Bach, Invention No. 14, BWV 785, m. 1.

same overall length. Thus, in Example 6-3, the quarter- and half-note impulses of m. 1 become half- and whole-note impulses in m. 2. The opening period flowers in the long unit from the second half of m. 4 to the downbeat of m. 6.

Kirnberger discusses variety in phrasing, including the relationships between regular and irregular phrasing. He remarks on what we would call subphrases ("rhythmic units"), which, without being fully separate from one another, are somewhat distinct and often articulated by shadings of harmony. These rhythmic units vary in length. "They can be of one to four, five, and even more measures in length, just as there are long and short lines in poetry" (Kirnberger, 408). Kirnberger observes further that the ear demands regularity in the number of measures in each phrase but indicates as well some typical instances where an irregular count is effective.

"Rounded playing" is a phrase Quantz uses in his treatise. It probably means giving follow-through to musical lines and finding the vital drive behind the linkage of varied subphrases and phrases. In other words, rounded playing is the opposite of conscientious but badly managed playing in which stops and starts damage the flow. An articulate but well-rounded performance presents all elements, local and large-scale, in due proportion, and is comparable to the long-line grace of a flawlessly performed athletic routine in which every detail

Example 6-3. Bach, Prelude No. 23, *WTC* 1, BWV 868i, mm. 1–6.

(head and hand movements as well as leaps and somersaults) is integrated into the overall choreography.

FIGURAL WRITING

A compositional technique frequently encountered in baroque music is construction of a movement from one or more short motives, often called figures. The word *figure* is used by analogy with "figures of speech," an important concept in spoken rhetoric. Rhetoric was used as the model for musical analysis in the baroque era. How the figural aspect is conveyed or treated in performance depends on the musical context and is discussed in chapter 12, which outlines the issues of musical rhetoric.

In the structuring of Bach's music from figures, we can find two basic approaches:

1. *Use of a single motive as the basis for an entire movement or a large section of a movement.* Examples are found readily in the *WTC*. The first twenty-four measures of Prelude No. 2, *WTC* 1, for instance, reiterate a motive in the right hand, and (roughly speaking) its inversion in the left, through many changes of harmony.

2. *Use of two or more motives in various vertical and lateral combinations.* Prelude No. 11, *WTC* 1, contrasts figures of sixteenth and eighth notes. These are heard in different vertical combinations (sixteenths in the soprano and eighths in the bass, and vice versa) and horizontal combinations: longer and shorter phrases that develop the motives in longer and shorter units. Prelude No. 12, *WTC* 2, contrasts the opening sigh figure (opening phrase) with a "busy" motive in sixteenths. These elements are presented in immediate juxtaposition, and then in various minglings through the course of the movement.

Naturally, the scansion of a piece is affected by the shape and accent pattern of each figure. Different figures may be of similar energy, or contrast with one another. Again, such small-level contrasts have to be brought out, not smoothed over.

TIMING IN THE *STYLUS PHANTASTICUS*

Freewheeling accent and timing, albeit with approximate signals from the rhythmic and metric notation, characterize the *stylus phantasticus* and passages in recitative style (as in the Chromatic Fantasia). The tempo is not strict, and the rhythms tend toward exaggeration rather than assimilation.

In the preface to his 1615 publication of toccatas, variations and other compositions, Frescobaldi described the free style of timing that was appropriate to these works. The most significant points for the modern player include:

1. *Freedom of tempo.* Frescobaldi compares the toccata's highly variable tempo to the performance of madrigals, whose tempo fluctuates according to the mood or sense of the text.
2. *Directions for the openings of toccatas.* The opening sections of toccatas are to be played slowly and arpeggiated. This point is important because it demonstrates the often unnotated flexibility of the free style. This slow treatment would not be otherwise inferred by the player from the notation; there are no specific signals to indicate a slow tempo.
3. *Application of ritardando to the conclusions of runs and cadenzas.* The latter, even when written in rapid notes, are played in a more "sustained" tempo than the notation suggests.

The tempo for this style was, to put it mildly, flexible.

Frescobaldi's pupil Froberger provided performance directions for some of his free-style pieces and for sections of stricter movements that change over to the free style. (Froberger admits free, toccatalike passages even to gigues.) Generally, he uses the word "discretion" to indicate the free style, but in the title to his lament for the deceased lutenist Blancrocher he elaborated on the meaning of this word: "Tombeau written in Paris upon the death of M. Blancheroche [*sic*]; to be played very slowly with discretion without observing precise measure" (*Tombeau fait a Paris sur la mort de Monsieur Blancheroche; lequel se joue fort lentement a la discretion sans observer aucune mesure*).

Some lines, especially virtuosic flourishes, form patterns that work against the notated metric pattern. Anthony Newman's book illustrates this feature with some famous passages from the Chromatic Fantasia, one of which appears in Example 6-4. The natural grouping of the note patterns would seem to take precedence over the metric notation. However, in some contexts the player may wish to consider how to project the delicate balance and tensions between the contrametric writing and the notated meter—a sort of super-syncopation. This is difficult but most rewarding when one is doing

Example 6-4. Bach, Chromatic Fantasia, BWV 903, mm. 65–68.

the most possible to bring out the elements that give such tensions to Bach's sinewy lines.

REITERATION OF NOTES

Another area in which the player can affect the accentual pattern is in choices of where to restrike sustained notes. The player is at full liberty to reiterate long notes that will not sustain on the instrument. The notation often presents only an ideal effect, which must be rendered according to the nature of the instrument at hand. Generally, the best places to renew are where renewal is least obtrusive, usually at the bar line (that is, at the bar lines that seem most apt) or beneath a heavy chord. However, renewing of notes can also help to create an accent. If upper chord members are dissonant to the bass, it can be effective to emphasize the dissonance by renewing the bass note at that point. The practice of reiterating sustained tones was very common. C. P. E. Bach takes it for granted when he warns the player not to restrike where the ear carries the imagination along and the literal re-sounding becomes counterproductive. The second Gavotte from English Suite No. 3 provides good examples of both contexts. Example 6-5 shows some possibilities for resounding the sustained bass G.

PHRASING AND DYNAMICS

Dynamics are of fundamental importance in bringing out phrase shape. Because of a kind of neutrality that arises from the piano's enormous flexibility, the earlier instruments give the player much more direct feedback than does the modern instrument concerning what works and what does not. In this sense, the limitations of the older instruments, compared with the piano, compel the player to hold more dialogue with them. Working within the same limitations with which Bach worked allows the player to narrow the field as to interpretive possibilities, as well as to open up new ones.

The harpsichord, again, gives the most direct feedback, because its dynamic rigidity forces the player to work with the nuances built into the keyboard textures. For example, the opening gestures of the Italian Concerto can be rendered very successfully in a strong-to-weak motion on the harpsichord because the heavy opening chord imparts a forward drive of energy to the rest of the first four measures. This shaping is entirely natural to the piano as well. However, the pianist may be able to render successfully an interpretation that is absolutely unconvincing on any harpsichord: playing the opening weakly and making a crescendo to the end of the first gesture. The dynamic flexibility

Example 6-5. Bach, Gavotte II, English Suite No. 3, BWV 808, mm. 4–16, with suggested restrikings.

(assisted by the basic massiveness of the piano's tone) allows the player to turn an inherently strong-to-weak motion into a weak-to-strong motion. It is true that one must be a highly skilled artist to make such an against-the-grain interpretation really convincing, but some acquaintance with the nature of harpsichords and harpsichord writing will prevent such a waste of artistic effort.

The opening of the Italian Concerto is a good example of a natural accent and of the way its shaping relates to the harpsichord's lack of touch-sensitive dynamics. It is natural to stress the opening chord with a tiny agogic accent, "stretching the time." "Agogic accent" is defined as musical emphasis made through duration rather than dynamics or other means. Agogics are essential to expressive harpsichord playing and must work in conjunction with other stresses and accents such as those produced by harmonies, texture, and range. What factors are inherently accentual? What features draw the ear? Especially important in instrumental terms is textural accent. The sonorities of the harpsichord and clavichord sometimes demand agogic stress in a given place, either for clarity in a very full chord or to help keep a texture clear. Texture and phrasing are interdependent in a way that is not characteristic of most piano writing (such as Beethoven and later).

Agogic accents must be kept in proportion to one another. If all are equally strong, the hierarchy of musical relationships is thrown off. Agogics require the same subtle grading as dynamics. When an inherent musical accent is clear and obvious, making a heavy performance accent can sometimes be redundant and peculiarly unattractive, such as a marked silence before a strong downbeat at a final cadence. Such a downbeat is inherently clear, and further underlining of it is usually counterproductive.

PLAYING COUNTERPOINT

It is extremely important to treat each individual line of a contrapuntal texture with the same independence of dynamics and articulation that it would receive in an ensemble of voices or instruments. During practice sessions, each individual part should be listened to, played (on its own and in combination with one or more other lines), and sung by the performer. Individual treatment of lines sometimes has to be compromised by the way the ensemble of parts moves together, but this is inherent in the nature of contrapuntal writing itself. Again, the clavichord is the best teacher for developing this kind of contrapuntal sensitivity: when all factors are managed successfully, the ensemble-like clarity can be astounding. (Albert Schweitzer quite rightly called the clavichord "a string quartet in miniature.") On this instrument one learns best the effectiveness of giving each polyphonic line its own dynamic shape, and this same goal should be sought at the piano.

Dynamic and articulatory inflection of a fugue subject can vary according to the way it is harmonized. (One might make a distinction here between very neutral subjects, such as the motto of *The Art of Fugue*, and tuneful subjects that are less open to varied renditions.) Thus, in *The Art of Fugue*, Contrapunctus V, D–C-sharp in the bass (Example 6-6, mm. 5–6) is weak-strong, the first-inversion dominant chord on C-sharp being more intense than the preceding tonic. However, when reharmonized in the soprano (mm. 8–9), moving from VI to V, the dominant has a sense of relaxation; the motion is strong-weak, and the dynamics might be varied accordingly.

Sometimes a fugue subject (and its subsequent harmonization) includes hemiola. Examples include the fugue of the Sinfonia from Partita No. 2 (Example 6-7a) and Fugue No. 15, *WTC* 2.

Example 6-6. Bach, Contrapunctus V, *The Art of Fugue*, BWV 1080, mm. 4–9.

A fugue subject need not always be especially emphasized. Often its appearances should blend with the overall continuity of line. A good example is the bass entry at m. 16 in Fugue No. 19, *WTC* 2. Examples 6-7b and c show two different versions that come from different manuscript copies; note that the version without the rest before the subject seems to presume blending rather than more explicit utterance. The subject itself is not always the important focus. What may be more important are other lines that it supports, interactions among several lines, a new harmonization of the subject, or use of the subject in creating a larger-scale phrase or period.

Articulations for the subject(s), countersubject(s), an so on cannot be chosen in a vacuum—that is, by studying only the first, unaccompanied entrance of a subject. Their articulation will depend on how they function in the harmonizations and as a bass line, as well as on their rhythmic relationship to the other parts. A good starting point is to think of any subject as a bass line, since it will often have that function. Most good fugue subjects are invented as pliable bass lines, not as tunes. Tunefulness is a happy by-product of functional factors. Generally, one must sort through all the expositional and developmental presentations of the different themes throughout the fugue and find what articulation will fit all of these different contexts. Note especially how a countersubject intertwines with the subject in rhythm and energy. The heart of a fugue is often the relationship between subject and countersubject. It is also important to consider what the various elements of a theme may be. For in-

Example 6-7a–c. (a) Bach, section 3, Sinfonia, Partita No. 2, BWV 826, mm. 1–4, with hemiola indicated; (b) Bach, Fugue No. 19, *WTC* 2, BWV 888ii, early (?) version, m. 16; (c) Bach, Fugue No. 19, *WTC* 2, BWV 888ii, later (?) version, m. 16.

stance, in Example 6-8 the subject has a rather neutral opening, followed by the typical brief rhythmic figure (*figura corta*) of long-short-short, in turn followed by a cadential figure with a trill. Each of these elements contrasts with the other, making perhaps a little crescendo and decrescendo of activity, from the low opening energy to the heightened energy of the *figura corta* to the cadence. The countersubject introduces further variety, with its play of sixteenths against the subject.

On the piano, midrange, close textures need clarity and rhythmic energy rather than big, visceral dynamics that readily clog them.

If the dynamics are kept constant, the ear listens for other factors: anything that changes. Hence, if the rhythmic approach to a given chord accents the chord, it will be heard as loud; if approached so as to minimize the chord,

Example 6-8. Bach, Fugue No. 23, *WTC* 1, BWV 868ii, mm. 1–4.

it will be perceived as softer. The harpsichordist must use this resource much of the time, implying dynamics by means of timing and articulation. In the interest of textural clarity, the pianist will find it advantageous to think in these terms as well. It is well to avoid dynamic extremes unless the music really calls for them. Poorly controlled dynamic shifts can cause the threads of the texture to be lost. The clear interrelating of different phrases and of simultaneous lines and their impetuses is the stuff of good playing.

No stringed keyboard instrument can sustain a long note over moving parts in the way a voice or melodic instrument can. For this reason, long notes (as mentioned in chapter 4) can sometimes be attacked on the piano and clavichord with a slight extra dynamic ictus, to draw attention to them and to help their sustain. Moving parts do not require this kind of treatment. In refining dynamic relationships in polyphony, it is useful to consider the image of a web of sound, in which every attack is vital, just as a spider's web is well supported at all the important points.

SUGGESTIONS FOR FURTHER READING

Butt, John. *Bach Interpretation: Articulation Marks in Primary Sources of J. S. Bach*. Cambridge: Cambridge University Press, 1990.

Kirnberger, Johann Philipp. *The Art of Strict Musical Composition*, translated by David Beach and Jurgen Thym. Chapter 4, "Tempo, Meter, Rhythm." New Haven, Connecticut: Yale University Press, 1982.

Lowinsky, Edward. "On Mozart's Rhythm." *Musical Quarterly* 42 (1956): 162–186.

Newman, Anthony. *Bach and the Baroque*, 2d ed. "Strong and Weak." East Norwalk, Connecticut: T. D. Ellis, 1994.

Chapter 7

METER, TEMPO, AND
TIME WORDS

M any baroque-era treatises on musical basics demonstrate clearly that time signatures were defined then as they usually are still today, with the strongest beat occurring at the bar line, a weaker beat following, and so on. Thus, common time nominally places the strongest accents at the bar line and the third beat of the measure; a weaker accent on the second beat; and the weakest on the last beat. Baroque theorists describe meters in these terms. The definitions were the same then as they are now, but the practical applications are somewhat different. In today's practice, we tend to treat beats and notes as being of equal strength except when notated otherwise. Only for well-understood conventions such as the style of a waltz, for instance, will a preconceived hierarchy of beat stresses automatically be provided by the player. In seventeenth- and eighteenth-century music, the hierarchy of accents within the measure was the player's point of departure. In the art music of the nineteenth and twentieth centuries, it became more or less irrelevant as the tendencies of musical phrasing increasingly overrode any constancy in the metrical background. Of course there are many exceptions to this sweeping generality: anyone playing a waltz or tango properly will render it with as much of a metrical hierarchy as a baroque passepied would receive. But, for example, the training of most orchestral musicians today produces players who will play "straight" through parts that are not marked with performance accents and dynamics. This approach is understandable, since most standard romantic repertory and twentieth-century literature of all kinds is very fully annotated with accents, dynamics, and the like. Today's metric notation provides, in practice, a neutral framework of pulses rather than an accentual hierarchy. When some baroque allemandes are read through modern lenses, common time can emerge as 16/16 time, with every sixteenth note more or less equally weighted. (This was not the meaning of 16/16 in Bach's time, incidentally.) Such a performance is often hailed as "objective." This neutral style of playing has often been mistaken for stylishness, which it certainly is not. It is a mask useful only for avoiding performance decisions.

Similarly, mechanical evenness of notes and dynamics is neither stylishly baroque nor especially musical. Yet, one often hears this kind of "classical" uniformity advocated for eighteenth-century music, when the same player would not dream of playing later music in so uninflected a manner. One of the specific intentions of the baroque terminology regarding "good" and "bad" notes was to avoid uninflected renditions. Just as the uniform underlying rhythm of a poem will be varied by the speaker, so the rhythms of eighteenth-century music generally require subtle modifications to bring out the shape of the phrase. I have heard performances (by pianists, harpsichordists, and organists alike) in which every short and offbeat note was played with precisely the same stress as the longer and onbeat notes: every beat, every embellishmental thirty-second note played with rigid evenness. The effect is heavy and anything but the cantabile Bach seems to have regarded as fundamental to keyboard playing. No singer would sing anything with such uniformity; it is against all proper musical instincts and highly unnatural for the voice. Then as now, the voice was regarded as the primary instrument and one to be emulated.

Unfortunately, metronome practice can pull the ear away from musical relationships and cause the player to stress the grammar (basic elements) unduly and not the rhetoric (expression) it serves. The metronome is best used to satisfy the grammatical needs: to check relative rhythmic values, the steadiness of pulse, and so forth. It is better not to use it for musical practice unless one can play freely against it, having learned to listen beyond the click to the large-scale, background values. This way, the bar line and the click still fall together at the major junctures. The metronome is also useful when searching for a *tempo giusto* for future reference. (*Tempo giusto* is normally defined as the most fitting tempo for a given movement. A useful amplification of this definition is to consider the *tempo giusto* as the pace that gives the strongest characterization to the different rhythmic levels, motives, and so forth. Eighteenth-century aesthetics generically extended this concept to the point of associating a *tempo giusto* with each different time signature.)

According to a still prevailing myth, eighteenth-century music is never as fast or as slow as later music. This notion stems from a feeling of complacency that seems to have characterized every musical era in Western culture for centuries: the music of preceding generations was always thought to be less varied and expressive than the newest music. We have enough accounts from the baroque era concerning ultra-slow playing of adagios, as well as of brilliant virtuosity, to lay that myth to rest.

While the baroque musician adopted the textbook definition of metric accents in actual practice, this was only a starting point. Many factors can change the accent pattern. The modern player has to begin from the baroque basis of strong and weak metric beats and then observe how the music's inherent stresses coordinate with those beats or override them. For example, a strong dissonance on a normally weak beat will upset the usual hierarchy or perhaps provoke an interesting tension with it.

Metric enunciation, while important, is only part of the basic grammar of baroque music. Full musical expression depends on less predictable factors. Let us look at an analogy from poetry. To give an effective reading of a sonnet by Shakespeare, one starts by recognizing the weak-strong, weak-strong pattern of the iambic pentameter that is the basis of the verse, thus: "Shall *I* com-*pare* thee *to* a *Sum*-mer's *Day?*" Reading the line this way follows the iambic (weak-strong) pattern from one syllable to another, but it also reduces the entire line to a uniform singsong. A sensitive reader will not enunciate that way but will accommodate other factors such as the relative strengths of various words and syllables in the line as a whole. The main stresses should probably fall on "-pare" and "Sum-." "To a" should doubtless be read right through without even a nominal stress on "to." Thus, at least two levels are present: an underlying meter, and a more diversified phrasing riding atop the metric basis. Musical phrasing and meter work in the same way.

TEMPO AND TIME SIGNATURES

Why does Bach provide nothing more than the few written tempo indications that appear in his clavier music? The reason is that a great deal of information is conveyed by time signatures, the prevalent note values in a piece, and the various styles (dance, recitative, and so on). What these styles signified for tempo and accentual patterns were often understood automatically. Tempo words were most often used to adjust the implication of the time signature as well as other aspects of pacing. Thus, Prelude No. 24, *WTC* 1, is marked andante, suggesting twice as many pulses as would be associated with the C time signature alone—a pulse in eighths instead of quarters. But the piece has a walking bass, which moves in eighth notes like a continuo cello line and is associated with a certain range of tempo, characteristically andante. The andante marking merely confirms the tempo that the bass line would have implied for the contemporary player, and Bach could easily have omitted it.

Variation VII of the *Goldberg Variations* (see Example 2-8a) illustrates how these functions of style and notation interrelate and why a time word may be required. In this movement, the style alone—featuring a persistent dotted figure—could mean one of two things. It suggests either a siciliano (rather slow, with a lilting dotted rhythm and a gentle character) or a gigue, with brisk tempo and a sharp, relentless dotted rhythm. Evidently Bach later realized that the notation did not give the player enough information and therefore annotated this variation in at least one printed copy of the work with the word *Giga* (gigue). This one word was the only clue needed by the contemporary player to be certain that the movement derives from the gigue. (Before modern scholars became aware of Bach's annotation, both interpretations were heard from twentieth-century performers.)

The basic principle of baroque metric notation is that larger beat values are equated with slower tempos and with emphasis, and shorter ones with faster tempos and lighter treatment. The time signature and the most prevalent note values are the main ingredients. Depending on what note values are most characteristic of a movement, the meaning of the time signature can be modified one way or another. The time signature can be further modified by time words, as just described. The most complete statement on this subject is given by Kirnberger, who approaches it by way of the dance. The importance of dance styles in relation to tempo and accent can hardly be overstressed. In Kirnberger's treatise on composition, he remarks that the aspiring composer "must have acquired a correct feeling for the natural tempo of every meter, or for what is called *tempo giusto*" (Kirnberger, *Die Kunst des reinen Satzes*, 376). He recommends study of every variety of dance, for each type makes a virtual case study of the meter(s) and note values associated with it.

By tempo, Kirnberger means not only speed per se, but the mood and style of a movement. He means also the diversity of note values and gestures, from a steady stream to constant change. He goes on to outline the relationship of time signature and tempo, which he later discusses in much detail:

Regarding meter, those having larger values, like alla breve, 3/2, and 6/4 meter, have a heavier and slower tempo than those of smaller values, like 2/4, 3/4, and 6/8 meter, and these in turn are less lively than 3/8 or 6/16 meter. . . . Regarding note values, dance pieces involving sixteenth and thirty-second notes have a slower tempo than those that tolerate only eighth and at most sixteenth notes as the fastest note values in the same meter. Thus, for example, a sarabande in 3/4 meter [which would often have thirty-second-note embellishments] has a slower tempo than a minuet [in which the fastest notes will usually be eighths], even though both are written in the same meter. Thus the *tempo giusto* is determined by the meter and by the longer and shorter values of a composition. . . . The adjectives largo, adagio, andante, allegro, presto, and their modifications larghetto [etc.] . . . add to or take away from the fast or slow motion of the natural tempo [that is, the basic tempo associated with the time signature]. (Kirnberger, *Die Kunst des reinen Satzes*, 377)

Generally, the most ordinary time signatures are the most neutral as to tempo, but they still indicate basic ranges. Kirnberger distinguishes the "greater" and "lesser" 4/4 meters. "Large 4/4" time—slow, emphatic, and weighty—is especially relevant to church music. It rarely uses sixteenth notes and is rarely encountered in keyboard music. The lesser 4/4 is used for all styles. In addition to its flexibility, it is faster in tempo than the ponderous "large 4/4" and much lighter in performance style.

The 3/2 meter is akin to the greater 4/4 in that it uses long note values and requires a slow tempo. Kirnberger likens this meter to 6/4, the difference being of course that the one has three beats and the other has two. He gives the example of a courante by Couperin that alternates 3/2 and 6/4 measures.

Kirnberger specifies 2/2, notated "alla breve," as being of frequent use in church music such as fugues and choruses. He calls it "very serious and emphatic," yet it is "performed twice as fast as its note values indicate, unless a slower tempo is specified by the adjectives grave, adagio, etc." (Kirnberger, *Die Kunst des reinen Satzes*, 386). Alla breve has one main and one subsidiary pulse. It has long been the custom to perform some of Bach's alla breve movements very ponderously. In reaction against this, sometimes they are now performed very briskly. Fugue No. 5, *WTC* 2, is a case in point. The question is, what range of tempo and what type of performance inflection will convey two rather than four beats to the listener?

Sometimes the alla breve signature is used in conjunction with another time signature to indicate fewer primary beats. Thus, Prelude No. 5, *WTC* 2, shows an alla breve signature modifying the 12/8 signature: there are two primary pulses of six eighth notes, not four pulses of three eighths.

Moving on to lighter duple meters, Kirnberger states that

2/4 meter has the same tempo as *alla breve* but is performed much more lightly. . . . 2/4 meter and the 6/8 meter that is derived from it are most often used in chamber and theater pieces. In their natural tempi, sixteenth notes and a few thirty-second notes in succession are their shortest note values. But if the tempo is modified by the adjectives andante, largo, allegro, etc., more or none of these note values can be used, depending on the rate of speed. (Kirnberger, *Die Kunst des reinen Satzes*, 386–387)

Pieces in 3/4 time must be heard as having three pulses: neither six per measure, nor one.

> Its natural tempo is that of a menuet, and in this tempo it does not tolerate many sixteenth notes, even less thirty-second notes, in succession. [Consider the first menuet from Partita No. 1, which moves primarily in eighths, or the second, moving mainly in quarters.] However, since it assumes all degrees of tempo from the adjectives adagio, allegro, etc., all note values that fit this tempo can be used, depending on the rate of speed. (Kirnberger, *Die Kunst des reinen Satzes*, 396)

Thus, when a sarabande is written in 3/4, the tempo can be inferred from the dance basis and the prevalent note values. The heavy embellishments of the Sarabande from Partita No. 6, as well as the dance title itself, signify a slow tempo.

A signature of 3/8 implies a much brisker tempo than one of 3/4. Thus, Bach's Sinfonia No. 10, so often heard at a dirgelike pace, would seem actually to be rather animated. The same is true of Invention No. 6, whose binary form, repeat signs, and style features strongly suggest a corrente—also very brisk. Kirnberger describes 3/8 in terms of a dance, as having "the lively tempo of a passepied; it is performed in a light but not an entirely playful manner" (Kirnberger, *Die Kunst des reinen Satzes*, 397).

Kirnberger derives 6/8 from 2/4, 9/8 from 3/4, and 12/8 from 4/4. The "natural" tempos are the same as if 2/4, 3/4, and 4/4 were played with triplet subdivisions, but the manner of performance is different. The eighth-note groupings in 6/8, 9/8, and 12/8 are played more weightily than the "light" triplets in 2/4, 3/4, and 4/4.

Some of the more unusual time signatures have even more specific meanings. A denominator of 16 means that the movement is to be played lightly and rapidly. Kirnberger states that 6/16 "differs greatly from 6/8 meter in the hurried nature of its tempo and the lightness of its execution." He cites Fugue No. 11, *WTC* 2 (Example 7-1a). If recast in 6/8 (Example 7-1b), "the gait is much more ponderous, and the notes, particularly the passing notes, are emphasized too much. . . . If this fugue is to be performed correctly on the keyboard, the notes must be played lightly and without the least pressure in a fast tempo" (Kirnberger, *Die Kunst des reinen Satzes*, 387–388). He describes accentuation in 6/16 and other "light" meters in terms of a violinist playing with the tip of the bow, a sound image to be emulated by the keyboard player.

A meter of 12/16 is similarly and "completely" different from 12/8. Kirnberger cites the fugues in Example 7-1. "The one at [Example 7-1c] designates a slower tempo and a more emphatic performance. . . . the sixteenth notes [at

Example 7-1a–d. (a) Bach, Fugue No. 11, *WTC 2*, BWV 880ii, mm. 1–4; (b) the same fugue rewritten in 6/8; (c) Bach, Fughetta in C Minor, BWV 922, mm. 1–3; (d) Bach, Fugue No. 4, *WTC 2*, BWV 873ii, mm. 1–2.

Example 7-1d] are performed quickly and plainly, without any emphasis" (Kirnberger, *Die Kunst des reinen Satzes*, 391–392).

Bach uses this sort of time signature with 6/16, 9/16, 12/16, 18/16, and even 24/16. It is most frequently found in gigue fugues, such as the concluding section of the Toccata in D Major (BWV 912), a gigue-derived movement in 6/16; several actual Gigues, such as those that conclude the English Suite No. 6 and Partita No. 4; and in the whirlwind figuration at the beginning and end of the Toccata in G Minor (BWV 915). Regarding Variation XXVI of the *Goldberg Variations*, in 18/16 time, Kirnberger remarks that it should be played "lightly, swiftly, and without the slightest pressure on the first note of each beat" (Kirnberger, *Die Kunst des reinen Satzes*, 397). The notation also appears in Prelude No. 15, *WTC 1*, using 24/16 time rather than triplets against the common time of the bass: the piece should course along rapidly and smoothly, with no enunciation of the "triplets" as such. Prelude No. 6, from the same volume, is written in common time with triplets, signifying perhaps a slightly slower or perhaps more accentual treatment, although Kirnberger remarks that triplets in 3/4, and presumably in common time as well, are to be played lightly (see below). Had it been written in 24/16, it might have been yet faster and lighter, and above all less accentual. Prelude No. 13, *WTC* 1, is written in 12/16 time. The time signature here probably indicates a reasonably quick tempo as well as a smoothly flowing performance without much accentuation.

Baroque usage of time signatures with a denominator of 16 is quite opposite in effect from the normal modern meaning of such notation, which tends to be understood as implying strong, albeit fairly equal, accents on every sixteenth note. This time signature today does not indicate the fleeting, light performance that eighteenth-century musicians associated with it.

Modification of a tempo indicated by a time signature seems to be the main purpose for time words in Bach's keyboard music. (He is more generous with them in ensemble works, perhaps because the players, working from parts rather than a full score, would often be unable to judge the tempo without the full picture.) Thus, Variation XV of the *Goldberg Variations*, a solemn movement in G minor, is notated in brisk 2/4 time. However, this signature is modified by the word "andante," which certainly indicates a slower tempo but also implies twice as many pulses. Thus, the movement would progress in eighth-note pulses rather than quarters. With the one time-word modification, the 2/4 meter provides just the accentual framework the composer desires.

The tempo suggested by a time signature can also be modified by slurred groupings that alter the accent pattern and even thus pull the performance toward a tempo different from what the time signature initially implies. The slurs in Example 5-6a maintain the quarter-note groupings implied by the C time signature, which could otherwise be understood to be modified to eighth-note groupings by the direction "largo."

Similarly, the baroque composer could choose from variously nuanced combinations of notational features with time signatures, each with slightly different implications for tempo and accent. The Courantes from French Suite No. 4 and Partita No. 1 are notated in 3/4 time with dotted figures that imply a sharper rhythm than would triplet groups of quarter note–eighth note, or notation in 9/8. As we know from Kirnberger, 9/8 meter would produce a heavier effect, with more stress on individual eighth notes:

Triplets in a 3/4 meter are played differently from eighths in a 9/8 meter. The former are played very lightly and without the slightest pressure [accent] on the last note, but the latter heavier and with some weight on the last note. The former [the 3/4 measure] never or only rarely permits a [new] harmony to be sounded with the last note, but the latter [in the 9/8 measure] do very often. . . . If the two meters were not differentiated by special qualities, all gigues in 6/8 could also be written in 2/4 [with triplets]; 12/8 would be a C meter, and 6/8 a 2/4 meter. (Kirnberger, *Die Kunst des reinen Satzes*, 396)

A contrary view is given by Bach's pupil Agricola. He attributed to Bach the view that triplet notation in duple or triple meter was no different from 3/8, 6/8, 9/8, and 12/8 except for matters of where and where not to assimilate dotted rhythms with the triplets (which Agricola allows only in very fast tempos, such as would apply to a corrente). Kirnberger commented, however, that the older notational nuances were disappearing. Agricola was apparently of the newer approach, despite his claim to represent Bach's viewpoint. It would seem unlikely that Bach would use such varied notational means if he saw no differentiation from one to another. Indeed, the argument that Bach employed the old notational convention is surely clinched by even a cursory examination of the enormous fugue that concludes the Toccata in G Minor (BWV 915). The gigue style and tempo, the length, and the complexity of the voicing negate any notion of a literal rendition with the short note of the dotted figure always coming after the triplet figure.

A 3/4 time signature with triplets and dotted values makes an apt middle-ground for a light Italianate corrente, with the stress and groupings midway between the heaviness of 9/8 and the extreme rapidity and lightness of 9/16 notation. In cases of fast tempos at least (correntes are rapid), the short notes of the dotted figures would be assimilated as eighth notes against the moving triplet groups of the other parts.

Another possibility for indication of tempo and accent is to modify one time signature with another. The first of the two signatures modifies the meaning of the second. In Prelude No. 5, *WTC* 2, which presents an alla breve signature in combination with a 12/8 signature, the former modifies the latter, indicating one primary pulse to the measure rather than two (as would be the case with 12/8 alone). The tempo must be brisk enough to allow this sort of enunciation. Of course, tempo is not the only aspect: a skillful player can project two or four pulses through the same tempo (at least, within a certain range of tempo) by various means. The same point applies to the ensuing Fugue: its alla breve signature indicates pulse groupings more than specific tempo.

Anthony Newman offers an opposite example, of C modifying 12/8 to indicate four accents rather than two, in *Jesus Christus unser Heiland*, BWV 626

(Newman, 41). He also offers a solution to the meaning of the Adagio overro largo movement from the Concerto in C Major for Two Harpsichords (BWV 1061). In Newman's interpretation, two groupings coexist in the movement (using a common pulse rate). "Adagio" refers to 6/8 with sixteenths, which makes two accents per measure. "Largo" refers to six accents per bar, with pairs of slurred sixteenths. The two styles are signaled by the tempo indication, "Adagio or otherwise Largo." As Newman points out, Bach "could hardly mean 'slow or otherwise slower'!" (Newman, 39).

To summarize: Bach's various choices and combinations of time signatures, niceties of rhythmic notation, time words, slurrings, and similar factors are not arbitrary. Each choice made from the various possible combinations is concerned with communicating a specific relationship of pulse, strength and number of accents, and range of tempo. The player must consider what the composer's options were in notating a piece in one way rather than another, and what the final choice indicates about performance.

METER AND THE *STYLUS PHANTASTICUS*

Occasional exceptions to the metric hierarchy for baroque music seem to be the *stylus phantasticus* and recitative, both of which are generally notated in common time. In the free style, the metric framework often functions simply as a neutral background for greatly diverse musical events—which is an elaborate way to say that a toccata will unfold in a more varied way than the typical allemande. Sometimes the major stresses do indeed coincide with the bar-line and half-measure beats, although the appropriate agogic style may so exaggerate them as to drive away a clear sense of pulse. The French unmeasured style (with its famous nonrhythmic and sometimes semirhythmic notation), which apparently derived from common time and the influence of the Italian toccata, uses a performance style that leaves the metric underpinning more implicit than explicit (see Troeger, "Metre and the Unmeasured Prelude").

TEMPO WORDS

Bach employed a wide range of tempo words in his works generally, but was quite reserved when it came to using them for the keyboard music. The player who is accustomed to Bach's taciturnity on the subject in, say, the *WTC* will be surprised upon exploring further to find such phrases as "Allegro ma non tanto," "Allegro e presto," "un poc' allegro," or "molt' adagio." However, these are exceptional cases (both in the baroque era generally and in Bach's works).

By far the most frequent directives are the familiar "largo," "adagio," "andante," "allegro," "vivace," and "presto" (see the reading from Marshall listed at the end of the chapter). This is apparently the order from slowest to fastest. It is important to remember that the literal meaning of the Italian words applied, as well as abstract meanings of tempo. Thus, "allegro," which means "cheerful," refers to mood as much as anything else, so that when two tempo words appear together, as in "allegro e presto," the two are not incompatible, in this case meaning "cheerful and fast."

The relative meanings of the six main tempo words are generally clear, except for the first two. Scholars differ on whether adagio is slower than largo or vice versa. It is not possible to know for certain, and in practice the matter remains subjective, but I will offer the following consideration. Quantz grouped all tempo markings into four general categories (see the reading listed at the end of the chapter). Two of his categories are "adagio cantabile," which includes moderately slow movements, such as Larghetto and Poco andante, and "adagio assai," which includes the movements Largo assai, Mesto, and Grave. He remarks that the differences within each category are slight, and that the mood aspects of the different words are the most significant. For Quantz, then, "adagio" seems to refer to slow tempo generally, with "largo" a mood-related detail. Walther defines adagio as "leisurely, slow" and largo as "very slow, as if expanding [*erweiternd*; perhaps, in this context, "broadening"] the measure." Walther, too, makes adagio the general designation and definitely places largo at the especially slow extreme. It is conceivable that for Bach, too, adagio was the more general term and that largo betokened a further slowness and perhaps heaviness or languor.

Walther's definition of andante is worth considering: "all notes executed precisely the same and alike (evenly), also each one distinct from the other, and must be played somewhat faster than adagio" (*alle Noten fein gleich und uberein (ebentraechtig) execurirt, auch eine von der andern wohl unterschieden, und etwas geschwinder als adagio tractirt werden Mussen*; Walther, 35). This description is important, as it shows that the designation *andante*, like the time-signature denominator of 16, smooths out the usual metrical and accentual hierarchy. In the case of the time signatures of $x/16$, a nonaccentual performance seems to be the most significant characteristic (even more significant than the fast tempo usually associated with these cases). With andante, there is an increase in accents, on both strong and weak beats.

Newman argues convincingly that the principle just discussed regarding andante applies to largo as well: that largo indicates more uniform accentuation of the strong and weak beats of the measure (Newman, 39). He cites such movements as Fugue No. 24, *WTC* 1.

In addition to these uses and the words' most ordinary meanings, a few tempo words had further meanings yet, which have to be understood from the musical context.

The word *adagio* was sometimes used as a generic term for "slower," meaning either a sudden change of tempo (but not necessarily slowing to a specifically adagio pace) or a ritardando. It could also (apparently) imply freer timing. Handel often indicates a ritardando at final cadences by "adagio," which was sometimes misinterpreted in nineteenth- and twentieth-century traditions of Handelian performance. Bach uses this indication only rarely in his keyboard works, but it does appear in the Toccata in C Minor. At m. 85, midway through the big concluding fugue and following a (free-style) flourish, a cadence is marked adagio (in the sense of a ritardando), followed by allegro to indicate Tempo I as the fugue resumes its ordinary pace.

Presto can indicate a generically faster tempo, signify an accelerando into a faster tempo (not a literal presto in the modern sense), or signal a return to a prior tempo.

The Prelude No. 2 from *WTC* 1 illustrates many of these functions. There is no tempo word heading the piece, but the C signature, the energy of the sixteenths, and the intensity of the harmonic changes all suggest something in the realm of "allegro," probably at least moderately fast. At m. 25, in an important manuscript copy from Bach's pupil H. N. Gerber, appears the word "adagio," omitted from most if not all modern editions. It may indicate a freer style of timing, as the figuration over the pedal G produces a change of mood after the relentless use of the one figure and its inversion up to this point. "Presto" at m. 28 conceivably restores the original tempo or, more likely, indicates an accelerando into the next passage. In either case, it probably calls for a single main pulse rather than two (as is usual with 4/4) in each measure. The adagio at m. 34 again suggests a ritardando or a general slowing down and loosening of the pace, not the "very slow" that it would nominally indicate to a musician today. The "allegro" at m. 35 presumably restores the original tempo. The style is freer than at the opening and the pacing might be as well, but the indication very likely restores two primary beats to the meter. Its contrast with the "presto" indication and the musical passages referred to by each would seem to confirm my suggestions regarding pulse and accent.

Prelude No. 10, *WTC* 1, uses the word "presto" at m. 23 as the texture shifts into two-part writing with a simpler rhythm than before. This is an equivocal situation. Bach may mean, literally, a very brisk tempo. But the indication more likely signifies an acceleration into a somewhat faster and certainly a less inflected pace, rather than a radically faster tempo.

TEMPO AND MUSICAL CONTEXT

Apart from the considerations of style, time signature, and the like that indicate an approximate range of tempo and accent, the individual player must decide on tempo in terms of the balance of the foreground of motivic, melodic, and contrapuntal activity with the background of harmonic motion and larger phrase shapes. Too much stress on the background can lead to overfast tempos that destroy the fuller meaning of linear activity. Too much stress on the latter can obscure the simpler, large-scale progressions and produce some bizarre treatment of surface detail. One view is like seeing a landscape from an airplane; the other is akin to using a microscope. A balance between foreground and background must always be preserved.

SUGGESTIONS FOR FURTHER READING

Badura-Skoda, Paul. *Interpreting Bach at the Keyboard*, 71–91. Translated by Alfred Clayton. Oxford: Clarendon Press, 1993. [A very useful discussion based in part on Marshall, "Tempo and Dynamic Indications."]

Cooper, Kenneth, and Julius Zasko. "Georg Muffat's Observations on the Lully Style of Performance." *Musical Quarterly* 53 (1967): 230–232. [Muffat on tempo.]

Kirnberger, Johann Philipp. *The Art of Strict Musical Composition*, 375–417. Translated by David Beach and Jurgen Thym. New Haven, Connecticut: Yale University Press, 1982.

Marshall, Robert L. "Tempo and Dynamic Indications in the Bach Sources: A Review of the Terminology." In *Bach, Handel, Scarlatti: Tercentenary Essays, ed. Peter Williams*. Cambridge: Cambridge University Press, 1985. [An excellent account of Bach's vocabulary of tempo and dynamic markings.]

Newman, Anthony. *Bach and the Baroque: European Source Material from the Baroque and Early Classical Periods with Special Emphasis on the Music of J. S. Bach*. New York: Pendragon Press, 1985; 2d ed., East Norwalk, Connecticut: T. D. Ellis, 1994; New York: Pendragon, 1995. [Newman has many fascinating insights into tempo issues. This is the first modern study (apart from Fritz Rothschild's pioneering effort, *The Lost Tradition in Music*) to take a serious look at Kirnberger's gold mine of information concerning meters and accent.]

Quantz, Johann Joachim. *On Playing the Flute*, 283–287. Translated by Edward R. Reilly. London: Faber, 1966.

Chapter 8

RHYTHMIC ELEMENTS

Baroque rhythmic notation sometimes has meanings different from those it would carry today. In this chapter I will consider some of these idiosyncratic "grammatical" aspects, as well as the expressive ("rhetorical") shaping of musical rhythm.

MUSICAL SHAPING

Precise and acute rhythmic expression is very important to baroque music. Rhythmic subtlety and forcefulness are often more convincing and far-reaching than superficial effects of color, virtuosity, or purely visceral energy. Rhythm can be ranked with dynamic shading in expressive importance. In fact, rhythm is often at the core of what dynamics and other elements can express. The same applies to rhythm and tempo: well-directed, poised rhythms and contrasts will drive a movement more effectively than will a merely faster tempo.

Differing rhythms and/or motives usually need to be characterized to the full. Small variations in rhythmic shape can create meaningful, even dramatic oppositions. The player should be ready to consider any changes in the rhythmic picture and to bring out their contrasts, however slight. Thinking in terms of the physicality of rhythmic gestures can heighten sensitivity to rhythmic diversity. So, too, can playing without dynamic variation (as an exercise, of course, not as a standard mode of playing), so that more of the expression depends on the sensitive expression of rhythmic contours. The most important reason the pianist should study the harpsichord is that the instrument forces the player to rely on rhythm as one of the primary sources of expression.

In every moment of a musical composition, especially works of such rhythmic subtlety as Bach's, one must be aware of how fine rhythmic inflections help project the shape of the phrase. Again, one phrases with time as much as with dynamics. Convincing agogic shaping requires careful listening and analysis: the player's concept of the phrase shapes must coordinate with all the elements built into the music. Only then can the player determine how best to realize the phrase shapes on the instrument at hand.

Rhythmic shaping involves minute degrees of rhythmic assimilation and exaggeration. Assimilation is apt for some embellishments and in some contexts with dotted figures, as discussed below. Exaggeration is relevant to fiery music generally, and often to dotted figures. Generally, baroque music depends upon very acute, sometimes minutely stressed or even exaggerated rhythmic enunciation. Without acutely realized rhythms, the characterization and opposition of different rhythmic shapes become difficult if not impossible to convey. In the interest of producing a smooth, long line, some players are in the habit of minutely rounding off rhythms, which is appropriate to certain contexts in the later literature. However, this tendency is quite inappropriate to eighteenth-century music. Even at very fast tempos, the full differentiation of different note values must prevail.

In deciding on rhythmic niceties, the player must consider notational nuances. What appears to be an anomaly may be of some significance. As already shown in chapter 7, the odd-looking mixtures of dotted versus triplet rhythms, so bizarre at first glance, in fact reflect a delicately graded notational scheme. If the notational conventions and details appear strange, one must consider what the composer's notational options were and on that basis find a rationale for what appears on the page.

FOREGROUND, MIDDLEGROUND, AND BACKGROUND

In music there can be said to be a foreground, a middleground, and a background. The proportions among all these must be maintained in performance. The foreground is the immediate, note-to-note, subphrase-to-subphrase aspect of a composition. The player who is unduly occupied with it can readily lose the sense of the larger phrase. He or she is in the position of someone looking at a large picture from one corner, nose almost touching the canvas. The painter of course works from close up, and the musician works out many issues in the same way, but both have to step back to maintain a feeling for the work as a whole. The middleground is comparable to the first stage in stepping back: it provides one with a sense of the local range of phrase and period. The background is the large scale of the composition, where the main segments of the piece relate to one another and to the whole. Awareness of it is like viewing a large picture from across a room. The player who maintains a sense of the overall musical composition can make the smaller elements cohere in their proper proportions to the whole. As Kirnberger would say, such a player has a sense of the phrases, sentences, and paragraphs of the piece. In addition, the surface-level rhythm is often governed by the underlying, large-scale note values of the middleground and background; but enunciation of the underlying values depends on manipulation of the surface rhythm. Reciprocal relationships exist among all three levels, and it is important to find the driving rhythmic forces of a work for each. Equally important is finding the *tempo giusto*, which both unifies and allows the fullest expression of the different rhythmic shapes and levels.

Intensity can die when a tempo, however steady it might be, merely pulses along without any expression of the music's rhythmic energy. Certain kinds of metronome practice can encourage such even but sapless playing. Mental subdivision of the beats and other values should be used only as a grammatical aid—to spell out uncertain rhythmic shapes, to check for constancy of underlying tempo, and so forth. It should not be an invariable approach. The player must be able to think and listen in terms of the large time units (the background level) that support the surface-level rhythm and the middleground activity.

The background of a composition, especially in regard to the overall phrase relationships, is often more apparent at faster tempos. Whereas a slow tempo promotes hearing a work "sentence by sentence," a rapid pace will make the various larger middleground units ("paragraphs") fall into place in the larger scheme. This background aspect has to be weighed against other factors, including foreground detail and clarity in the middleground, in making final choices of tempo and other elements. With the right choices, a sense of the background can be maintained without excessively fast tempos. The conductor Bruno Walter once commented that younger conductors need to rely on faster tempos, while older, experienced ones can afford a slower pace. It seems likely that he meant that with experience comes the ability to keep the larger picture vivid while working in more detail—the detail allowed by a slower tempo.

Coherence among the foreground, middleground, and background is all-important. For instance, surface details should be shaped according to the player's sense of their role in relationship to the larger groupings. It is possible to enunciate individual motivic statements and other surface details without reference to how these details cohere in larger units—an approach that can produce mannered playing or even overall inertia. It is helpful to think in terms of projecting like a public speaker: the audience has to take in the overall argument and not lose sight of the main points because of excessive detail in the presentation. Similarly, the audience listening to a musical work has to hear the overall structure and drive of the piece, and to hear the details in due proportion to those larger aspects.

It is often productive to think in terms not only of the contrasts of rhythmic shapes and motives, but also of the different roles of the various note values in a piece. Each may tend to a certain characterization. The fastest values, for instance, may drive forward, with a brilliant quality; an intermediate level may present a quite different energy. Both the fastest and intermediate values often reflect the large groupings that underlie them. The longest notes are often pregnant with forward motion, and they have to be approached and inflected in terms of that implied energy, just as a great actor can dominate the stage in silence and without motion. I say "approached," because a note is prepared by the conduct of the motion toward that note, not by the sounding of the note itself. Thus, the offbeat notes can prepare the enunciation of a downbeat, and fast notes lay the ground for longer notes. (Ralph Kirkpatrick has discussed these matters in a memorable passage from his book *Domenico Scarlatti*, 318–319.) The player must find the rhythmic motivations in a work. Which elements drive the music forward? Which are more serene? How do the different phrases and motives relate to the common metric pulse? What is the *tempo giusto* that will support these contrasts? Finding the energy of each phrase can assist in the grammatical aspect of keeping a unified tempo: through inner musical coherence rather than by outward mechanical (for example, metronomic) procedures. A sense of comparative stasis in some phrases, contrasted with high energy in others, requires that both moods be given their due. For instance, the sequences in Sinfonia No. 15 are foils to the bravura passages of thirty-second notes.

Rhythmic impulses can vary from a single beat to a full measure or more. The Sarabande of English Suite No. 2 provides an illustration (Example 8-1). Bach begins with a chordal passage in which the separate quarter values are all weighty to some degree, then shifts to a lightly supported melodic figure that sweeps across full measures. A sensitive performance will project this diversity of impulse.

Example 8-1. Bach, Sarabande, English Suite No. 2, BWV 807, mm. 1–8.

CHARACTERIZATION

Contrasts, whether of beat groupings or other features, are constantly found in Bach's music. They must be understood, absorbed, and projected by the player. This subject is a particular focus of chapter 12.

It is important to seek out and express all the types of energy that are inherent in a work, rather than foist onto it an external notion of energy (for example, equating mere loudness or speed with vitality). Most often the variations in energy are expressed through diversity of rhythm, of harmonic intensity, and of overall progress of the formal structure. Other clues to energy and mood include dance types and their associated moods; styles of ornamentation and embellishments; choice of key; and discernible styles, such as programmatic, motoric, or imitation of other media (lute, trio, and so on). Particular types of energy were typically associated with certain commonly used musical figures. For instance, appoggiaturas (especially in affective slow movements) had something languishing about them, while dotted figures in certain contexts were typically proud and fiery.

There can be considerable diversity of rhythm and even motive within a phrase. Bach frequently writes a long line made up of small, often diverse units, whereas Liszt may write a long line made up of far fewer subphrases. Much of the energy of a baroque line often comes through small-range contrasts: variety of rhythmic shapes or even strong oppositions of character, such as energized motives heard in opposition to languishing or "drooping" motives. Sometimes these contrasts are very subtle, and the mainstream tendency is to move through the phrase without differentiating them; but considerable energy and expressive force can be released when the full diversity of motivic type is brought out. A few illustrations are given in Example 8-2. In the Air from French Suite No. 2, the intensity of the opening rising sixteenths receives a local-level response by the eighth notes, a descending figure of considerably less energy. The whole phrase can be played in an agitated manner. However, bringing out the contrast with the eighths is not only more interesting in itself, but also gives more meaning to the ensuing phrase. Prelude No. 4, *WTC* 1, is often played with a fair degree of uniformity throughout, but this work in fact contrasts a drooping opening figure with an energized arpeggio-plus-dotted-note figure. Realization of this basic contrast enlivens the subsequent development of the material. Sometimes, however, the contrasts are between phrases, as in the Polonaise of French Suite No. 6. Here we find smooth, lyrical areas in opposition to relatively boisterous pairwise groups. Similarly, Prelude No. 12, *WTC* 2, juxtaposes a "sigh" figure in eighth notes with the forward drive of the sixteenth-note passages.

Contrasts, then, should usually be brought out. If, in trying to follow your original interpretive idea, you find that you are smoothing out an inherent contrast, give up that idea. Bring out the contrast instead, and base part of your (new) interpretation on that. The one alteration might suggest further changes, to the point where you find that you have achieved an entirely new, and much more evolved, concept, which is always stimulating for both you and your listeners (because your performance is based on a vital idea). Suppose, for instance, that you start with a notion that the third section of Bach's Toccata in E Minor is sad and quiet throughout. It is possible on the piano to play the percussive tremolo in m. 8 of this work in accordance with this thought—but not on a harpsichord. Its response is not calculated to a quiet rendition of a tremolo; the lack of touch dynamics and the ictus of the rapid succession of plucks require a bold and disruptive treatment. The harpsichord can teach a simple, pragmatic lesson of far-reaching consequences: if a contrast seems unavoidable, bring it out. (To put it with rule-of-thumb crudity, "If you can't help it, do it on purpose.") The resourceful player will always make a virtue of necessity and in the process can learn interesting musical effects. If one kind of treatment seems questionable, find a different way to approach the problem. Measure 8 of the toccata contains a deliberate interruption (called just that—"Interruptio"—in rhetorical analysis) that should be brought out as a contrast, rather than smoothed over. This is a very straightforward illustration, but the principle applies to even the most subtle of contrasts.

Example 8-2a–c. (a) Bach, Air, French Suite No. 2, BWV 813, mm. 1–3; (b) Bach, Prelude No. 4, *WTC* 1, BWV 849i, mm. 1–3; (c) Bach, Polonaise, French Suite No. 6, BWV 817, mm. 1–4.

RHYTHMIC FUNCTIONS

A fundamental question in realizing any musical work is: which notes are relatively active, and which comparatively inactive? Similarly, what is the function of a rhythmic pattern or rhythmic value in its particular context? Long notes often have great power in their stasis, and the player can project the function of a long note by the way it is prepared and (on the piano and clavichord) by the dynamic level assigned the note and the other notes heard against it. One can sculpt vivid proportions. The player's imagination must transcend the limits of the keyboard and encompass both note function and suggestions of other media. For example: a long held note can be imagined to swell slightly, as on a violin or by the voice, and this image can help shape the rest of the note's musical context. If the long note eventually resolves from a dissonance to a consonance, the dynamics should be contrived to suggest the diminuendo into the resolution, even if the sound of the first note has in fact died back. A rhythmic pattern should be characterized so as to make its maximum impact, and for strong differentiation from contrasting rhythmic figures. Even motoric pieces, in which the surface rhythm is continuous, nonetheless can show a great diversity of groupings. The final fugue of Bach's Toccata in E Minor is a good example.

Bach sometimes provides layers of the same rhythmic figure. That is, the same basic impulse may appear within the beat and also across the measure. In the Sarabande from Partita No. 1, the dotted figure (so characteristic of French-style sarabandes) is heard on both larger and smaller scales (see Example 2-3). This excerpt provides a good example of different levels of foreground activity.

RUBATO

Rubato was nothing new in the classical and romantic eras. Many discussions of strong and weak notes and beats by baroque-era authorities refer to small "stretchings" of the time in the strong areas. The point also arises in notation. Froberger, who was famous for what we would call his rubato style and for general rhythmic delicacy in performance, often begins a scalar run with a dotted figure. This notation almost certainly signifies an agogic accent rather than a literal rendition. It might also have been intended to suggest an accelerando, which Frescobaldi advocated for virtuosic scale passages.

"Agogic accent" is defined as durational accent, as opposed to a dynamic or metrical accent. ("Durational accent" can also refer to holding notes to their full notated length, without any rubato treatment, in a context where other notes are detached.) An agogic accent can take two forms. Within an overall strict time frame, the accent is made by elongating the accented note and subtracting time from the next. This approach is a major component of the classic definition of rubato as a rhythmically flexing line rendered against a steady accompaniment (a generally apt approach, for instance, to the Andante of the Italian Concerto). Durational accent is sometimes indicated in the notation, and it can even suggest the larger-scale rubato discussed below. Example 8-3 compares the opening of Partita No. 6 in two versions. The earlier shows a single value in the written-out arpeggio; the later version puts a durational stress on the first note, reminiscent of Froberger's notation.

Agogics can also involve "stretching" the overall time slightly by pushing and pulling the metric beats. In some ranges of tempo and relative note values, the bar line or another group division may act as the pulse, while the beats are

Example 8-3a, b. Bach, Toccata, Partita No. 6, BWV 830, mm. 1–2: (a) early version; (b) final version.

somewhat flexible. This is similar to the relationship between the freedom of a rubato line and a steady accompaniment, only on a larger scale. Agogic accents can also take extra time that is not made up subsequently; the "stretch" is simply absorbed into the overall shape of the phrase. The strength of the agogic accent, the musical context, and what may be called the rhythmic fingerprint of the individual player are all determining factors.

A highly inflected rubato is often appropriate to complex embellishments, to the *stylus phantasticus*, and to recitative style.

Agogic accents are frequently used for stress and shaping on the harpsichord and clavichord, these instruments being deeply dependent upon varying densities of sound to make dynamic variations. The accents can often be made by arpeggiation: breaking chords or intervals (the latter is termed *suspension* or "fringing") provides an artful way of consuming the added time of the accent. Ornaments can be added to create accents; in fact, this is often the function of notated ornaments.

Agogic accents can be a technical aid. Sometimes a trifling, musically appropriate agogic accent will considerably facilitate an awkward jump or change of position.

FINAL CADENCES

The frequently encountered modern habit of pausing on the penultimate chord before resolving to the final chord, and/or minute delaying of the final chord, may be considered a mannerism with no historical, and certainly no musical, justification. Except in some highly dramatic, extroverted cases, the more obvious a musical gesture, the less specific underlining it requires. The final cadence of dominant to tonic is nothing if not obvious, however delicately realized by the composer, and does not usually require special emphasis. A more elegant way to inflect a cadence is to make appropriate agogic inflections in the passage leading up to the cadence (rather than in the cadence itself). One can put on the brakes, so to speak, by making slight agogic accents on the chords and beats that naturally take stress. These are usually the primary metric beats. Properly prepared in this way, the final cadence virtually takes care of itself. Such use of agogic accents on primary beats is more stylish and effective than either a steady ritardando or an artificial punctuation of an already obvious cadence.

RHYTHMIC NOTATION AND PERFORMANCE PRACTICES

With the foregoing musical considerations in mind, let us look at some conventions of notation and performance that were taken for granted by Bach's contemporaries. These topics include strong and weak elements, notated agogics, rhythmic inequality, and dotted notation. All of these grammatical issues must be approached by the player in terms of the particular musical context to which they apply. A baroque-era writer would say these treatments must be rendered with "good taste."

Georg Muffat gives a good summation of the baroque view of "good" and "bad" notes, which we today more readily call "strong" and "weak." The good notes, or principal notes, are those that "seem naturally to give the ear a little repose." They are proportionally longer (including dotted notes) and fall on the principal beats; when notes are of equal value, they are the odd-numbered notes—those that, again, fall on the main divisions of the measure (Cooper and Zasko, 239).

One performance practice that goes beyond habits of notation is inequality: playing notes that are written equally with deliberate and finely calculated unevenness. Inequality was an accepted practice, in one form or another, throughout the seventeenth and eighteenth centuries. Various types of inequality are described by French, Italian, Spanish, and German authors, and evidence appears in musical sources from England as well. Bach's works in the French style are perhaps eligible for the French approach to inequality, though how relevant it actually is to Bach's music remains an open question. The subject of inequality is of general importance, however, in that it gives some insight into baroque-era agogics. The quotations that follow emphasize German writers who assimilated the French practice, since their understanding of it may reflect Bach's own.

The most thorough descriptions of rhythmic inequality (*notes inégales*) are those given with great consistency by many French authors of the later seventeenth and early eighteenth centuries. Most often, the use of inequality has several requirements:

1. The rhythmic value eligible for alteration is the prevailing note value, which is usually half the value of the metric beat (e.g., eighths in 3/4 time; often sixteenths in common time).
2. The passages open to inequality show fairly uniform movement in the appropriate rhythmic value(s).
3. The notes generally move by step rather than by leap.
4. The mood is usually more "gracious" than energetic.

Inequality is appropriate only to certain circumstances. It is not to be applied when more than two notes are placed under a slur, probably because the rhythmic alteration would undermine the larger-scale impetus signaled by the slur. In addition, the French would sometimes simply specify, in a performance direction, that notes were to be rendered equally: this direction would of course apply to notes that were otherwise open to unequal treatment. An alternative notation to ensure equality was to put dots or dashes over or under the note heads. To modern eyes, dots and dashes give the visual impression of staccato or staccatissimo, but in the baroque era they sometimes meant only equality of emphasis. Detachment could assist equality of stress, but "equality" dots do not necessarily call for it. (François Couperin, for one, used dashes to represent detached notes, dots to show equality.) In German practice, at least, a tempo marking of andante also negated use of inequality, for "andante" itself indicated equal emphasis of the pulse and its subdivisions (see chapter 5).

French-style inequality most often uses a long-short (L-S) pattern, the lengthened notes falling on the metric beats and subdivisions. The degree of inequality is variable, from mild to sharp, depending on the mood and expression. Most often, the inequality is subtle, with a slight rubato being placed on the odd-numbered subdivisions of the beat: not usually a fully dotted rhythm, although the style was sometimes notated with dotted figures. Pieces that use written-out dotting to convey *notes inégales* are usually more gentle in nature than those (such as overtures) that require exaggeration of the dotted rhythm. The one notation is used for two different rhythmic styles. Written-out dotting to convey *notes inégales* is one of the comparatively rare instances in which slight rhythmic assimilation, rather than exaggeration or sharp profiling, is required. It is up to the player to recognize by style and context whether a movement requires literal or exaggerated rendering of the dotted notes or assimilation of them to the style of *notes inégales*.

Sometimes a short-long (S-L) style was used, but this seems to have been much less frequent than the L-S pattern. In French music, S-L treatment seems to apply exclusively to stepwise descending notes. When such notes are slurred in pairs, the S-L style seems to be especially appropriate, and Couperin makes this correlation in his ornament table of 1713. However, the L-S style was by far the more common and is described with great consistency in an overwhelmingly extensive range of writings from the period.

Quantz, working at the court of Frederick the Great, where the French culture was carefully emulated, describes L-S inequality in his treatise of 1751. He remarks in a much-quoted passage:

> You must know how to make a distinction in execution between the *principal notes*, ordinarily called *accented* or in the Italian manner, *good* notes, and those that *pass*, which some foreigners call *bad* notes. Where it is possible, the principal notes always must be emphasized more than the passing. In consequence of this rule, the quickest notes in every piece of *moderate tempo*, or even in the *Adagio*, though they seem to have the same value, must be played a little unequally, so that the stressed notes of each figure, namely the first, third, fifth, and seventh, are held slightly longer than the passing, namely the second, fourth, sixth, and eighth, although this lengthening must not be as much as if the notes were dotted.

Quantz goes on to describe the standard candidates for inequality: notes of half the metric beat, or less if more rapid notes are prevalent. He continues, referring to the measures shown in Example 8-4a:

> For example, if the eight semiquavers are played slowly with the same value, they will not sound as pleasing as if the first and third of [each group of] four are heard a little longer, and with a stronger tone, than the second and fourth. (Quantz, 123–124)

Quantz makes an exception to this style for rapid passagework, in which agogic stress is to be applied only to the first of every four notes rather than to pairs of notes; and he remarks that eighths in gigues are to be equally stressed rather than L-S. (French authors, by the way, sometimes except the allemande, rather than the gigue, from use of inequality.)

Quantz also cites the usual rules that dots and slurs cancel inequality where it would otherwise apply. For him, too, the slur rule obviously applies only to slurred groups of more than two notes, as his example shows slurred pairs of notes.

Elsewhere Quantz remarks, of a passage of notes slurred in pairs, that "the first of each two must always be heavier than the following one, both in duration and volume" (Quantz, 223). This is one of the few descriptions of inequality to mention dynamics. It should be noted that the goal of unequal rendering of notes is not rhythmic alteration per se, but use of agogics to put emphasis on the principal notes and to deemphasize offbeat and passing tones.

Quantz gives a very accurate account of French-style inequality, and his remarks about dynamics are as significant as they are unusual. He stresses that the inequality is not as strong as actual dotting would be, and he is careful to point out that inequality applies only to the more prevalent note values in a movement. Also of interest is the fact that for Quantz, S-L inequality does not seem to be associated with slurred pairs (used in his example). These points are important, in coming from a significant figure in mid-eighteenth-century German music.

Earlier, in 1698, Georg Muffat described inequality, among the many other features of French performance, with particular reference to the French court and Lully's orchestra. Muffat had spent years in France and was well acquainted with the practice. He says that it applies to notes of uniform value in such contexts as "sixteenth notes in four-beat measures, eighth notes in two-beat or *alla breve* measures, or notes that divide a beat in half in slightly quick triple meters." He describes the practice simply as dotting the odd-numbered notes at the expense of the time of the even-numbered notes (Cooper and Zasko, 232).

Muffat's description of playing inequality in terms of the longer note's being "dotted" oversimplifies matters slightly. Many French authorities of the period describe inequality as requiring "a little more time and stress on the first [onbeat] of two notes of equal value . . . without, however, dotting it or detaching it" (Brossard, 294). This approach is confirmed by the earliest known attempt at notating inequality. Guillaume-Gabriel Nivers, in his *Second livre d'orgue* (1667), represents inequality in several settings of "Lauda Sion" by means of pairwise sequences of ♩. ♪ ♩. ♪: a 3:2 proportion. Sometimes inequality is represented by ordinary dotted notation, as in the organ music of Gigault

(1685), who remarks that one can vary the sharpness of the rhythm to animate one's playing. Music written with pervasive dotted notation, from France, England, and Germany, and even the music of Domenico Scarlatti (e.g., the Sonata in G Minor, K. 8), may be subject to this sort of varied treatment rather than the persistent sharpened rhythm that is often associated with written-out dotting. These decisions depend on the style and mood of the piece.

Inequality can apply to either slow or brisk movements, apparently for the sake of graciousness in the former and for liveliness in the latter. Its application should be flexible and feel convincing to the player. If your attempts at inequality feel forced and unnatural, work with it until it becomes meaningful. Even so celebrated a virtuoso as Ralph Kirkpatrick remarked that he had to "make peace with the doctrine of inequality." The best general advice I can offer is to root inequality in agogic accents—to treat it as a kind of stylized rubato. (This approach is suggested by Quantz's association of inequality with what the player is to do in a very brisk tempo: not to apply pairwise inequality, but to place an agogic accent on the beginning of each four-note grouping.) An indiscriminate application is meaningless, for the music to which inequality applies is constantly varied in its utterance.

Italian inequality seems to have favored S-L (Lombardic) treatment, perhaps in a rather sharp rhythmic style. This rhythm is often fully notated in highly characteristic passages in works, for example, by Frescobaldi and Froberger. However, the player could also apply S-L inequality to notes written evenly. Frescobaldi describes this practice as applying to sixteenths against eighths, where the player is to render the second note of every pair of sixteenth notes as dotted. Frescobaldi mentions that the tempo should not be especially fast. The direct relevance of Frescobaldi's comments to Bach's music is, of course, remote, but I mention the passage to indicate another important trend distinct from the French style: use of Lombardic rhythm on sixteenths (in the almost invariably common-time meter of seventeenth-century toccatas). This is a trend at least initially important to the *stylus phantasticus*, which flowered in Italy.

Opinions vary on what movements or passages in Bach's music are candidates for treatment in French-style inequality. One would expect that French inequality would be most applicable to Bach's dance suites, which are generally of French inspiration. Bach must, almost certainly, have been aware of the practice.

A well-known example of S-L inequality in Bach's music appears in the Italianate slow movement of the D Major Harpsichord Concerto (BWV 1054). I call it inequality because this oft-quoted passage amounts to an example of "written-out performance practice." The harpsichord version is a transcription of the Violin Concerto in E major (BWV 1042). In the course of making the arrangement, notes written equally but slurred in pairs in the violin original become S-L in the harpsichord version (see Example 8-4b). The change in notation was probably made to allow the four-note slurrings that appear in the harpsichord version. These permit more nuance (with shadings of overlegato) in the harpsichord and preserve a sense of the quarter-note pulse, which might be lost when the violin notation, rendered on the harpsichord, is shorn of the violin's dynamic flexibility.

Example 8-4a, b. (a) Quantz, illustration of three passages to which inequality applies; (b) Bach, Adagio e piano sempre, Harpsichord Concerto in D Major, BWV 1054, mm. 23–24.

Inequality has nothing to do with overdotting. These are two different rhythmic treatments that apply to different contexts. Overdotting refers to the exaggeration of written-out dotted rhythms. Inequality refers to the mildly uneven rendering of notes written in equal values. Inequality rarely sounds fully dotted, let alone exaggeratedly dotted. A crossover point in notation, which sometimes causes confusion, is the use of dotted notation to suggest *notes inégales*. In this case, style and context must determine whether mild inequality or overdotting is intended.

VARIABLE DOT

The durational dot (as opposed to the articulatory dot) in baroque rhythmic notation is extremely flexible in meaning. The rendition of rhythms notated as dotted figures can vary greatly depending on the context. Dotted notation served for everything from sketched inequality to triplets (that is, the dotted figure would be assimilated to triplet notation), to literal performance, to exaggeration of the notated values. Another important consideration is that the notation is often mathematically imprecise. Thus, within a quarter-note value, a dotted eighth may be followed by three or five thirty-second notes, when of course only two thirty-second notes really "fit." Baroque notation is extremely pragmatic in this regard, and the player can readily see the intended sense. Similarly, flourishes sometimes have an extra note, or one fewer, than called for by the value-count of the measure. Modern editions often adjust this notation, though it is better left to the player's taste and discretion (see Examples 8-5a and b).

Another convention, most often applicable to overtures and other pieces of brisk mood with pervasive dotted motives, requires that the upbeat to a dotted figure be rendered as short as the short note of the dotted figure. In this practice, for example, the opening of Bach's Partita No. 2 must be played with short upbeat figures, the eighth values converted to sixteenths or less. A related convention is that of assimilating slower upbeats with faster ones. Thus, the written text (Example 8-5c) would be rendered as in Example 8-5d. Research by Graham Pont indicates that, although the assimilation of upbeats was a common practice, exceptions were possible (Pont, "Handel's Overtures," 317).

Overdotting or double-dotting (called *pointé* style by the French) is perhaps the most famous and controversial of eighteenth-century performance practices. Many authorities from Bach's era describe the sharpening of dotted rhythms, and they sometimes appear in the actual notation, as in Example 8-6a.

This treatment most often applies to overtures and other movements of grand, fiery spirit, particularly when the dotted rhythm is pervasive—movements such as Variation XVI of the *Goldberg Variations* or the opening of Partita No. 4. Thus, when Kuhnau wants to evoke the boasting and pride of the giant Goliath in the opening movement of his Biblical Sonata "The Battle between David and Goliath" (1700), he uses a dotted figure as his primary material (Example 8-5b), and here overdotting would be applicable. Dotted rhythm was considered evocative of pride, nobility, and courtly pomp. The French overture style is a preeminent instance of the latter.

Although dotted figures in overtures and other genres were often overdotted, Quantz states that a dotted eighth and sixteenth played against a group of eight thirty-second notes should be rendered literally. Whether Bach had this rule in mind when he penned a movement such as Fugue No. 5, *WTC* 1, is uncertain. Literal rendition of dotted figures of course applies to a wide range of ordinary instances. Overdotting or underdotting is applicable mainly to the various contexts described here.

Example 8-5a–d. Bach, Variation XVI, *Goldberg Variations*, BWV 988: (a) m. 6, original notation; (b) m. 6, Henle edition; (c) m. 3 as written; (d) m. 3 as played.

Example 8-6a, b. (a) F. Couperin, Passacaille, Ordre 8, mm. 50–52; (b) Kuhnau, "Le bravate di Goliath," Biblical Sonata No. 1, mm. 1–3.

"Underdotting" is a modern term used to denote rhythmic assimilation rather than exaggeration. It applies when the dotted figure serves as shorthand for a triplet figure, as in Fugue No. 10, *WTC* 2. This notation was a substitute for a triplet group. That is, a dotted eighth and sixteenth represent what today would be written as a triplet group of a quarter note followed by an eighth note. This caught on only slowly as the eighteenth century progressed. Assimilation of such dotted formulas is often required. For instance, in the corrente of Partita No. 1, the rapid tempo of the dance makes a literal rendering of the notation absurd (with the short note of the dotted figure coming after the third note of the triplet groups). Similarly, the brilliant and rapid fugue that concludes the Toccata in G Minor obviously requires assimilation of the dotted figures to triplets. The reasons for this kind of notation are discussed in chapter 7.

A long-short rhythm can sometimes be altered to a dotted figure. A written-out example, with the alteration applied throughout the movement, is found in two versions of the chorale setting *An Wasserflüssen Babylon* (BWV 653 and 653a). Of course, the difference between the two versions should probably be considered more than ornamental. One version uses an eighth value followed by two sixteenths, the other a dotted eighth and two thirty-seconds. Similarly, notes written evenly could be performed L-S (not necessarily in terms of French inequality, although the dividing line is impossible to ascertain). Perhaps most cases in which today's player should make such an alteration of the rhythm would involve individual contexts requiring rubato rather than outright, thorough-going reshaping of a fundamental motive, but the degree to which such pervasive alterations were normal in the baroque era cannot be determined. Some eighteenth-century printed texts have even note patterns altered by hand to dotted rhythms. Changes of this type are not consistent, but vary in the course of a movement, as an aspect of rubato rather than inflexible application of a principle. These altered scores seem to bear out the point that performance subtleties should accord with musical context rather than rules of uniformity. Graham Pont has done invaluable work on the subjects of overture style and rhythmic alterations.

Probably the most usual alteration of even notes to dotted figures is as an intensifying ornamentation. Two eighth notes may be altered to a dotted eighth followed by a sixteenth, or an eighth note followed by two sixteenths may become a dotted eighth followed by two thirty-second notes. Bach's written-out embellishments to several sarabandes include instances of this practice (see chapter 9). As with the Froberger example discussed earlier, these cases may be ways of notating an agogic accent rather than full dotting, let alone overdotting. Again, these areas can sometimes be open to slight rhythmic assimilation rather than exaggeration. No one solution is necessarily more "correct" than another.

TWO AGAINST THREE

A rhythmic pattern of two against three is fully possible within the parameters of Bach's style, although some modern commentators have asserted the contrary. Several works (both for solo keyboard and for ensemble) make this indisputably clear, however. (Frederick Neumann has discussed this point admirably.) In Example 8-7, motives in triplets and duplets are presented at first separately, and subsequently in combination. Instances such as this make it clear that two against three is indeed part of Bach's musical language.

Example 8-7. Bach, *Allein Gott in der Höhe sei Ehr, Clavierübung* 3, BWV 675, mm. 38–39.

SUGGESTIONS FOR FURTHER READING

Caswell, Judith. "Rhythmic Inequality and Tempo in French Music between 1650 and 1740." Ph.D. diss., University of Minnesota, 1973. [The first half of this study contains translations of all the texts relating to French inequality.]

Cooper, Kenneth, and Julius Zasko. "Georg Muffat's Observations on the Lully Style of Performance." *Musical Quarterly* 53 (1967): 239. [Muffat on strong and weak.]

Neumann, Frederick. *New Essays on Performance Practice.* "Problems of Rhythm." Ann Arbor, Michigan: UMI Research Press, 1989.

Pont, Graham. "French Overtures at the Keyboard: 'How Handel Rendered the Playing of Them.'" *Musicology* 6 (1980): 29–50.

———. "Handel and Regularization: A Third Alternative." *Early Music* 13 (1985): 500–505.

———. "Handel's Overtures for Harpsichord or Organ: An Unrecognized Genre." *Early Music* 11 (1983): 309–322.

———. "Rhythmic Alteration and the Majestic." *Studies in Music* 12 (1978): 68–100.

Chapter 9

ORNAMENTATION AND
EMBELLISHMENT

Players accustomed mainly to ornaments as they were notated in the nineteenth and twentieth centuries tend to find baroque ornament signs a confusing, bristling jungle. But here, as elsewhere in life, much depends upon mental habit. Players who become accustomed to a few basic signs and their meaning will soon find themselves comfortable with Bach's range of signs as a whole.

Bach's keyboard ornamentation has received nearly as much written commentary as the four Gospels. All that I propose to do here is to give an account of the basics for each ornament: signs and other notation, interpretation according to the usual contexts, and a few pragmatic suggestions. I unequivocally recommend further reading, suggested at the end of the chapter and in the bibliography. Full coverage of this subject can extend into an infinitude of detail that will surprise the novice, who is advised to absorb it in units.

Why are the ornaments shown by signs at all? Why are they not written into the text in "normal" notes? There are many reasons: the signs keep the basic line clearer; they save time that would otherwise be spent in writing notes; since each ornament uses the same basic formula, reading the ornament as a sign instead of in multiple notes is that much easier; and the signs allow more flexibility in the exact rendition (the "realization") as to speed, rhythmic delicacy, and the number of notes in a trill or mordent.

The little table of ornaments that Bach drew up for his son Wilhelm Friedemann (Table 1) is perhaps the most often-reproduced page of eighteenth-century music manuscript. A few minutes spent with it can banish much perplexity. For instance, those who are confused by old editions that revise the meaning of the short trill (✚) into an inverted mordent (♩♩♩)

174

can feel reassured upon seeing Bach's own example of the sign's realization (♪♪♪♪.). The interpretation as an inverted mordent is not the standard (as Bach's realization should make reasonably clear), but is an occasional exception to the rule, chosen by certain editors and performers to be the norm as they would like to see it.

Bach's table leaves several issues unresolved. Are the ornaments always and invariably on the beat? Are they always to be realized precisely as in the table—three repercussions in a short trill, one in a mordent, and so forth? When should a suffix be included? The answers to these questions (respectively, no, no, and it all depends) always depend upon musical context, as do matters such as the speed and duration of trills and other ornaments.

Perhaps the most important thing to understand concerning ornaments is that, while they are stereotypical in shape, they are not to be played stereotypically. The speed, the particulars of rhythm, and the number of repercussions are not supposed to be invariable. The signs were developed for ease of notation and to allow variety in the rendition of what would otherwise look too uniform in full notation. For instance, the mordent sign (♩) tells you, fundamentally, to play the written note, the note just below it, and the written note again as a rapid figure (♪♪♪.). The sign does not tell you just how rapidly to render the ornament, whether to crush the notes together or play the figure lingeringly, or how many repercussions to play. (More than one repercussion is possible if the player's taste judges this to be musically suitable.) All these divergent possibilities are options, and choices must be made in terms of the movement and phrase in which the ornament is found. Here as elsewhere, context is all-important. The interpretation of ornaments must never be perfunctory; they must suit the line, the harmony, the mood, and the instrument. Different instruments require different shadings for the ornaments in a given passage.

One can often decide how to realize any specific ornament by asking, "What is the ornament's role in this context?" Playing the passage without the ornament will frequently show what it is doing there: how it amplifies the functions of the basic notes, how it provides some accentual or rhythmic function, or how it forms part of the line. Is it melodic, harmonic, accentual, sustaining, an extension of the surface rhythm to its fastest elements, a combination of some of these, or something else yet? A trill, for instance, can create a sustained vocal effect or provide an accent; appoggiaturas create expressive dissonance; and sometimes ornaments assist in creating a crescendo of rhythmic activity. Mere reproduction of the pattern shown in a table of ornaments is not the same as musical realization of the ornament—it is only the beginning. The ornamentation is always part of the melodic and harmonic picture and must be worked out with that in mind. The ornaments are integral to the musical conception.

When in doubt about an ornament, or indeed many about musical issues, ask yourself, "How would I sing it?" No good singer would adopt a mechanical realization of an ornament.

Ornaments should not be omitted at whim, if they are authentically Bach's. However, not all of the surviving sources for Bach's music were supervised by the composer. Some works, such as the English Suites, are known only in manuscript copies made by Bach's pupils. Others, for example the French Suites, are known in their final, revised form only from pupils' copies. In such cases, one or another manuscript will sometimes present ornaments that do not appear in other copies. Those that most likely stem from the composer himself will be the ornaments common to all or most of the sources. The extras may still be appropriate (indeed, they are important evidence regarding baroque performance practice), but in these cases the player has discretion as to what to include and what to omit. (Therefore it is important to use an edition that indicates what the different sources present. See Appendix A.) Works extant in a fair copy by Bach (such as *WTC* 1) or in a printed version that he supervised (notably, the four parts of the *Clavierübung*) represent the other side of the coin. In these cases, while there are places where it can be appropriate to add further ornaments, nothing should be left out. There are recordings by famous artists in which many ornaments are omitted. The fame of the players notwithstanding, these performances should never serve as models for the treatment of Bach's texts.

VARIABILITY IN ORNAMENTS

Bach's ornament table in the *Clavierbüchlein* appears in Table 1. It amounts to a somewhat simplified selection made from the famous table of ornaments by Jean Henry d'Anglebert (published in his *Pièces de clavecin* of 1689). Bach copied out d'Anglebert's table (his copy is reproduced in Badura-Skoda, 325) and in the course of time adopted what he required from it. (The main omissions were d'Anglebert's arpeggiation formulas.) Although incomplete, the table shows the basic shapes of most of Bach's keyboard ornaments. I will first discuss the general contents of the table and then go into more detail in discussing each ornament separately.

One and the same ornament can be shown by various signs or with some or all components fully written out as notes. For instance, even in Bach's table, two different signs for the same ornament appear at the end. The ornament

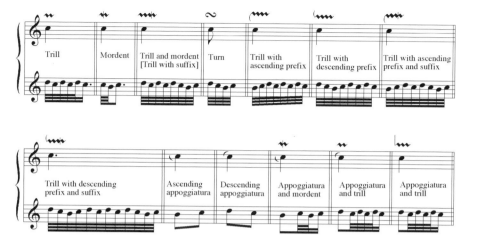

Table 1. Bach's table of ornaments.

table uses signs because its function is to explain the common signs, not to show every written form of every ornament. Thus, a trill can be represented by a sign or by the indication *tr*. A trill with a suffix can be represented by a sign that includes the suffix indication (the vertical line at the end of the sign) or by the sign and written-out notes to show the suffix. A turn can be either shown by sign or fully written out.

The short trill, beginning on the upper note, is shown with three repercussions, ending on the main note, which is sustained slightly at the end. This differs from d'Anglebert's illustration of the basic trill, which fills up all the time value of the note with repercussions. Bach shows perhaps the most usual rendering, with the slight pause on the main note at the end; but it is the shape, not the number of repercussions (which will of course vary according to note length and other circumstances), that is important. Remember that the short trill is misrepresented as an inverted mordent in some old editions; indiscriminate use of this form is perhaps the most glaring grammatical error commonly heard. (The inverted mordent, or *Pralltriller*, has its uses—see below—but these are limited.) Whatever the exceptions to the rule might be, the basic form starts on the upper note, and usually on the beat, rather than before; the notation suggests that the repercussions should occupy most of the note value. Again, the signs are a stenographic convenience, but their realization has to be flexible. Of course, flexibility is one thing, stark alteration another. I have heard playing in which the prefixes and suffixes were deliberately removed from some of Bach's trills (for example, at the opening of the Fantasia in C Minor, BWV 906—taking all the wildness out of the passage). Elaborating the existing ornamentation appears to have been a standard eighteenth-century practice; simplifying it was not. Elaboration can range from replacing a simple trill with a more complex one (with a prefix, for example) to thoroughgoing embellishment, as will be discussed later in this chapter.

The trills with prefixes and suffixes are represented in the table by their basic shape, not an unvarying prescription. Bach's illustrations fill up the note values with thirty-second notes, but in actual practice the repercussions of the main part of the trill depend upon the interpretation of each particular case. The prefix or suffix is invariable; the middle part is ad libitum.

As the notation for the trills, mordents, and appoggiaturas shows, the time of the ornamenting notes is subtracted from the value of the basic note over which the sign appears. Therefore, the point of departure seems clearly to be rendition on the beat, not ahead of it. (C. P. E. Bach's unequivocal preference for onbeat ornaments may well stem from his father's taste.) At least in some cases where an ornament was to be realized ahead of the beat, Bach wrote it out. This kind of exception is sometimes pointed to as evidence of a supposed tendency to before-the-beat performance. However, it seems at least equally valid to see these cases, which require writing out in full, as exceptions that prove the rule of onbeat realization. To be sure, Bach occasionally writes out a standard treatment: note all the onbeat short mordents in the Fantasia in C Minor, BWV 906. David Schulenberg has suggested that, in this chromatic piece, the mordents are written out to ensure the correct accidentals for the auxiliary notes (Schulenberg, *The Keyboard Music of J. S. Bach*, 122). (It was not Bach's practice to write in accidentals above or below ornaments. If these appear in an edition, they are editorial.)

Appoggiaturas are represented in the table only by small hooks, which are not always reproduced in modern editions. These appear frequently in Bach's scores, but he more often uses a small note slurred to the main note, a notation that does not appear in the table. Also, the table shows the appoggiatura modifying only a duple-value note; it gives no example of ternary division. Bach includes the combination of appoggiatura and mordent (shown by d'Anglebert as well), a formula particularly beloved of the French keyboard school.

Also missing from the *Clavierbüchlein* table are acciaccaturas, the slide (shown either by notes or a sign), arpeggio signs, and the short style of appoggiatura, as well as a separate sign for the long mordent with multiple repercussions (included by d'Anglebert); but Bach used one and the same sign for both long and short mordents. He doubtless explained this and the other finer shadings of the notation to his son orally, in the same way that he abandoned writing out a full guide to thoroughbass. (The last pages of the 1725 *Clavierbüch-lein für Anna Magdalena Bach* include fifteen rules for thoroughbass playing, followed by the written comment that the remaining considerations lent themselves better to oral than written instruction.)

THE TRILL

If its creator had known how much ink would be spilled on the topic (including here), the trill might never have been invented. Regarding the trill in Bach's era, the main topics of seemingly endless discussion in modern times center on before-the-beat versus on-the-beat realization, and whether to begin on the main (written) note or the upper (auxiliary) note. My own position on these matters is somewhat biased toward the middle of the road, and I will try to outline the issues fairly and briefly.

Trills serve many functions in keyboard music. They can sustain, accent, suggest dynamics or vocal effects, and end a rhythmic crescendo (as they do so often in Mozart's music). Harmonically, a trill can be a kind of animated appoggiatura, by virtue of the dissonant auxiliary note. The dynamic emphasis can be put on the main or the upper note of a trill on both the piano and the clavichord. The same effect can be managed to some extent on the harpsichord by timing or articulation: by judicious rhythmic and metric adjustment, the performer can make a trill stress either the dissonant auxiliary note or the consonant main note. More or less emphasis falls on the main or the auxiliary note according to the way the note is placed on the metric subdivisions.

Trills were not used primarily to make up for the lack of long-term sustain in stringed keyboard instruments. The organ can prolong a note indefinitely, yet French and German organ music of the period is copiously supplied with trills and other ornaments.

The trill can function as the rhythmic activation of one very long note. This concept can greatly help to shape a trill's rendition. It also suggests that the trill should accelerate, however slightly, to maintain and increase the intensity through the "single" note's duration.

A "short" trill sign (⁓) can signify a long trill, as can *tr* or a longer wavy line. Notation was not altogether exact and exclusive, particularly in manuscripts. Again, the player must always take the context into consideration when deciding on details of the realization.

Most of the important French tables of keyboard ornaments show the trill unequivocally beginning on the upper note. This is also the case with German tables, including one by J. C. F. Fischer, whose music was known to Bach. The only written-out realization of a trill sign that we have from Bach, who took French ornamentation as a model, shows the same thing. As already discussed, it would seem that beginning with the upper note, and beginning on the beat rather than before, make a reasonable norm from which to work. There are of course exceptions. Foremost among these is the case of short trills on offbeats. In the course of a line, these are often most gracefully played ahead of the beat, frequently as inverted mordents. This way they have a melodic and connective function, rather than an accentual one. Short onbeat trills can be highly accentual. C. P. E. Bach and others recommend a "snap" at the end of short trills, by which is meant playing the last two notes as rapidly as possible, a characteristic that can apply to both onbeat and prebeat treatments. It is conceivable that Bach's realization of the trill in his ornament table reflects a snapped trill, of which the slightly sustained main note at the end is characteristic.

When the main note of a trill is preceded by a note a step above, the auxiliary note of the trill can be tied over (Example 9-1a). This effect, with the repercussions beginning momentarily after the beat on which the trill would otherwise start, must not be confused with a main-note trill starting on the beat. However, there is no reason not to use the latter formula if it works gracefully in the context. A representative candidate for this approach is shown in Example 9-1b, with a main-note trill on the G-sharp that does not repeat the opening A.

Approaching the trilled note from the note a step above the main note of the trill does not require tying over the upper note, nor does it mandate beginning the trill from the main note. There is no reason not to start the trill afresh if repeating the upper note is effective in the context, as in Example 9-1c, from Invention No. 1. Certainly a main-note start is possible, but reiterating the C at the trill's opening allows a clearer, more even delineation of the four eighth notes. Decisions of this kind have to be based on what makes sense in regard to accent, rhythm, harmony, and other contextual elements.

An afterbeat or "suffix" can be added by the player when it is not written in by the composer. A suffix is effective when it moves smoothly into the ensuing note. Short (often accentual) trills do not usually require it; this is particularly true, as C. P. E. Bach indicates, when trills are added to descending stepwise passages. Depending on the context, many long trills do not require a suffix either. Note that suffixes make a trill more weighty, in that they stress the arrival point, and less "passing" or merely decorative in effect.

As mentioned, trill afterbeats are sometimes shown by a vertical line in the trill sign (as in Bach's table), sometimes written out as sixteenths, sometimes written as thirty-seconds or other values. This is another case in which the notation is not always literal, but merely shows the shape. In at least two well-

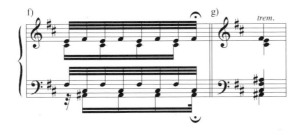

Example 9-1a–f. (a) Formula for trill with auxiliary note tied over; (b) Bach, Sarabande, Partita No. 3, mm. 1–2; (c) Bach, Invention No. 1, BWV 772, mm. 1–2; (d) Bach, Grave, Overture in the French Manner, mm. 8–9; (e) ribattuta formula; (f) Bach, Adagio, Toccata in D Major, BWV 912, m. 1, final version; (g) Bach, Adagio, Toccata in D Major, BWV 912, m. 1, early version.

known instances, Bach includes a rest before the afterbeat: in Prelude No. 10, *WTC* 1, and in the opening Grave of the Overture in the French Manner (Example 9-1d). This is presumably an unusual effect but could be adopted when it seems appropriate.

One ornament symbol has given rise to some uncertainty and speculation. It looks like a short trill with ascending or descending prefix and suffix (,) and appears in some non-autograph Bach sources, notably the Prelude and Courante II of English Suite No. 1. In the Prelude it is found on eighth-note upbeats in a reasonably brisk tempo. In this context, interpretation as even a short trill with prefix and afterbeat is difficult and clumsy, and quite unlike Bach's usual use of elaborate trills. However, as a mordent sign modified by an appoggiatura hook, the sign would be equivalent to the "appoggiatura plus mordent" of Bach's table. This realization accommodates the context of the English Suite Prelude very naturally, as well as the ornament's other appearances in the Courante. On the other hand, the Gigue by Dieupart from which Bach evolved this Prelude (see Example 2-8b) uses a short trill with afterbeat where Bach used the sign in question, which may suggest that the sign after all signifies some form of trill with afterbeat.

In the Italianate trill called the ribattuta, the first two repercussions are in dotted rhythm (Example 9-1e). This ornament was used by the organist Dietrich Buxtehude, whose music was studied and admired by Bach. How relevant this formula may be to Bach's writing is questionable, but the ribattuta can make a lovely effect in appropriate contexts, as for instance in the slow movements of the transcriptions of Italian and Italianate concertos.

When parallel fifths or octaves would result from the usual realization of trills or other ornaments, adjustments have to be made to avoid them. Usually one ornament must be realized ahead of the beat or delayed slightly until the other part or parts have shifted.

THE TREMOLO

Usually written out in thirty-second notes, the tremolo is an ornament that only rarely occurs in Bach—among the clavier works, most notably in the Toccatas in D Major and E Minor. As with written-out realizations in ornament tables, the player need not feel obligated to follow the precise number of repercussions notated. The notation is even more approximate in the early version of the D Major Toccata (see Example 9-1f).

THE MORDENT

The mordent is shown in Bach's table with only one repercussion, but multiple repercussions are appropriate when there is space and if it is rhythmically and melodically apt. The single repercussion is more incisive. Mordents can be played quickly at various degrees of speed and accent; they can also be rendered slowly, such as with some lingering on the first note. Although the basic form is with the notes connected, there is no reason not to articulate them to some degree for a more aggressive, brilliant effect. Fast mordents were sometimes played with the main note sounded once and sustained, while the auxiliary note was quickly touched and released against it. This is a rapid, light way of suggesting a three-note figure while sounding only two notes: a nip, not a bite. (The term *mordent* comes from the Italian word meaning "to bite.") The latter approach is like playing an upper-auxiliary grace note almost simultaneously with the main note, but holding the upper rather than the lower note. The effective result is a glancing, very fast and light mordent.

The accentual nature of the mordent, and the appearance of its realization in Bach's table of ornaments, would seem to preclude prebeat performance in most instances, but it is certainly an option.

THE TURN

Bach's table shows the turn only in the form that begins from the note above the written note. In musical uses, it occurs as shown in the table, modifying one note (usually played on the beat); it can also appear as a figure sounding between two written notes, played after the principal note has been sounded. Though fundamentally a rapid, legato formula, it has to be played according to context. (E. W. Wolf, writing in 1785, mentions detached rendering of turns as an option, which makes their effect more brilliant; this treatment may have been idiosyncratic to the time Wolf was writing.) Bach often writes out the turn in full-sized notes, as in the Andante of the Italian Concerto and in certain of the *Goldberg Variations*. He probably did this to ensure the rhythmic pace that his notation shows, as opposed to the turns being played so quickly as to isolate them from the overall flow (see Examples 9-2a and b). Such cases are suggestive for realization of the sign notation elsewhere: the turn can be integrated into the predominant moving values. Bach uses the turn in varied contexts and often integrates it into the melody, even with the first note tied over from before (Example 9-2c), so it was natural to write out the line in full rather than to rely on signs. This choice was probably easier in the long run, and it afforded more control over the final performance. C. P. E. Bach remarks that the turn is nearly always played quickly; he compares it to "a normal suffixed trill in miniature." This assertion makes even more understandable his father's decision to write out what are, in effect, slower turns. The written-out turns suggest that this ornament can sometimes be rendered more slowly than the son's comment would indicate.

THE SLIDE

The slide is a rising three-note formula, represented by the sign ⌣. It begins two steps below the principal note and follows the formula shown in Example 9-2d. Like the turn, it can be notated by sign or in full notes. The slide is basically legato and gracious, rather than brilliant. It seems to be an onbeat formula but is sometimes written out before the beat (Example 9-2e). Therefore, context rather than rule should probably govern its realization. As with other ornaments, its rendition should be varied in accordance with the immediate circumstance.

ONE-NOTE GRACES

Like the trill, the appoggiatura and related single-note ornaments have produced enormous quantities of written commentary. A fundamental problem is that one-note graces of a melodic nature can be rendered either ahead of the beat or on the beat, and one-note graces of a harmonic nature (appoggiaturas) are played only on the beat, yet are notated in precisely the same way as the melodic ornaments. Whether a particular grace is one or the other can only be determined by context, and the decision is not always cut and dried.

One-note graces are most often notated either with small notes that modify the full-size written note, or with hooks—small curving lines near the head of the note being modified (see Table 1). Their notation draws attention to their function, their dynamics and timing being different from the other notes.

The appoggiatura has an important harmonic role. It is a dissonant note, played on the beat, that resolves to the consonant note. Occasionally it is fully written out, probably when Bach wanted one particular realization and no other. Whatever the notation, the appoggiatura is always slurred to its resolution.

In his ornament table, Bach used the term *Accent* for the appoggiatura: he called an ascending appoggiatura a "rising accent" (*Accent steigend*), the descending form a "falling accent" (*Accent fallend*).

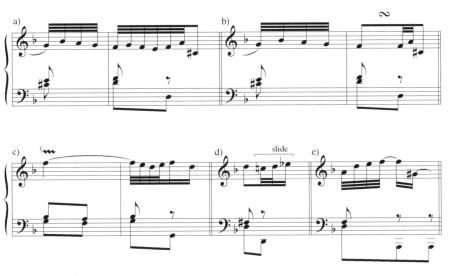

Example 9-2a–e. Bach, Andante, Italian Concerto, BWV 971: (a) mm. 11–12 as written; (b) mm. 11–12 with sign notation; (c) mm. 17–18 (tied-over turn); (d) m. 45 (slide formula); (e) m. 42.

There are two basic varieties of appoggiatura: the short and the long. The rule with the long appoggiatura is that it occupies half the value of a duple-value note (as shown in Bach's table, where the realizations show two eighth notes for an appoggiatura and its resolution) and two-thirds the value of a ternary-value note (not shown in the table). Thus, an appoggiatura modifying a dotted quarter note takes a quarter-note value, and the resolution—the written note—takes the remaining eighth-note value. When the main note is tied over or is followed by a rest, the appoggiatura can occupy the full time of the first note, since the resolution then takes place on the following tied-over value or rest. When the context does not allow time for such treatment, the appoggiatura's duration is shortened. In fact, the context most often does not allow such treatment, as in the opening of the Loure of French Suite No. 5. Following these rules in such a case makes nonsense of rhythm and harmony.

The dissonant appoggiatura must resolve before the harmonic picture has shifted so that the resolution is not compromised (Example 9-3).

The short appoggiatura is played on the beat, very quickly; its duration is from very brief to perhaps roughly one-quarter of the resolution note. (This treatment should not be confused with the standard crushed grace note of later

Example 9-3. Bach, Prelude No. 4, *WTC* 2, BWV 873i, mm. 21–22.

piano styles.) There are many contexts where the short appoggiatura is the only logical and satisfying solution, if the rhythm and/or harmony do not admit the formula of the long appoggiatura.

Frederick Neumann took the view that most of Bach's one-note graces were to be interpreted as short appoggiaturas or prebeat melodic graces. Certainly there are many contexts in which these are the most valid solutions. However, he stresses this view to the extent that he discounts Bach's own ornament table. The player must be sensitive to context and keep the various possibilities in mind. What do we know for certain? For one thing, Bach emulated French ornaments in his keyboard music; he knew the ornament tables of d'Anglebert and Dieupart at least. Both of these, and Bach's own, show the same realization of an onbeat, half-value appoggiatura. For another, many contexts in Bach's music make musical sense with the long appoggiatura. Additionally, C. P. E. Bach, in his *Essay*, comes out flatly against prebeat one-note graces, perhaps in a reflection of his father's general attitude. However, some contexts in Bach's music require short appoggiaturas or prebeat interpretations, for instance to avoid parallel fifths.

It is conceivable, from what we know (and there is much that remains unknown on this subject), that Bach may have taken the onbeat model of the long appoggiatura as a standard treatment while also recognizing the exceptions of short appoggiaturas and prebeat graces. Today's player must take all these possibilites into account. Yet we can make some general observations on the treatment of appoggiaturas, long or short. Appoggiaturas are always slurred to their note of resolution; there is no exception to this rule in performance, whether the notation shows the slur or not. There is a firm rule of dynamics that is generally applicable to dissonances moving to resolutions, and certainly to appoggiaturas: the dissonance is relatively loud, the resolution is soft. This inflection was strong. And in coordination with its dynamic shape, the appoggiatura can be strengthened by agogic emphasis. If it takes nominally half the value of the resolution note, that "half" can be prolonged slightly.

One-note graces that serve a purely melodic function were sometimes played ahead of the beat. This was possible even when the written notes were slurred to the following note rather than the prior one, a notation identical to that of an appoggiatura. Eighteenth-century authorities particularly cite one-note graces, occurring between descending notes a third apart, as open to pre-beat rendition. A classic case in Bach's music is in the theme of the *Goldberg Variations*. Example 9-4a shows the music as written. The grace notes in m. 2 could be played ahead of the beat, in accordance with the usual rule that such graces between descending intervals of a third were to be played as prebeat graces. On the other hand, C. P. E. Bach and F. W. Marpurg disallowed pre-beat performance and insisted on short appoggiaturas. (Thus, there were differing views about interpretation in the eighteenth century as well as today.) The downward slide figures in m. 4, written on the beat, and the crowded context for a prebeat realization of the ensuing appoggiatura on the second quar-

Example 9-4a–c. (a) Bach, Aria, *Goldberg Variations*, BWV 988, mm. 1–4; (b) d'Anglebert, ornament table (1689), acciaccaturas; (c) Bach, Scherzo, Partita No. 3, BWV 827, m. 28.

ter-note value of that measure would seem to coordinate with an onbeat inter-pretation of m. 2.

An extremely important one-note grace was the acciaccatura. One form of this ornament has already been cited: a mordent with both notes sounded simultaneously and the lower note released. (Again, this is not the same as the later grace note that precedes the main note, although both ornaments use crushed notes.) C. P. E. Bach considered this form of mordent to be unusual and applicable to detached articulation only. Whether it is relevant to J. S. Bach or not remains an open question. A more significant form is the passing acciaccatura. When breaking a chord, a dissonant note (usually one falling between chord members a third apart) is played but immediately released, whereas the chordal members are held. Other notes as well can be crushed in this manner (see Example 9-4b). This ornament adds considerable fire and color to chords, lends them more powerful accentuation, and can help in the timing and rhythm of extended arpeggiations. As to the last issue, C. P. E. Bach writes: "All chords may be broken in many ways and expressed in rapid or slow figuration. . . . In the interests of elegance the major or minor second may be struck and quitted below each tone of a broken triad or a relationship based on a triad. This is called 'breaking with acciaccature'" (*Essay*, 439).

Bach, like the French, sometimes notates the acciaccatura with slanting lines between the written chord members. A famous example appears in the opening chord of the Sarabande from Partita No. 6. A chord with acciaccaturas indicated by slanting lines did not require an arpeggiation sign as well; an appropriate breaking of the chord was understood. However, acciaccaturas were sometimes played simultaneously with the rest of the chord and appar-ently held through for some time, without arpeggiation necessarily being involved. This was a typical Italian continuo practice that gave the harpsichord rhythmic authority (and an effect of heightened volume). This style appears in solo music as well, most notably certain sonatas by Scarlatti (see K. 175 in A Minor and K. 215 in E Major for two famous examples), whose incredible dis-sonances derive from rather normal Italian continuo style. This style of disso-nant acciaccatura, written out in normal-looking notes, explains the famous dissonant chord in Example 9-4c, a case in which Bach wrote out the acciac-catura in the Italian manner, as a chord member.

ARPEGGIOS

Broken chords are of great importance on the harpsichord, as they provide much flexibility in sonority and musical effect. It is not surprising that the

French school, which gave particular emphasis to both ornamentation and the harpsichord, developed the most complete notation for variety of arpeggio treatment. D'Anglebert's table, like many others, shows chords broken from above, from below, and with various acciaccaturas. Even further variety is found in French unmeasured preludes, whose notation allows uninhibited clarity in showing broken-chord treatments. Bach did not include an arpeggiation sign in his ornament table, probably because he used only a single, undifferentiated sign. It may have been open to varied interpretations and hence would have been difficult to account for in the table. Both upward and downward breaking were very much part of the common vocabulary of keyboard playing, and there is no reason not to use either, whether in realizing a sign for a broken chord or in arpeggiating where no sign appears.

Bach rarely writes in arpeggiation signs. Their frequent appearance in Prelude No. 8, *WTC* 1, is completely without parallel in his other keyboard works. This does not mean that he never employed arpeggiation unless the sign for it appears; indeed, it was an understood keyboard resource. The notation may suggest that he felt the need of particular accents in the Prelude: on the harpsichord particularly, arpeggiation can accentuate a chord.

Breaking a chord can soften or increase its impact on the harpsichord or clavichord, depending on the speed and rhythmic placement of the break. Especially on the harpsichord, slower arpeggios usually have the greater weight, so the speed or slowness of a broken chord can suggest more or less accent. These elements become very flexible and subtle on the harpsichord and clavichord because of the clarity of the sound and the pinpoint accuracy of each note's attack. Therefore, broken chords and more elaborate arpeggiation can be useful in making agogic accents. The speed of the break and the rhythm of the breaking can allow much variety of accent, which can be as useful on the piano as on the earlier instruments. As mentioned, acciaccaturas can also be a resource for accent and timing in broken chords.

It is important to break a chord smoothly, regardless of whether the break is slow or so fast as to be almost imperceptible. An arpeggiation must either be evenly paced or move in a graceful arch of increasing or decreasing energy, slowing or accelerating through the pattern. Straggling notes in irregularly paced attacks must be avoided. Often, for clarity's sake the bass must be louder than the middle parts of the chord. Thus, after the bass is sounded, the next note is much softer; following that, a crescendo can be made to the soprano part (a point is also mentioned in Badura-Skoda, 453). Such treatment is crucial on the piano, and often on the clavichord, to avoid opacity of sound. On the harpsichord, rhythmic placement must stand in entirely for such dynamic arching.

Whether an arpeggiated chord is written vertically, as a block, or its full rhythm is realized in notation (as in the first Prelude from *WTC* 1), the established practice was to sustain all the tones of arpeggiated passages. Thus, the detached or even staccato rendition sometimes given to the right-hand notes of Prelude No. 1, *WTC* 1, is a major departure from eighteenth-century style. Bach did not trouble with the cumbersome notation of tying over the upper-staff sixteenths. His notation shows the rhythmic and figural pattern, and he could expect the player to understand the convention of full legato for arpeggiation.

As Nicolas Lebègue points out in his collection of 1677, in terms of unmeasured preludes, a given chord can be sounded more than once. Lebègue mentions that in harpsichord style one "separates [that is, arpeggiates] or repeats chords rather than holding them as units as is done on the organ" (Lebègue, n.p.). A chord can, for instance, be sounded with a quick break or none at all, then immediately reiterated more slowly and meditatively. This sort of treatment is most natural to contexts allowing some freedom of pace, as in "improvisatory" areas of toccatas or at any climax with a fermata. In the latter instance, this technique can help to make a grand accent (see Example 9-5).

BLOCK-NOTATED CHORDS

J. S. Bach wrote a number of keyboard pieces in which chords to be arpeggiated are notated in vertical blocks of whole- and half-note values, and sometimes with quarter-note values as well. These include the Praeludium in C Minor (BWV 921), the Praeludium in E-flat Major (BWV 815a; originally part of French Suite No. 4), the Fantasia of the Fantasia and Fugue in A Minor (BWV 944), the early version of Prelude No. 3 from *WTC* 2 (BWV 872), and the Chromatic Fantasia (BWV 903). The degree and kind of elaboration that was expected of the performer remains an open question, but it is likely that some latitude of approach was expected. Similar passages occur in music of Bach's contemporaries, including works of J. C. F. Fischer, and in music of the next generation, notably by W. F. Bach and C. P. E. Bach. Fischer's Preludes No. 6 and No. 8 from his *Musicalisches Blumen-Büschlein* (1696) are particularly beautiful pieces, with passages strongly reminiscent of the arpeggio sections of Bach's Chromatic Fantasia.

The basic approach to arpeggiation of block-notated chords is a rhythmically uniform sweep up from the bass and down again, as indicated in the first arpeggiated chord (this one written out) of the Chromatic Fantasia. Passing tones (represented by quarter-note members of some half-note chords in the

Example 9-5a, b. (a) Bach, Fugue No. 20, *WTC* 1, BWV 865, mm. 79–81; (b) Bach, Contrapunctus VI, *The Art of Fugue*, BWV 1080, mm. 72–73.

Chromatic Fantasia) can be accommodated in the downward sweep. (An excellent summary of approaches to arpeggiation from the Chromatic Fantasia is provided in Schulenberg, *The Keyboard Music of J. S. Bach*, 126–127.)

Sometimes, block chords are written in whole notes or quarter-notes rather than the prevailing half-note notation. Whole-note chords are usually restricted to the opening of a succession of chords. The rhythmic value clearly suggests a metric proportioning in the arpeggiation, however free in general, as well as the possibility of multiple upward and downward soundings of the chord. Full chords written in quarter-note values could be contrasted with the half-note chords by playing them only bass to treble, while the half-note chords are played bass to treble and down again. Other possibilities are suggested in C. P. E. Bach's *Essay*. Apropos of a specific example, he remarks that "in performance each chord is arpeggiated twice. . . . The tones of the slow, fully gripped chords, which are played as arpeggios, are all of equal duration" (442). He also directs twofold arpeggiation of each chord in one of his other fantasias. (This style may relate to Lebègue's description of chord repetition and breaking; it allows considerable freedom in time and in the pacing of the arpeggiation.) The same principles hold for fully notated passages with elaborate chordal figurations ("figurated chords") in C. P. E. Bach's fantasias. If most of the chords, usually notated in half notes, are to be broken twice, then quarter-value chords and quarter-note passing tones that appear in half-note chords are presumably sounded only once. This treatment could apply to the notation in the Chromatic Fantasia and other works of J. S. Bach. What looks like a realization of this kind of treatment appears at the start of Mozart's famous Fantasia in D Minor (K. 397), which begins with a twofold iteration of each broken chord and later moves to single statements of each chord. The chords are slightly elaborated but if written as block chords would, presumably, begin with halves and move to quarters.

Figurated arpeggio patterns (more elaborately patterned than simple up-and-down motion) are a further possibility for J. S. Bach's block-notated chords, although this style may pertain more to C. P. E. Bach's generation than to Sebastian's. Certainly, the period manuscripts that include written-out arpeggios for the Chromatic Fantasia show nothing more elaborate than straightforward up-and-down movement. Badura-Skoda discusses the figurated approach and provides some interesting illustrations (457–464).

A rendition using a regular rhythmic pattern sometimes has to add acciaccaturas to the chords containing fewer notes, in order to accommodate the pattern.

ELABORATION OF FERMATAS

Eighteenth-century sources tell us that fermatas, then as now, indicate a pause. However, they add that it is sometimes appropriate to improvise a flourish, or even a brief cadenza, at these points. Where should these be added, if at all, in Bach's music? One manuscript source of the Toccata in F-sharp Minor includes a short passage (not found in the other manuscripts) to introduce the long sequence before the final fugue. Such brief connective flourishes are occasionally appropriate and may be improvised or prepared by the player.

There are many instances in which Bach, with his usual thoroughness, has written out the appropriate flourish. Two examples appear in the Harpsichord Concerto in D Minor (BWV 1052): at m. 109 of the first movement, and at m. 74 of the second. These are brief gestures (respectively four measures and one measure), eruptions in thirty-second notes of the accumulated energy of the preceding passages. The third movement of this concerto reaches its peroration with what is essentially an orchestrally accompanied cadenza that includes a transitional passage, complete with trills and fermata, marked adagio. A further cadenza or flourish added at the fermata would be completely redundant. Therefore, a fermata, with or without trills and the word *adagio*, does not necessarily signal the need for an added passage, but sometimes requires merely a pause and free timing of the written-in flourish. Here as elsewhere, the musical context must decide what is required. The transition to the fugal section of the Prelude to English Suite No. 6 is a case in point: we find a brief, dramatic pause before the very active fugue commences, but after such a thorough preparation that the balance of elements would most likely be upset by additional passagework. On the other hand, the fermata over the chord that prepares the final tutti of the Presto to the F Minor Concerto, BWV 1056, is an obvious place for an interpolated flourish. The flourish amplifies the climactic moment rather than disturbing any inherent contrasts.

Concertos and toccatas are not the only candidates for flourishes. The *WTC* contains several movements with fermatas that might suggest decoration. Prelude No. 14 and Fugue No. 10 from *WTC* 2 are cases in point, although the bass motion following the fermata in the Prelude is probably sufficient in itself as a bridge. Other movements have a more elaborate flourish composed in: for instance, the concluding two measures of Fugue No. 2, *WTC* 2, in which the fugal texture breaks off to allow a dramatic (and rather organ-like) free-style preparation of the final cadence. Even more dramatic is the interruption of thirty-second notes before the conclusion of Fugue No. 15, *WTC* 2. Such passages require freedom of timing both intrinsically and to underline the contrasts of the events unfolding. Even *The Art of Fugue* contains a passage or two that suggests or requires a cadenza. There can hardly be a question about the need for a flourish before the final cadence of the Canon alla Decima. One of my own solutions for this passage appears in Example 9-6a.

Perhaps Bach's most famous examples of written-in fermata flourishes are those toward the ends of Preludes Nos. 5 and 6 of *WTC* 1 (see Examples 9-6b and c). Prelude No. 22, *WTC* 1, could conceivably include a short connective flourish after the chord with the fermata (m. 22), but this is a case where a simple pause is perhaps as effective as any extra notes could be: "the rest is silence."

CONVENTIONAL ADDITIONS OF ORNAMENTS

It is difficult to suggest general approaches for the addition of graces, which are perhaps most usually required for lightly varying the repetition of a section. Once one begins tabulating the possibilities, the list grows indefinitely. The best guide is study of Bach's own ornamentation. What is the context and function of each ornament? What kinds of ornaments fall on downbeats, on offbeats, on important strong and weak areas? Close study of a few movements in terms of those questions will go far toward providing a sense of "what goes where."

There are some standard contexts in which ornaments may be found and to which they may often be added. Trills, turns, and mordents can appear as

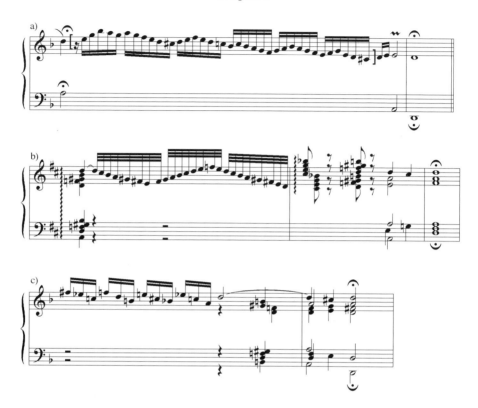

Example 9-6a–c. (a) Troeger, suggested flourish to conclude the Canon alla Decima, *The Art of Fugue*, BWV 1080; (b) Bach, Prelude No. 5, *WTC* 1, BWV 850i, mm. 33–35; (c) Bach, Prelude No. 6, *WTC* 1, BWV 851i, mm. 25–26.

accents on important notes. Short trills often form a melodic ornament on off-beat notes. Very long notes are sometimes sustained by a trill, sometimes sounded afresh (without a trill), or sometimes most effectively left alone. Trills are most often approached from above, not from below, although there are exceptions. Mordents are approached from above or below; they most often appear on downbeats and other accented notes, and sometimes as an extra decoration upon the resolution of an appoggiatura. Turns can appear as a connective formula between notes a step or a third apart. Appoggiaturas can be used to intensify a harmony. Slides can be effective in approaching a note reached by leap. The discussion of *doubles*, below, offers many practical examples of added graces.

Some of Bach's works that survive in multiple copies by his students contain numerous ornament signs (such as trills and mordents) that are not directly traceable to the composer. It is the fashion among both editors and performers to dismiss these from serious consideration, and indeed, they often seem excessive to modern taste (for instance, in the Gigue of French Suite No. 2, whose lavish ornamentation appears in the Neue Bach-Ausgabe and Bischoff editions, among others.) However, no one denies that such zealous applications of ornaments were often made by members of Bach's circle. Were the works really played with such unrestrained ornamentation? We find the same abundance in some other German pieces from the same era (Example 9-7).

Example 9-7. Böhm, *Vater unser in Himmelreich*, mm. 1–3.

It is conceivable that the heavily ornamented versions might imply a very rapid, short way of rendering trills and mordents so that they functioned mainly as tiny accents rather than as distinct (and heavier) ornaments. This treatment would accord well with the two-note rendering of mordents discussed above and the use of snapped inverted mordents for short trills. Perhaps such a light approach characterized the rendition of many ornaments in a way that has not yet been assimilated by modern players.

It is also (barely) possible that the heavily ornamented movements contain most of the ornaments that might be appropriate, and that these texts served

Bach's students as working examples of where ornaments could conceivably be added, without the expectation that all of them be played in any one rendition.

Although the ornaments shown in some nonautograph sources are by no means obligatory, it is not the player's option to pick and choose from among those that certainly stem from Bach. The modern practice one sometimes encounters of omitting written ornaments and playing them upon the repetition has no historical precedent known to me and is scarcely appropriate to Bach's carefully considered scores.

BACH'S NOTE PICTURE

Bach wrote out most of his major works in full, and only rarely do more notes need to be added. For example, a comparison of the Sarabande of English Suite No. 4 with Bach's other sarabandes will suggest that this movement is exceptional in requiring the addition of some further graces. Bach was unusual in his time for being so complete in his notation. Johann Adolph Scheibe, in his famous criticism published in 1737, even saw this habit as insulting to the player, who should know what to add to a plainer note picture: "Every ornament, every little grace, and everything that one thinks of as belonging to the method of playing, he expresses completely in notes; and this not only takes away from his pieces the beauty of harmony but completely covers the melody throughout" (*New Bach Reader*, 338).

What Scheibe means is that the player should be credited with knowing what to add to what is written out: such knowledge is part of the "method of playing." Bach writes out all the detail, which for Scheibe is an insult to the player's knowledge, and also adds to the difficulty of seeing the forest for the trees: with the melody "covered" throughout, it is hard to distinguish the essential notes from the embellishments and thus to sort out the different functions in performance. In fact, playing a skeletal version of the line and texture of a fully realized composition can answer many questions.

Scheibe's remarks are usually attributed to personal anger toward Bach, but his little diatribe suggests what was probably a prevalent attitude about the player's role. François Couperin took the same road as Bach: he wrote out everything, and even went so far as to declare in the preface to his third book of *Pièces de clavecin* (1722) that he was tired of hearing ornaments added and subtracted by players and that his pieces were to be played precisely as he had written them. (Berlioz, in a note to the performers, says much the same thing regarding his opera *Les Huguenots*.) Thus, we find major composers resisting the usual performer's license. In Bach's case, the ornaments and embellishments are often so organically tied to the motives themselves that it is understandable that the whole had to be written out; this is often the reason that the framework should not be elaborated in any other way.

EMBELLISHMENTS

Embellishment is the word used for all musical filigree apart from the ornamental formulas usually indicated by signs rather than written out in notes. Embellishments tend to be connective, linking important notes, whereas ornaments tend to fall on, and emphasize, important notes.

Baroque embellishments range across the spectrum of freedom of timing. The rhythmically freer gestures, although often written in strict values, can be almost as loose in performance as many of the figurations that Chopin and Liszt write in small notes. The written rhythm gives the general shape, which nonetheless may flex to greater or lesser extent. Sometimes some degree of rhythmic assimilation (reducing the sharpness of the notated rhythms) is called for.

What might be termed the lateral density of embellishments (and of ornaments and musical textures generally) is a dynamic function that builds energy. That is to say, the multiplicity of coruscating notes in small values can accumulate considerable power. The harpsichord shows this instantly. On the clavichord and piano, some of the energy buildup can be reduced by dynamic gradations; on the harpsichord, this is done mainly by rhythmic adjustments.

Baroque notation in general includes enormous contrasts between skeletal notation—showing only the barest essentials, to be embroidered by the player —and movements that are notated with utter completeness. Composers used skeletal notation because of the frequent need for haste in providing music for one occasion or another. The composer could depend on the performer's skills to provide what was missing, and indeed the performer's virtuosity depended in part on improvisation.

Paul Badura-Skoda gives a very fine demonstration of background fundamentals versus embellishmental options by offering an interesting treatment of the Sarabande from Bach's Partita No. 1. He reduces it to sparse notation in the style of Handel, then offers new ways of elaborating the foreground: as a choral Kyrie, as a cello solo, and as another keyboard version (Badura-Skoda, 511–518). As he says, Bach happened to want a specific treatment of the foreground (which is naturally part of the compositional process). Handel's plain, chordal-style sarabandes imitate an orchestral type of sarabande; Bach is doing something more intimate.

Though Bach was criticized for taking away the player's prerogative by showing every detail, the reason for his thorough notation lies deeper than an impulse to control. As mentioned, his embellishments are often motivic in nature, so that musical development is ongoing from the largest to the tiniest levels of the composition. Naturally, with the "extra notes" elevated to full participation, they have to be fully written out. Thus, certain sarabandes are in one or another style of *double* (a heavily embellished variant of a movement; see below). These sarabandes, which lack either a separate *double* or a simple version, draw on the style of a *double* to develop the basic material. Partita No. 2 presents an example in its Sarabande, which is modeled on a type of *double* characterized by evenly flowing notes. In fact, it goes even further, for its *double*-like elaboration exhibits tightly figural writing: a highly integrated, structural use of the *double* style. The Sarabande of Partita No. 6 is in an "encrusted" style, with flourishes that are sometimes motivic in nature. At the time of their composition, Bach's ornate sarabandes were probably regarded as unusual. It is up to the modern player to be aware of the basis on which Bach evolved such movements and be able to render them accordingly, giving freedom to the embellishments while balancing their rubato aspect with the motivic functions.

Motivically based embellishments (such as those in Variation XIII of the *Goldberg Variations*, which makes extensive use of a turn figure) sometimes require a more or less straightforward rhythm. Perpetual inflection of the figuration becomes pointless. Others (certainly many scale and arabesque figures) are much freer in nature. Indeed, in the latter, the rhythmic notation is often only approximate: sometimes more accurate, sometimes less. The player must bear in mind what conventions were available for the notation of such freedom.

Sometimes the embellishmental note values do not work out with mathematical accuracy. Fine-level rhythmic accuracy is not the point; rubato is. The French went further: for their approach to the notation of very free music, rhythmic notation was at first dispensed with altogether. Example 9-8 shows a passage as written with great exactitude by Froberger (who combined this exactitude with directions to play freely) and as a contemporary French musician would have notated it. The unmeasured notation of the latter approach has a strong relationship with several measured genres and their rhythmic formulas. The writing is nowhere near so chaotic as it first appears to today's musician. Obviously, Bach's approach to notation of music in the free style derives from Froberger rather than the French school; but Example 9-8 should suffice to convey a warning against overly strict renditions.

The important task of assimilating embellishments into the larger phrase often involves a certain freedom in rendering the figurations, and such rubato

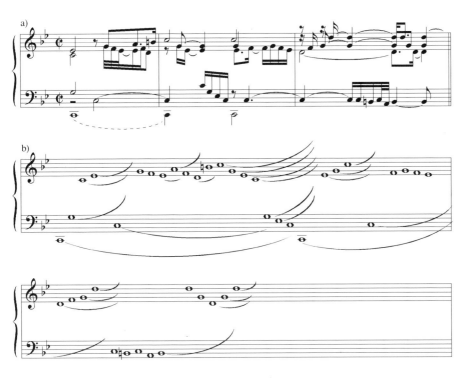

Example 9-8a, b. Froberger, *Tombeau de M. Blancrocher*, mm. 1–3: (a) original notation; (b) as it would appear in French-style unmeasured notation.

was indeed part of the eighteenth-century approach. Without such freedom and sweep, the ear is drawn to the smallest level of rhythmic division rather than to the larger values of the subphrases and phrases. I well recall once looking up a certain Froberger toccata in a library copy of a modern edition. The piece moves in large gestures governed by half-note, whole-note, and larger values. All the runs and flourishes are decorations over these large groupings, very rubato in nature. Someone who had got hold of quite the wrong end of this particular stick had written at the top of the first page, "Count sixteenths." To render the freer range of embellishments in terms of strict beat subdivision is often to miss their point altogether; the grand sweep of certain gestures becomes divided up into small groups of notes like pinpricks. (A good example of a piece to which this is inappropriate, and in which it is often done, is Bach's "Great" Fantasia in G Minor for organ.) Leaving the embellishment level to its proper function (rather than promoting it to the foreground with pedantic and indeed irrelevant attention to small subdivisions of time) allows the basic line to emerge more clearly.

VARIED REPETITIONS

In the eighteenth century it was obligatory for the performer to take repeats. Indeed, it was considered better to omit one or more entire movements from a suite than to omit repetitions within a movement. Since the music was generally new and had not been heard before, repetitions were necessary so that the audience could get a firm grasp on the material. They would have been particularly necessary in Bach's case, as his music is especially elaborate and concentrated. Since this music has a "classic" status today and is usually well known to at least some of its audience, repeats are no longer universally considered to be indispensable in all circumstances.

Nevertheless, some if not all repetitions should be observed in modern performances. They need not be perfunctory. Indeed, they can contribute to the overall projection of energy in the performance. Usually it seems to me most effective to take all repeats and give a more intense and/or detailed rendition in the repetitions. The first time through can be geared to giving the listener a large-scale view of the material, which is intensified and sometimes seen as if through a microscope upon second hearing. Or, in some cases, the reverse may be preferable: one emphasizes the finer details the first time through and brings out the larger sweep on the repetition.

It was expected of the eighteenth-century performer that he or she would, to some extent, ornament and embellish a movement upon repetition. Again, since Bach most often writes out all the necessary details, the performer may feel as though adding anything is an intrusion, but variety can nonetheless be achieved. There are several possible approaches to the repetition of a section:

1. Change the overall dynamic level. The harpsichordist might play on a different registration; the clavichordist or pianist might play more softly or more strongly.
2. Render the accents and contrasts more strongly, play the written ornaments more richly, or otherwise lead the listener's ear in an intensified or even alternative approach to the section just heard. Even if no extra notes are added, the repeats in a movement provide a good opportunity to play even more expansively and/or with greater contrasts and impetus than in the first time through. A parallel to this that was commonly accepted in the baroque era is the way an orator

becomes more and more forceful in the course of a speech (see chapter 12). Low energy should never follow high energy, as one can learn from listening to any effective public speech.

3. Add a few or many ornaments and/or embellishments, basing these choices in the accents and phrasing of the movement itself.

4. Play (either as the repetitions or perhaps additionally) a full *double*. There were at least two distinct styles for such wholesale variation (discussed below).

A good basis for elaborating repetitions is to shape the embellishments so as to highlight any interesting contours or other aspects of the phrases, to render important accents even more fully, and to bring out any other details or alternate approaches that could not be accommodated in a single reading. The dynamics created by the extra activity, and the effect of the new rhythms on the phrasing and motivic development, have to be considered. An undifferentiated, arbitrary thicket of faster notes will accomplish nothing musically.

It is usually unnecessary to embellish passages Bach has already written out in full. Imagine, for instance, adding anything to the opening gesture of the Toccata in D Major. Most fully embellished dance movements can still accommodate discreet additions upon repetition, especially when these increase the intensity. With full-fledged *doubles*, of course, the field is wide open.

Really skeletal writing of course requires extensive improvisation—for example, in some movements by Handel and many Italian works (such as violin sonatas), which are often notated in barest outline with a figured bass (sometimes not even figured) and a bare-bones line for a soloist to use as a starting point. In complete contrast, the best-known baroque keyboard music tends to be fully realized already, and yet sometimes receives extensive additions on the basis of baroque "practices"—practices that apply more readily to truly skeletal texts. The modern player should compare complete and incomplete texts so as to have a firm idea of the overall eighteenth-century terrain: for instance, a sarabande by Bach at his most ornate and one by Handel at his plainest. On the other hand, it was not out of the question to add even more to an already full note picture. "Good taste," constantly invoked by baroque-era commentators, must determine the boundaries.

BACH'S *DOUBLES*

Bach has given us several examples of dance movements with expanded ornamentation and embellishment. Sometimes these are simply specified as "the graces of the same sarabande [or other movement]"; sometimes he uses the term *double*. These movements are:

Praeludium et Partita del TuonoTerzo, BWV 833: Sarabande; Double
Suite in A Minor, BWV 818: the sarabande is entitled "Sarabande Simple" and is followed by a more ornate version entitled "Sarabande Double."
Partita in C Minor, BWV 997: Gigue; Double
English Suite No. 1, A Major: Courante II, Double I, Double II
English Suite No. 2, A Minor: Sarabande; Les agrémens de la même sarabande
English Suite No. 3, G Minor: Sarabande; Les agrémens de la même sarabande
English Suite No. 6, D Minor: Sarabande; Double. (This *double* includes first and second endings, which suggests that it be played independently following the performance of the sarabande proper.)

A special case appears with Courante II of English Suite No. 1. This movement is provided with not one but two fully written out *doubles*. Whether both of the two Courantes in the suite were to be played in a single performance is an open question. Equally unclear is whether both *doubles* to Courante II are to be played in one and the same rendition. My own solution is usually to use Double I for the repeats of the Courante proper, then to play Double II afterward, with or without repeats of its own. This approach (also suggested in Ferguson, 32–33) prevents the one movement from dominating the suite disproportionately. If I were performing Courante II by itself, I might at least play the two *doubles* separately. One could also choose to omit either Courante I or Courante II from a complete performance of the suite. This would probably have been an eighteenth-century player's choice.

The two *doubles* illustrate two different approaches. The first adds miscellaneous flourishes and embellishments to the basic movement, in both bass and upper parts. The principal alteration in the second *double* is made to the bass line, now a walking bass rendered in a more or less even flow of eighth notes. It is more than likely that Bach provided these two *doubles*, as well as others, not as an invariable requirement in performance, but as models for improvising or composing *doubles* for other movements.

As an example of utilizing the lesson provided by Double I of Courante II from English Suite No. 1, I provide here an excerpt from my own *double* for the Courante of Partita No. 2 (Example 9-9). This treatment greatly amplifies the sixteenth-note motion of the original and includes some imitation among these gestures. At m. 10, a passage in sixteenth notes in the original text is turned into an imitation by the tenor embellishment that just precedes the sixteenths.

The embellished versions of the Sarabandes from English Suites No. 2 and No. 3 are particularly useful models for ornamentation and embellishment. In the Sarabande from English Suite No. 3, we find added to the basic text:

Arpeggiation signs
Accented passing tones
Acciaccaturas
Appoggiaturas, appearing both as small notes and as full-sized notes
    (for example, the sixteenths in m. 6). Note the change to
    Lombardic (S-L) rhythm in the soprano of m. 8.
Combinations of appoggiatura and mordent
Trills
New or different suffixes and prefixes to trills that appeared in the
    simple version

Embellishments include flourishes leading into a stressed beat or measure, generally in thirty-seconds and often including sixty-fourths; or division-style transformation of a line in eighths to one in (primarily) sixteenths. Slurs are added largely to reinforce the embellishmental functions of note groups.

In the Sarabande from English Suite No. 2, we find much of the above as well as:

Appoggiaturas (written out in m. 8 and paired notes in m. 25 ff.)
A new dissonance and resolution (m. 14)
Embellishments of a circling or *échappé* variety, as at the opening and
    in mm. 21 and 23
Division-style embellishments
Use of Lombardic rhythm: for example, to break the pattern at the
    final cadence
Mordents and trills
Slide figures in written-out notes, after being notated as a sign in the
    simple version

In neither movement is the left-hand material significantly altered.

A standard technique for *doubles* in the seventeenth and eighteenth centuries was to create a continuous, more or less uniform rhythmic flow using a subdivision of the metric beat: eighths or sixteenths, for example, when the beat is a quarter note. The *double* to the Sarabande of English Suite No. 6 is a

Example 9-9. Troeger, suggested *double*, mm. 1–12, for Bach, Courante, Partita No. 2, BWV 826.

typical example of this technique. The meter is 3/2 and the surface rhythm is movement in eighth notes, which serves as the basis for thoroughgoing arpeggiation of the original voicing. Much of the original voicing is preserved, whether or not it happens to be swept into the flow of eighth-note movement. Its essentials are retained even when, toward the end, the general texture is reduced to simple upward arpeggios.

(Example 9-9 continued)

As we saw, Bach extended this principle of *double* construction even to making a walking bass the source of the uniform rhythm, in the second *double* from Courante II of English Suite No. 1.

The *double* to the Sarabande in the early Suite in A Minor (BWV 818) uses a flow of sixteenth notes in the right hand against eighths in the left, but with a dotted rhythm at the start of some phrases. This is a rather stiff example of a *double*, and in fact Bach later rewrote this movement (and added a Prelude and Menuet to the suite) in the version now designated BWV 818a. In the later Partita in C Minor (BWV 997; not to be confused with Partita No. 2 of *Clavierübung* 1), the *double* makes a virtuosic cascade of sixteenths out of the rather moderate 6/8 gigue and raises the range of the upper line—a quite radical *double*.

A standing question concerns whether Bach's *doubles* are intended to be used as the repeats of the basic movement or are to be played afterward, as separate segments. Occasionally a new tempo is specified for a *double*, as in the one marked Presto that follows an Allegro assai by Jean Marie Leclair in his Sonata in A Major for Violin and Basso Continuo, Op. 9, No. 4. The *double* in Bach's early Praeludium et Partita del Tuono Terzo is marked Allegro, although, as Schulenberg remarks, the tempo may be constant and the marking refer to the general sense conveyed by the faster notes that characterize the *double* (Schulenberg, *The Keyboard Music of J. S. Bach*, 36). However, such tempo markings, taken in conjunction with the repeat signs often provided with *doubles*, suggest that *doubles* were played subsequent to the movement proper, rather than as ordinary embellished repetitions.

Occasionally in modern performances, a simple version is "reconstructed" for a lavishly embellished movement or one written in the style of a *double*, and the original version is played as the repetition. It hardly seems likely that Bach's contemporaries would have done this. Since Bach's writing of the embellishmental surface is closely entwined with the fundamental motives, lines, and harmony, "deconstruction" is a highly arbitrary procedure. However, as a way to recognize the extreme sparseness of means by which Bach creates lush harmonies, an attempt to render a *simple* from, say, the Sarabande of Partita No. 2 is extremely salutary, and I recommend the exercise.

SUGGESTIONS FOR FURTHER READING

Badura-Skoda, Paul. *Interpreting Bach at the Keyboard.* Translated by Alfred Clayton. Oxford: Clarendon Press, 1993. [Includes a list of Bach's ornaments, showing all signs used for each type of ornament (307–310). Well worth examination.]

Neumann, Frederick. *Ornamentation in Baroque and Post-Baroque Music, with Special Emphasis on J. S. Bach.* Princeton, New Jersey: Princeton University Press, 1978. [The exhaustive book on Bach and baroque ornamentation. The scope and presentation of the author's research are breathtaking, but his assertions as to practical performance must be approached with caution. Neumann wrote this massive book with a particular bias. He wished to show historical and musical evidence to support such things as prebeat realizations of one-note graces and other ornaments, trills beginning on the main note, and similar matters. He considered that the twentieth-century revival of historical performance was too rigid in applying the general rules described by so many seventeenth- and eighteenth-century authorities. In amassing evidence for a more liberal view he performed a valuable service, but in his enthusiasm (and iconoclasm) his commentaries often tip the balance too far in the opposite direction. I strongly recommend that the student utilize Neumann's encyclopedic work, but with more attention to the facts presented than to their interpretation.]

Chapter 10

KEYBOARD FINGERING

In this chapter I will summarize what we know of Bach's approach to keyboard fingering, relate it to aspects of baroque and modern-era keyboard technique generally, and offer some practical observations.

Modern piano technique often involves indiscriminate application of scale fingering and other standard patterns without reference to metrical and rhythmic groupings. This practice can run counter to musical values, especially in earlier music. But as mainstream players know, it is often important to finger according to the groupings of meter and rhythm, particular stresses, and the like, and this is a concept basic to many earlier fingering techniques. So the novice may feel reassured: not all the early techniques feel radically different from modern standards. Some of them are readily adapted and will be found to be very helpful. On the whole, the aspects of historical fingering relevant to discussion here involve fingering by groups that lie under the hand, changing position through many kinds of finger crossing and/or thumb passing, occasional use of alternating hands, and sometimes just lifting the hand. These approaches allow a closed hand position to be more readily maintained, which is an advantage on any keyboard instrument and often crucial to good tone production on the clavichord.

The fingering on early keyboard instruments relates to technical approaches based in finger motion. The aspect of modern keyboard technique that involves depressing a key by motion originating in the hand, wrist, or arm is irrelevant here.

Bach's lifetime spanned major changes in keyboard fingering. Most early keyboard technique based scalar fingering and change of hand position in finger crossings: for example, stepwise motion in the right hand 3-4-3-4 ascending, 3-2-3-2 descending; left hand 2-1-2-1 ascending, 3-4-3-4 descending. By the time C. P. E. Bach published the first part of his *Essay* in 1753, he was able to present what we would call modern scale fingerings as the norm. J. S. Bach's practice seems to have embraced both techniques. The few sources of information available imply that his approach was extremely flexible. Indeed, even C. P. E. Bach did not completely discard the older style.

C. P. E. Bach's comment (quoted in chapter 3) that his father made greater use of the thumb than ever before may well be true, as far as German baroque practice is concerned, but his description of earlier fingering as using the thumb only when absolutely necessary is one of those exaggerations that often creep in when an innovator is being praised. Perhaps German fingering was at times as pedantic and limited as the younger Bach describes, but extant fingerings from sixteenth-century Spain and England include what could be called standard modern scale fingerings that appear in the sources side by side with finger crossings. The thumb was used freely: indeed, the many full chords in much earlier literature could not possibly be played without it. However, it was probably with Bach's generation that, as the son describes, the thumb gained greater importance in German practice. As he exaggeratedly put it, the thumbs "rose from their former uselessness to the rank of principal finger." Certainly, the thumb is of crucial importance to modern fingering and of a more limited role in the older style.

Whether Bach inclined more toward the older or the newer techniques, his choice of fingering seems to have been motivated by economy of motion as an ideal. Contorted, awkward, and inconsistent motions were to be avoided. Forkel mentions that in Bach's technique, "no single finger has to be drawn nearer when it is wanted, but every one is ready over the key which it may have to press down. . . . No finger must fall upon its key, or . . . be thrown on it, but only needs to be placed upon it." Good fingering in both older and newer techniques will guide the fingers to the smooth shifts of position necessary to this ideal. The crossing of fingers, a technique that surprises the newcomer, can often help in making smooth changes. For example, the third finger of the right hand is the principal finger in the right hand's finger crossing, and when it is used as the basis for shifting upward or downward, its position keeps the entire hand centered on the keys with which the hand is immediately occupied.

The only examples of fingering we have from J. S. Bach himself are found in two small pieces in the *Clavierbüchlein vor Wilhelm Friedemann Bach*. These are the opening Applicatio in C Major and the Praeambulum in G Minor (generally known as No. 11 of the set of Twelve Little Preludes). The Applicatio (excerpted in Example 10-1a) is only an exercise in fingering and shows a good many techniques. It includes within its eight measures:

1. Finger and thumb crossing in scalar passages: right hand 3-4-3-4 ascending, 3-2-3-2 descending, left hand 1-2-1-2 ascending. In this way, Bach places 1, 3, and 5 on metrically accented notes: the good fingers on the good notes, as a baroque musician would say.
2. Use of the fifth finger of both hands to play extreme notes and in scalar passages.
3. Transfer of a single finger from an offbeat to a downbeat note and vice versa ("finger skipping"). This occurs where the right hand plays a three-part texture (m. 4).
4. Trills fingered with 5 and 4 of the right hand. This feature seems quite advanced for a beginner such as W. F. Bach, but Forkel tells us that the father put his students through a preparatory regimen of exercises before they were allowed pieces to play. The students would also have had musical preparation: certainly they would have been reading notes and singing from the first.
5. Use of consecutive fingers on scalar passages in inner voices, as in the outer parts, rather than finger skipping.

The finger skipping does not require large gaps in sound or heavy articulation of downbeats; it can be managed smoothly on the basis of structured legato, by releasing the first note only immediately before sounding the next and making a clean, swift transfer.

There are no grounds for associating rhythmic alteration or "automatic articulation" with pairwise fingering if the player is accustomed to this approach. Naturally, these fingerings seem awkward and irregular to a modern player trying them for the first time.

If the fingering of the Applicatio seems archaic in its use of finger crossing, that of the Praeambulum (excerpted in Example 10-1b) could well be the product of a modern conservatory. It is distinguished first and foremost by what is now called harmonic fingering, whereby the notes of broken chords are fingered as they would be if played simultaneously as block chords. The first and fifth fingers are in frequent use in both hands, on naturals or accidentals as the chords require.

Both of these examples show (once one accepts the finger crossing of the Applicatio) utterly natural fingering that is careful not to strain the hand, shows no clumsy shifts, and seems to be concerned with the most direct and practical way to deploy the fingers. Again, this approach is consistent with Forkel's description of Bach's efficient technique.

Bach's practicality concerning keyboards, described by his student Agricola, may have some relevance to the technique and fingerings just described.

Agricola states that Bach preferred narrow keys to wide ones and short keys to long ones, the latter in part because short keys allow readier access to the upper manuals of a four- or five-manual organ. (Short manuals compress the front-to-back dimension of the console.) Agricola supports these comments by remarking that "anyone who is in the habit of placing his fingers properly will know that he need never stretch a finger out straight in playing. Why then does he need such long manuals?" (*New Bach Reader*, 365). A long-held modern myth insists that thumb-under technique is awkward on instruments with short keys (especially short natural keyheads), but Agricola obviously did not think so, and many players, including myself, can confirm his opinion. Indeed, thumb-under technique was known even in the sixteenth century.

One other example of keyboard fingering comes from Bach's circle, a manuscript of the earliest version of the Prelude and Fugue No. 1, *WTC* 2, made by Johann Caspar Vogler (Staatsbibliothek Preussischer Kulturbesitz Mus. Ms. P. 804, pp. 235, 238–239; first printed in the Bach Gesellschaft edition, 36: 224–225). Vogler annotated the movements with rather complete fingerings, which have been discussed at length in several articles. In summary:

1. The fingerings allow the player to preserve a relatively closed hand, a tendency that is very helpful to clavichord playing. This consideration includes a few nominally odd fingerings that balance the hand as the player negotiates a fairly broad span of notes. Such fingering is useful on the clavichord and strongly implies this instrument, as it serves little purpose on other instruments (see Example 10-1c).
2. As in the Applicatio, a single finger (including 1 and 5 in either hand) is often transferred between conjunct notes, with the second note usually falling on an accented beat.
3. Transfers of position are sometimes made in the wholesale way described above (see Example 10-1d and e).
4. Most important, pivots on the thumb are used on an equal footing with a wide variety of finger crossings. Examples (all on conjunct notes) include right hand ascending 2-3-4-3, 4-2, and descending 5-4-5, 5-[4-3-]5, 5-5-3-5, 1-3, 4-5; left hand ascending 2-1-2-1, 5-4-5, and descending 1-2-1, 1-2-3-4-2.

Although we have few examples of Bach's fingering, we have a reasonable number of illustrations of his way of "handing" a passage. The division of a line between the hands is sometimes indicated by the groupings of note stems, allocated to the hands by upward (for the right hand) and downward (for the left) beaming. Well-known examples are found in scalar passages from the Chro-

Example 10-1a–e. (a) Bach, Applicatio, BWV 994, mm. 1–4; (b) Praeambulum in G Minor, mm. 1–6; (c) Bach, Praeludium in C Major, BWV 870a/i, m. 8; (d) Bach, Fughetta in C Major, BWV 870a/ii, m. 10; (e) Bach, Praeludium in C Major, BWV 870a/i, m. 9.

matic Fantasia (see Example 6-4) and in Prelude No. 21, *WTC* 1. This latter
example we have in Bach's own fair copy.

There can be more than one way of dividing a line between the hands. In
scalar passages, the change from one hand to the other is usually made on an
offbeat (as in passages in Example 10-2), a procedure that is likely to be technically and musically more graceful than onbeat changes. When moving from
one hand to the other in, say, a scalar sweep, it is often most fluent and graceful to have the new hand take over using 2 or 4, rather than an outer digit (1 or
5). Interchanging the hands in a single passage need not break the flow of the
line, unless the exchange is managed clumsily, and wholesale attributions of
articulatory effect to alternation of hands are unwarranted. (Indeed, in the
unlikely event that one wished to approximate a *glissando* effect, playing a long
scale with alternating hands would be far smoother than playing with a single
hand and conventional fingering.) Nonetheless, certain fingerings and hand-
ings will help to group notes one way or another and can assist in making certain kinds of emphasis. For instance, the hand division in Example 10-2a suggests weight on the first note of every four-note group. In Example 10-2c, both
scalar and arpeggiated motions change hands on the offbeats.

Often Bach's fair copies of his works show no stemming to indicate hand
distribution, but the technique appears in copies of his works made by his students. Instances of this technique of note division should be carefully considered and applied to similar passages for both technical security and musical
clarity. I would hazard, in general, that scale passages, properly divided between
the hands, were intended for ease of playing and to allow a smooth flow. Indeed, it seems clear that the passage from the Chromatic Fantasia was intended
to produce a virtuoso effect. Arpeggiated and other disjunct passages are prone
to various weightings made by the different possible handing patterns. In
Example 10-2b, the onbeat division of the figuration would seem to be the
only logical possibility. Sometimes the hands alternate notes, in imitating the
cross-string technique of violin passages (see Example 10-2d). In such cases, the
weighting of notes implied by the handing should be considered carefully. This
subject is admirably discussed by Peter Williams in the reading cited at the end
of this chapter.

Sometimes the technique is useful simply to provide a moment of ease in
the course of a complex movement. For example, midway through the Gigue
of Partita No. 3, the inverted theme after the double bar can be divided between
the hands, when the fugal texture is reduced to a single line (Example 10-3a).
The technique can also provide rhythmic thrust at the start of a fugue (Example 10-3b). Such fingering cannot be maintained beyond the opening statement, but it is very helpful to establish the proper momentum.

Example 10-2a–d. (a) Bach, Fantasia in A Minor, BWV 922, m. 1; (b) Bach, Toccata in F-sharp Minor, BWV 910, m. 2; (c) Bach, Toccata in G Major, BWV 916, mm. 1–3; (d) Bach, Allegro, Sonata in D Minor, BWV 964, mm. 45–47.

The notation in polyphonic textures usually reflects the voice-leading rather than the distribution between the hands, but there is no reason not to reallocate the notes for ease of playing. Sometimes such redistribution is unavoidable.

C. P. E. Bach remarks that "tones repeated at a moderate speed are played by a single finger, but alternating fingers are employed in fast repetitions. Only

Example 10-3a, b. (a) Bach, Gigue, Partita No. 3, BWV 827, mm. 25–27; (b) Bach, Fugue No. 5, *WTC* 1, BWV 850ii, mm. 1–2.

two fingers should be used at a time" (*Essay*, 73–74). François Couperin required a change of finger on repeated notes in a context such as an anticipation. This technique allows a more connected, fluid sound quality.

Finger substitution is unavoidable in many passages as the hand shifts from one position to another. The technique appears in the Vogler manuscript and in at least one example from Kirnberger; it is very common in the many fingerings we have from François Couperin. Substitution, so commonly used by organists, harpsichordists, and clavichordists, and so often avoided by pianists, is frequently necessary on the piano for clarity in polyphonic textures. Use of the sustaining pedal must be entirely free from the need to compensate for lazy fingering; otherwise, both textural clarity and the freedom to make proper pedaling effects are compromised. One of the greatest of pianists, Chopin, used a great deal of finger substitution. A contemporary observer, Alfred Hipkins, compared his piano technique to organ playing in this regard.

One should never strain to hold notes literally when they cannot be so held. It is better to release a note slightly early, changing a quarter note to an eighth, for instance. These cases are rare (I am not suggesting a casual approach); but Bach writes for musical logic first and for the hands only secondarily, although he shows wonderful ingenuity in accommodating the requirements of both aspects. Occasionally there are passages that cannot be held by an ordinary hand. They were probably rendered by releasing one or two notes early (see Example 10-4a). Chords that do not lie under two hands can be negotiated by means of a violinistic arpeggiation, in which the lower notes are released before the highest are reached. This is especially effective in a violin transcription, as in Example 10-4b.

Example 10-4a, b. (a) Bach, Adagio, Sonata No. 3 for Harpsichord and Violin, BWV 1016, harpsichord part, mm. 7–8; (b) Bach, Praeludium, Partita in E Major, BWV 1006a, mm. 134–136.

There is a prevalent notion that *The Art of Fugue* does not really fit under two hands, but in fact it does so nearly as readily as the *WTC*, with occasional awkwardness. The only movements that do not accommodate two hands are the two pairs of mirror fugues, whose contrapuntal exigencies forced even Bach to drop the two-hand capability. In fact, he came very close in Nos. 13a and 13b, in which perhaps a half-dozen notes exceed the range of the hands. The composer prepared duet versions of these two movements. The other pair of mirror fugues (Nos. 12a and 12b) are readily divided for two players, each taking two of the four parts.

The duets in the *Goldberg Variations* feature a few passages in which the hands cross on the harpsichord's two keyboards. Playing these as written on the piano is usually uncomfortable. There is no reason not to redistribute the notes between the hands for greater facility and security. However, one must take care that the notes are articulated so as to maintain the integrity of the contrapuntal lines. (Bach himself might have expected such management: one of the knottiest of the duets, Variation V, bears the indication "for one or two manuals" and contains several passages that can barely be played on a single keyboard without some redistribution of the notes. Of course, Bach's designation might also be an invitation to play some portions on one keyboard and some on two.) Such redistribution might also be necessary for the well-known voice crossing near the end of Sinfonia No. 15 (mm. 26–28). The duets of the *Goldberg Variations* are intended for two-keyboard performance, but the Sinfonia, perhaps equally intended for one or two manuals, is notated as it is to maintain the clarity of the voice-leading. While there are many single-line passages in Bach's and other music in which the note beaming is divided to show hand allocation, polyphony cannot often offer such directions in its notation. Certainly, in his fair copies, Bach rarely does anything in terms of showing hand allocation that might compromise the clear notation of the polyphony. Realization of the texture on the keyboard is left entirely to the player.

Bach's keyboard music is often conceived in an abstract, or at least non-keyboard, idiom for which any fingering that works should be the choice. In fact, the textures are usually so dense that how and where to apply the little we know of Bach's style of keyboard fingering is a matter of emulating the principles outlined here, rather than direct application of patterns.

I will close with some practical considerations.

Always avoid any fingering that strains the hand. A fingering that feels eccentric (even once mastered) should probably be discarded. However, this proviso should by no means discourage one from experimenting with what we know of period fingering. At least some aspects of early fingering readily become both practical and comfortable and often simplify problems.

To summarize my impression of relevant historical fingering, I would suggest that it involves fingering by groups that lie under the hand and changing position through many kinds of finger crossing and/or thumb passing, or sometimes just lifting the hand. With this approach, a closed hand position can more readily be maintained.

On any keyboard instrument, it is necessary to cultivate a relaxed, squeezing, sometimes weighted touch (well taught by the clavichord), as opposed to angular pushing of the keys without follow-through. The latter both feels and sounds as if the player were trying to push forward through the music, just as one might try to start a train engine by pushing it along the tracks. Pushing the keys without adequate follow-through often results when students first react to the newness of controlling the music without pedal, through the fingers alone.

Ralph Kirkpatrick was in the habit of fingering at first to allow (so far as possible) a completely legato rendition, and afterward to develop whatever articulations that he decided the music required. Certainly this approach allows flexibility, but it can create its own obstacles. I would suggest that developing a generic fingering far in advance of interpretative decisions can be counter-productive in that it conduces to ready-made performance decisions. Wanda Landowska carefully worked out fingerings that sometimes forced effective realization of her articulatory decisions: for example, a fugue subject consisting of detached notes might be rendered entirely by one thumb (that is, before other voices joined in). In conjunction with historical techniques, a happy medium between these two approaches might be a good point of departure: fingering for general fluency, but with articulatory choices or requirements firmly in mind and given priority over mere ease of performance.

SUGGESTIONS FOR FURTHER READING

Ahlgrimm, Isolde. "Current Trends in Performance of Baroque Music." Translated by Howard Schott. *Diapason* 73, No. 4 (April 1982): 1–14.

Faulkner, Quentin. *J. S. Bach's Keyboard Technique: A Historical Introduction.* St. Louis, Missouri: Concordia, 1984.

Lindley, Mark. "Early Fingering: Some Editing Problems and Some New Readings for J. S. Bach and John Bull." *Early Music* 17 (1989): 60–69.

Sachs, Barbara, and Barry Ife. *Anthology of Early Keyboard Methods.* Cambridge, England: Gamut, 1981. [An invaluable compilation and translation of seven early keyboard treatises.]

Troeger, Richard. *Technique and Interpretation on the Harpsichord and Clavichord.* Chapter 3, "Fingering." Bloomington: Indiana University Press, 1987. [A brief general survey of the history of keyboard fingering plus practical considerations.]

Williams, Peter. *Playing the Organ Works of Bach: Some Case Studies*, 92–98. New York: American Guild of Organists, 1987.

Chapter 11

CONTINUO ACCOMPANIMENT
AND ENSEMBLE PLAYING

A little learning, as the saying goes, can be a dangerous thing. However, one must never take the negative attitude that letting something alone will, by a void, produce the right solution. A story told by the harpsichordist and musicologist Putnam Aldrich will illustrate:

> In 1949 . . . I was engaged to play the solo harpsichord part in Bach's Fifth Brandenburg Concerto. The conductor, Pierre Monteux, guaranteed that this was to be an absolutely authentic performance: he conducted from the Bach-Gesellschaft edition. At a preliminary rehearsal with the flute and violin soloists, I began straightway realizing the figured bass of the opening tutti. The conductor interrupted: "What are these chords you are playing? Bach wrote no chords here!" I tried to explain that the figures under the cembalo part stood for chords, but he said, "If Bach wanted chords he would have written chords. This is to be an authentic performance. We shall play only what Bach wrote!" And in an aside to the other musicians he said "You see, musicologists have always their noses in books and forget to look at what Bach wrote." At any rate in the opening tutti [the lack of chords] is not too serious. . . . But in the second movement, scored for three solo instruments, the effect of the harpsichordist's playing one note at a time with the left hand only was nothing short of ludicrous. Even Monteux began to suspect that something was wrong. At the dress rehearsal he said to me in a whisper, "In this movement you may add a few discreet chords." (Aldrich, *Notes*, 466)

I was informed by a relative of Aldrich's that, to the end of his life, he would turn red with rage when he thought of Monteux's staggering combination of ignorance, arrogance, and rudeness.

This anecdote rather neatly illustrates three things: the limits of "authenticity" when it is in the words and not the spirit (to say nothing of the understanding); a sometimes-encountered mainstream attitude toward research; and the fact that even soloists have to realize a continuo part from time to time.

Most pianists admit that the piano is not the most effective continuo instrument. It does not blend naturally with the sonorities of strings and winds in the effortless way the harpsichord does. If a pianist is performing the Fifth Brandenburg Concerto with a piano, he or she has no option but to play the continuo areas discreetly, using such chord voicings as are most transparent and graceful. (Bringing in a harpsichord to play continuo would only compound the blending problems with the piano.) However, when the task is continuo accompaniment rather than solo playing and a decent harpsichord is available, the pianist or organist should take advantage of the situation and use that instrument rather than a piano. (Of course, the organ is suitable for much continuo playing.)

Some advice for the nonharpsichordist who is called upon, on short notice, to play continuo on a harpsichord:

1. Whatever the particular harpsichord is like, do not be intimidated by either elaborate gadgetry (older modern instruments sometimes have multiple pedals to change the registers) or the lack of it. Find a setting with two 8' stops and stick to that. Avoid use of the 4'. It tends to go out of tune and its brittleness does not blend with the ensemble as well as do the 8' stops. The 4' should be reserved for the accompaniment of really loud sections or movements. Unless the 16' stop is absolutely necessary (for example, to produce any volume of sound at all from a bad instrument), avoid it except for special coloristic purposes.

2. If the instrument has two keyboards, the upper one usually has only a single 8' stop; it can be used for extended soft passages.

3. In any case, the dynamics are in the chordal voicings you select and how fully you sustain (and how soon you release) the notes. As C. P. E. Bach put it so pragmatically, the continuo player plays "in one, two, three, four, or more parts" (*Essay*, 175). A strict four-part accompaniment is more typical of the organ than the harpsichord. The latter uses a variable, sometimes almost impressionistic texture, varied in density according to the dynamic requirements of the

ensemble as a whole. Although "basic continuo" is in four parts, one must, as C. P. E. Bach implies, do whatever works, from playing nothing or the bass alone (*tasto solo*) to full chords in both hands.

4. For *pianissimo*, play only the bass line or even remain silent altogether, if the harpsichord seems intrusive in a delicate ensemble texture.

5. Do not feel obligated to accompany where the harpsichord seems superfluous: for instance, when a fugal exposition takes place among strings and the harpsichord. In such cases, even playing the bass alone can be more intrusive than supportive.

6. Normally, base yourself in four parts (three in the right hand, the bass in the left) that never rise above the highest solo line; generally, c" or d" can be regarded as the limit.

7. Avoid doubling dissonances, leading tones, and other vital parts, especially when these are exposed in a solo instrument. If such tones are fully accounted for elsewhere, play the root and fifth of the chord.

8. Avoid doubling other parts. Alternatively, double them altogether. This approach is especially relevant to early baroque choral music accompanied by the organ.

9. If you are not fluent in reading figured bass and depend upon a written-out continuo part, adapt the written realization to your needs as freely as you feel confident in doing. There is nothing sacrosanct about an editor's continuo realization.

10. Legato is suited to lyrical movements. A detached style most effectively provides rhythmic impetus in the ensemble.

11. Note the harpsichord style in concerted works that have a fully written out keyboard part. In accompanying passages, a continuo style of rapid two-part writing is characteristic (for example, in the first movement of the Concerto in D Minor, BWV 1052); this style alternates with real solo passages.

12. Bach was noted for his elaborate, obbligato-style continuo realizations (see chapter 3). There is no reason for the knowlegeable player to shy away from this often full-voiced and/or polyphonic way of accompanying (see Example 11-1). Such examples are often the best models for the more flamboyant style of accompaniment.

13. Articulated arpeggiation on the harpsichord can sound like rapid "musketry fire" (as Saint Lambert described it in 1707). The piano lacks this quality, but one can try to approximate it where appropriate.

14. Long cadenzas are altogether out of place, although one still hears inappropriate cadenzas, extended beyond any reasonable proportion, in some performances of baroque music. Models can be found

Example 11-1. Bach, Andante, Sonata in B Minor for Flute and Harpsichord, BWV 1030, mm. 1–3.

in Bach's music (see chapter 9). Improvisations at fermatas are generally meant to be brief flourishes rather than developmental cadenzas in the classical and romantic sense.

15. Less is nearly always more.

These considerations apply generally to piano continuo as well. For the piano, the chord voicing should be as clear and lightly textured as is compatible with the needs of the ensemble. The primary function of continuo playing is rhythmic punctuation and support to the group. It need not even be directly audible to the audience.

Recitative is of course free in timing, according to the expression of the words. One can treat the chords with various durations and arpeggiations as the expression requires. The harpsichord was of course used to accompany secular vocal music and was sometimes heard in church music as well. The organ was, however, the primary instrument for the accompaniment of sacred music. In secco ("dry") recitative, in which the singer is accompanied only by keyboard and one or more bass instruments, Bach most often notates the bass line in the conventional manner, with what look like long-held whole and half notes. There has been considerable debate over the years as to whether such notation was to be followed literally or treated in the "short style" described in many eighteenth-century sources and occasionally notated by Bach. (A good account of the history of this debate, and a very reasonable resolution of it, can be found in chapter 3 of Lawrence Dreyfus's *Bach's Continuo Group*.) In the short style of accompaniment, the long notes are played as quarter notes (perhaps with slight variation of duration, according to the expression) followed by rests.

Thus, the chords punctuate the singer's line and sketch the harmony, but are not held through.

In playing concertos and other concerted works, whether with piano or harpsichord, it is important to elicit from the ensemble a light, articulate (but still singing) string tone; observation of hemiolas and other irregular accents; a chamber-music feeling rather than an orchestral mentality (the flexibility of the music needs chamber-style intimacy and give-and-take within the entire group); and coordination among the group members of strong-weak phrasing patterns and use of agogic accents. (Mainstream orchestral players are often resistant to such approaches, as well as to the use of a different, lighter sound on their instruments.)

Keyboard players are not the only musicians who have an accompanimental role. This function was expected of other instrumentalists as well. A special style, virtually extinct since 1800, was cultivated by eighteenth-century violinists and flutists: playing with extreme softness to accompany the harpsichord or fortepiano (or even the clavichord; by "extreme softness," I mean just that). In music written in this style, it is the keyboard player who has the important material. Mozart's flute sonatas contain many examples. (When these were recorded around 1960 by Jean-Pierre Rampal and Robert Veyron-Lacroix, Veyron-Lacroix was required to give up the harpsichord's right-hand part, which was taken over by Rampal in his misunderstood role as solo flutist. The harpsichordist was reassigned the far less interesting accompanimental part, which Mozart had expected to be rendered gently and unobtrusively by the flute.)

Bach's sonatas for various instruments with harpsichord do not, to any large extent, require the accompanimental function from the nonkeyboard parts. However, the composer did obviously expect that the two instruments would share equally. It is absurd to hear the violinist's line in a three-part fugue played as a solo line, drowning out the other two parts that are supposed to be heard in the harpsichord. An example of such an ensemble fugue is the second movement of the Harpsichord and Violin Sonata in C Minor. (Note the order of instruments as presented in the original title.) Pianists, with their potentially powerful sound, have more reserve ammunition for such circumstances, a point envied by harpsichordists. Of course fugues, to sound like fugues, notably require an equable balance among the parts. On the other hand, something like the opening movement of the C Minor Sonata consists of a melody that the violinist is at liberty to play as fully as he or she prefers; the harpsichord part is nothing but a written-out version of a certain perpetual-motion style of accompaniment (which was one standard way of realizing a thoroughbass accompaniment). Yet again, when the harpsichord has the main line and the violin accompanies with double-stopped intervals, the virtuosity is not in the double-stopping, but in the extreme *pianissimo* with which, courteously, the violinist subdues his or her part to the needs of the harpsichord's line.

In short: in Bach's ensemble works with obbligato keyboard, all players must take note of the overall nature of each movement and indeed every passage.

SUGGESTIONS FOR FURTHER READING

Dreyfus, Lawrence. *Bach's Continuo Group: Players and Practices in His Vocal Works*. Cambridge: Harvard University Press, 1987.

Lunde, Nanette. *The Continuo Companion*. 2d ed. Eau Claire, Wisconsin: Skyline, 2001.

Troeger, Richard. *Technique and Interpretation on the Harpsichord and Clavichord*. Chapter 6, "Accompaniment." Bloomington: Indiana University Press, 1987.

Williams, Peter. *Figured Bass Accompaniment*. 2 vols. Edinburgh: Edinburgh University Press, 1970.

PART III

SPECULATIVE MATTERS

Chapter 12

MUSICAL RHETORIC

R hetoric is the art of using language effectively in writing and particularly in oratory—that is, public speaking. It is often defined primarily as the "art of persuasion," but as a discipline it is more directly concerned with the effective organization and presentation of one's ideas. The study of rhetoric was part of the educational curriculum in earlier eras and was adopted for musical analysis by many music theorists in the seventeenth and eighteenth centuries. They developed a very complete analogy between musical structures and the selection, arrangement, and development of ideas and emotions in oratory and writing. This way of looking at musical organization, with its appeal to both the intellect and the emotions, seems to have been natural, to some degree or other, to the musical thinking of composers throughout Europe until at least the early nineteenth century. I present a synopsis of the concept here because grasping only a few basics about the rhetorical model for music can greatly open up a player's sense of both logical development and dramatic contrast. Furthermore, an understanding of rhetoric allows one to look at baroque music in the same terms that were understood—indeed, taken for granted—by the original composers and performers.

Rhetoric is not to be confused with grammar. Grammar refers to basic constructive elements (for instance, sentence structure), whereas rhetoric is concerned with the higher goals of the constructive elements—their expressive use in larger formal structures. To illustrate this contrast in regard to music: if reading or playing a rhythmic pattern is troublesome, one will break it down into smaller units and spell it out to learn its grammar. To play it expressively (the rhetorical aspect), one usually thinks in terms of larger time units, to hear the pattern in relation to other parts of the phrase and larger segments. Learning the basic patterns of Bach's ornaments is grammatical; musically integrated, expressive use of them is rhetorical. François Couperin drew on this well-known analogy in the preface to his little treatise *L'art de toucher le clavecin*:

> The Method that I give here is unique, and has no relationship with tablature [i.e., notation], which is nothing but a science of numbers; but I treat here (by demonstrated principles) all things concerning fine harpsichord playing. . . . As there is a great distance from grammar to declamation, there is also an infinity [of distance] between tablature and the art of playing well. (Couperin, n.p.)

In short, Couperin tells the reader that he is not presenting the basics (grammar), but the higher flights of art (rhetoric).

How seriously to take the rhetorical analogy, and how widespread its use was in the baroque era, remain points of contention among scholars. Certainly it is possible to develop some overreaching theories and analyses. However, it seems unquestionable that the rhetorical-musical relationship existed, if only as a general point of departure in terms of finding musical subject matter, and for at least some aspects of organization, motivic use, program music, and performance.

Bach's position in this area has been questioned also, down to taking seriously the sniping remark by his sometime enemy Scheibe that Bach was unable to write a decent letter. The notion that Bach had such a perfunctory education does not seem to be borne out by the facts (see Christoph Wolff's biography) or other circumstances. To begin with, Bach attended a school (the Ohrdruf Lyceum) of high reputation that students came from far around to attend. His standing as a student was among the very highest: anywhere from first to fifth in his class. His progress was very far beyond average, and he was the youngest in his class by four years when, at fourteen, his study at the Lyceum ended. Bach continued his education at St. Michael's school in Luneburg, quite possibly (as Wolff suggests) with the intention of subsequent university study, as was expected of St. Michael's students. There he was taught "religion, logic, rhetoric, and Latin" (Wolff, *Johann Sebastian Bach*, 57). Rhetoric was a standard course of study in the seventeenth and eighteenth centuries, and one hardly needed to be a classical scholar to understand its general concepts and applications. (Indeed, many experts in one or another field are limited in their powers of verbalization, yet understand elaborate verbal and other constructs. I know several musicians, phenomenally gifted improvisers, who fit precisely this description.) Furthermore, it was not unusual for a church cantor such as Bach to teach Latin and rhetoric as part of his general duties. It is true that because of his schedule Bach often engaged a substitute, but he was obviously competent to do the work. Bach's friend Johann Abraham Birnbaum, who taught rhetoric at Leipzig University, described in 1739 Bach's thoroughgoing comprehension of the relationship between music and rhetoric:

> The elements and merits, which the working out of a musical composition has in common with the art of rhetoric, he understands so completely, that one not only listens to him with satiating pleasure when he directs his profound conversation to the similarities and correspondences of both [rhetoric and music]; but one admires, as well, their clever application in his works. (*Bach Dokumente* II, 352)

These well-known comments come in the course of Birnbaum's 1739 rejoinder to Scheibe's attacks on Bach. Although they may exaggerate the degree of Bach's verbal elaboration on the subject, there is no reason to assume that Birnbaum's statement is a whopping lie. Indeed, it is hard to reconcile such an idea with Bach's seeming general probity, or with the likelihood that such friends as Bach and Birnbaum were discussing possible relationships between their respective, much-loved disciplines.

While the "art of persuasion" has been called the weapon of dishonest lawyers and politicians at least since the days of Aristophanes, the negative aspect is by no means rhetoric's only facet. Like any intellectual tool, it can be used for a variety of purposes. Indeed, the extremely transparent and crude rhetoric of many modern politicians has given it an undeserved bad name, particularly since obvious lies, dodges, and coverups are referred to in popular usage as rhetoric. (Perhaps today's speechwriters need classical training to give a more elegant form to their chicanery.) In its more positive aspect, rhetoric involves the coherent organization and development of facts and ideas and their effective presentation. The ultimate intent is to persuade or convince the audience to take the speaker's viewpoint. Naturally, effective presentation involves performance. In early treatises, the speaker is often advised to become more agitated in the course of the presentation, in order to work up the audience's sympathy and sense of participation.

It is a commonplace to say that music is a language, but (unlike musicians before 1800) we rarely develop this idea. The rhetorical analogy takes it seriously, and enables one to look at music as discussion and argument: the contrast and resolution of opposites (or, as scholars of the past might have phrased it, thesis and antithesis leading to synthesis). The rhetorical analogy puts the opposition(s) into both analytical and dynamic terms, thereby helping the player grasp the inherent contrasts and developments of the music. Kirnberger gives a good summary of the analogy between rhetoric and music. Writing in 1777, he says that

> a musical composition, like a speech, consists of several periods (or sections). And as in a speech these periods are constructed of sentences, these in turn of words, which are made up of longer and shorter syllables, so the musical period likewise consists of phrases, these of motifs (or phrase members), which are made up of longer and shorter notes that either are only passing in effect or have their own characteristic stronger and weaker accents.
>
> If a speech is to achieve its proper effect, it must be delivered well; and likewise, a musical composition attains its beauty only through a correct and good performance. (Kirnberger, *Recueil*, 66)

Kirnberger is only one of a multitude of music theorists who found in rhetoric a ready-made model for handling a wide variety of structural and syntactical variations. (I quote him in particular because he was close to Bach and speaks very clearly on the subject.) For one thing, the rhetorical discipline was already fully formed as far back as classical antiquity; for another, every educated person was well acquainted with it. Nothing was more logical than for musicians to adopt it wholesale, and it is taken for granted in musical analysis in sources from England, France, Italy, and Germany at least. German scholars, in particular, threw themselves into certain details of the model.

Traces of this major interdisciplinary phenomenon survive in much of the language we still apply to music. (These have been extended in recent times to the application of Noam Chomsky's syntactical theories to musical analysis.) Many words common to verbal and musical analysis are still in frequent use: "phrase," "imitation," "parody" (as in "parody Mass"), "development" (of an idea, musical or otherwise), "syntax," "cadence" (referring to the typical patterns of someone's speech or writing, for instance, as well as to musical "punctuation"), "exposition" (whether in formal writing or in fugues and sonatas), "theme," fugal "subject," "antecedent and consequent" (or "question and answer") phrases, "embellishment," "variation," and of course a host of poetic and musical rhythmic patterns, including trochees, iambs, anapests, and so on. It is not unusual to speak even today of a contrast recognized in the eighteenth century: music based in regular and related phrases is called "verse," and that based in irregularities is "prose." Examples could be, respectively, a menuet and a toccata. Dances, with their relationship to the ballroom, naturally begin with a basis in regular groupings, and this is particularly true of menuets. The *stylus phantasticus* is typically full of irregularities and unexpected turns. Even music that is based in regularity can often be termed musical prose; many of Haydn's sonata movements qualify for this description, for the composer expands sometimes simple material into wonderful irregularities of phrase and structure.

THE RHETORICAL MODEL IN BRIEF

The discipline of rhetoric provides a large-scale, very flexible vocabulary of possibilities for devising a speech or other verbal presentation. Classical rhetoric analyzed from the ground up what a writer, and particularly an orator, does. Writing and speechmaking boil down to five categories: invention, arrangement, style, memory, and delivery. (In music, these could be invention, form, style, memory, and performance.) I will omit memory from this discussion, as it does not relate to analysis. The four remaining categories, complete with their Latin names, are:

1. *Inventio (invention)*. The writer decides on a topic and the data to be adduced and discussed. The musician decides on basic musical "topics" (*topici*): tonalities, themes (and contrapuntal combinations), motives (figures), meters, rhythms, and genres: for instance, a baroque composer could always rely on the style of a gigue as the basis for a bouncy, cheerful mood. For vocal music, a prime consideration is of course the choice of a text to set.
2. *Dispositio (disposition, arrangement)*. The writer arranges the subject matter in a cohesive, orderly fashion. Musically, the "disposition" of material involves the formal layout of a work.
3. *Decoratio (decoration, elaboration; we would say "style")*. This facet concerns the most apt choice of words (specific turns of phrase, similes, metaphors, analogies, imagery) by which to present and develop the material. Through the centuries, classical and medieval rhetoricians often went to extravagant lengths to identify the multitudinous devices of artful language, discussing and cataloging the possibilities in attempts to be comprehensive. Generically, these are called "figures of speech," or merely "figures." A common example is simile: directly comparing one thing to another. Another example would be *noema*, a technique beloved of politicians: deliberately obscure wording. Any musical device (still called a figure, without any evocation of historical usage, as late as the first edition of *Grove's Dictionary*) can qualify as a figure. This is the area where many musical commentators, like their

rhetorician colleagues, often went to great lengths in cataloging motivic types, musical techniques, and so forth.

4. *Elocutio*. Delivering the speech; musically, performing the music.

Both the writer/speaker and the composer must find or invent the thematic material, decide on its formal arrangement, select appropriate (verbal or musical) techniques, and see to the effective performance of the finished product. The baroque composer required knowledge of the common vocabulary of topics (such as genres and motivic types) that could be drawn on, and such information is of immense significance for a performer's understanding of styles and particular pieces. Historically, the various theorists' discussions of decoratio allow much insight into how musical elements were regarded, despite the fact that these writers' various enumerations of devices, although similar in method and intent, show many divergencies. For today's performer, however, it is the elaboration of item 2, the disposition or organization of material, that is of especial importance, for here the logical development of the music relates to its dramatic impact. Consideration of the general nature of motives and their contrasts (under decoratio) is also extremely relevant.

The terminology that appears here is consistent with that used in teaching rhetoric in the baroque era, as well as in classical antiquity. The reader who is new to this subject should not feel intimidated by the new vocabulary or by the density of material regarding figures of speech (decoratio), which indeed intimidates everyone at first except seasoned classical scholars and philologists. Begin by getting a grip on the main divisions of a speech (the dispositio) and understand, at the outset, that the figures under the general heading of decoratio are nothing but a varied assortment of verbal techniques used to make a speech effective. In music, the "figures" are musical techniques and motives. Any technical names will do for them, of course; but the function of a device or formal procedure has to be vital to the player and organic to the composition as a whole. The rhetorical model (with or without Latin labels) provides a context for such vitality.

I will now consider the rhetorical model more fully as it applies to music.

INVENTIO; LOCI TOPICI
(INVENTION; FINDING TOPICS)

It is important for the modern musician to realize that the notion of "originality" was quite different in the eras before romanticism, compared to what it became during the nineteenth century. The baroque musician did not look continually to innovate in form, let alone to change the very nature of the musical language. In the nineteenth century, originality in these realms became increasingly emphasized through, first, a sense of expansion, as the "romantic rebellion" identified itself with newness partly for the sake of newness, and later through a sense of "where do we go from here?" as tonal language itself seemed to be verging on entropy. In the twentieth century, particularly, so many theories of new musical languages came into being—from serialism to aleatory music, from neoclassicism to Harry Partch—that innovation, in and of itself, has long been regarded as a hallmark of vitality. It was not so for the baroque composer, who found enormous variety within a wealth of established forms and genres. A composer's originality could be judged by what new aspects he or she could bring to known compositional types and procedures. Bach's originality is perhaps best demonstrated by the fact that his music developed nearly every style of his time to a point beyond which it could scarcely go. However, of "originality" in the romantic sense he demonstrated very little. He did not smash every form in searching for something new. He expanded them all by bringing new ideas and more thorough development (and these of the highest quality) to the established forms and procedures. The same could be said of Beethoven, a transitional figure between classicism and romanticism, who fundamentally changed little; his music extended the classical style to its ultimate expression.

A composer, then, had a repertory of forms and styles to draw on in creating a piece of music. On the large scale, one could choose a genre with a particular character as the basis for a movement in a corresponding mood. Thus, one of several gigue styles might be selected as the starting point for composing a joyful movement, an allemande for a serious movement. For example, in *WTC* 1, Bach took what is clearly an "allemande grave" topic for Prelude No. 12 and a sarabande model for Prelude No. 8. On the smaller scale, various types of motive were in common use, and anything from one to many might appear in a composition. In Prelude No. 1, *WTC* 1, Bach takes a single, simple figure of neutral emotional significance—an upward arpeggiation pattern—and creates with it one of the most memorable movements in keyboard history. More dramatically, to express "crowding" in the "Gathering of Friends" movement of the *Capriccio upon the Departure of his Beloved Brother*, the polyphonic device of stretto (overlapping thematic entries) is used in a programmatic way: the entries all crowd and tumble upon one another. Many composers chose the descending chromatic bass motive (figure) to express grief; two famous examples from Bach are Variation XXV of the *Goldberg Variations* and the Crucifixus of the B Minor Mass. Many topical references were so well established that a single sonority could cue the audience. For example, a French harpsichordist at court or in a salon had only to play an 8-5 diad (octave plus open perfect fifth, heard in so many musettes) for his listeners to realize immediately that the music was about to evoke pastoral scenes. Of course, a composer can introduce any number of topical references into a piece of music. Leonard Ratner has provided a fine illustration of the different musical topics that crop up in the course of a symphony movement by Mozart, a multitude of themes and motives that reflect musical and nonmusical associations: rustic, military, and so forth (Ratner, 281).

In addition to considerations of idiom, invention involves the finding of themes, motives, and techniques that are appropriate to whatever kind of development the composer has in mind: varied harmonization, stretto, and so forth. It is well known that Bach, upon hearing a theme, could immediately recognize the compositional techniques that were natural to it. C. P. E. Bach reported:

> When he listened to a rich and many-voiced fugue, he could soon say, after the first entries of the subjects, what contrapuntal devices it would be possible to apply, and which of them the composer by rights ought to apply, and on such occasions, when I was standing next to him, and he had voiced his surmises to me, he would joyfully nudge me when his expectations were fulfilled. (*New Bach Reader*, 397)

It is hardly surprising, especially in view of their pedagogical purpose, that Bach retitled the inventions according to the rhetorical term. In the first version, each piece bore merely the neutral title "Praeambulum." By calling them inventions, he draws attention to these pieces as models of different musical techniques.

Tonality itself can function as a topic. It seems to be fairly clear that Bach associated certain characteristics of mood and/or symbolism with certain keys. This assertion is borne out by comparison of various works in the same keys, although there are naturally exceptions to every case. Thus, Bach frequently uses G major for a brilliant, often virtuosic character. The *Goldberg Variations* alone demonstrate this point, but note also both G Major Prelude and Fugue pairs from the *WTC*. F major also tends to brilliance, as the Italian Concerto and both fugues in that key from the *WTC* suggest. D major is festive, redolent of trumpets and kettledrums, as in the orchestral style of the Overture of Partita No. 4, the Fugue in D Major from *WTC* 1, and the Prelude in D Major from *WTC* 2. B minor is tragic and often majestic: think of the Overture in the French Manner (originally in C minor) and the Prelude and Fugue No. 24 of *WTC* 1 (to say nothing of the B Minor Mass). E-flat major is lyrical and/or majestic; examples include the Praeludium, Fugue, and Allegro; the "St. Anne"

Prelude and Fugue; and Prelude and Fugue No. 7 from both books of the *WTC*.

DISPOSITIO (ARRANGEMENT)

Authorities from antiquity and later divide the dispositio into anywhere from three to seven sections:

1. *Exordium (literally, beginning)*. An opening gesture to attract the audience's attention and establish a rapport with it.
2. *Narratio (narration)*. Narrative of the past history of your topic, as in a legal defense.
3. *Propositio (proposition)*. The proposition you will argue for; your own view of the topic.
4. *Partitio (division)*. A brief outline of how you will approach the topic. (The partitio, not surprisingly, can blend with the propositio.)
5. *Confirmatio (confirmation)*. Justification and development of your proposition.
6. *Confutatio (confutation, refutation)*. Addressing and rejecting other viewpoints.
7. *Peroratio (peroration, climax)*. The climax and stirring close of the speech.

These sections can sometimes overlap, blur into one another, and even be put into a different order. However, the order as given is logical and underlies most cohesive presentations. The speaker need not employ all these functions. For instance, one may dispense with the exordium and/or peroratio, or a confutatio may not be relevant to the subject matter.

How does this outline work in an actual speech? And what are the meanings of these oratorical functions in music? Here is an outline for a short speech, divided into exordium, narratio, and so on, together with the range of equivalent musical functions.

1. *Exordium (which is dispensable)*. "Good evening. It is a pleasure to visit your beautiful city." The opening is merely to break the ice, to get the audience's attention and sympathy. To ingratiate myself, I might make complimentary remarks about objects of civic pride, or tell a joke about some local issue—or about my real topic, to introduce it unassertively and casually. Musically, this could be a prelude or intro-

ductory section, which is not necessarily related thematically to what follows. However, like the verbal speech, it can also give the first utterance of themes (or germs of themes) that will be more fully stated in the next segments. For example, the opening page of Beethoven's Piano Sonata in C Minor, Op. 111, offers the germs of thematic material that will shortly be presented in the exposition proper.

2. *Narratio.* "Since our country was founded, American justice has been a cornerstone of our democracy." That introduces the topic (the judicial system) and gives some of its history without exposing my bias on it yet. Or I might tell an anecdote (narration) that leads into my topic or my view of it. Musically, this segment would apply mainly to vocal music with a narrative. It is also relevant to cyclic works: the summary of movements 1–3 that commences the fourth movement of Beethoven's Ninth Symphony is an example.

3. *Partitio.* "I will be discussing today's judicial system in regard to the following main topics," briefly outlining the course of the discussion to come. Musically, the equivalent would likely be a summation of all the thematic material to be used in the movement, before its development begins at all. For instance, the opening ritornello of Bach's Concerto in D Minor, BWV 1052, is an epitome (another rhetorical term, filed under decoratio) of all the material to be developed in the movement. Bach in effect states, "Here is the material we'll be working with."

4. *Propositio.* "The judicial system needs reform." With this proposition, my own slant on the subject is announced. Musically, the propositio is a statement of themes or other important material, for instance an exposition in a fugue or sonata. In a speech, the partitio and propositio can blend. Certainly their musical functions are essentially identical. The term *partitio* is applicable in the case of a more thorough presentation of the motivic and thematic material, as just described regarding BWV 1052.

5. *Confirmatio.* This involves confirmation of the proposition by developing it: that is, repeating and analyzing it to consider and prove its validity. My speech would list the reasons that the judicial system needs reform, perhaps further developed by citation of particular cases. Musically, this involves thematic restatement and any developmental procedures: fragmentation of themes, modulation, contrapuntal elaboration, sequence, and so forth. The techniques used for development belong to the division of decoratio in the overall framework. Of course, in both speech and music, some elements from decoratio may

be used at any point, but it is in the meat of the developmental discussion (in words and in music) that these devices come into greatest prominence.

6. *Confutatio.* To strengthen my own viewpoint, I summarize viewpoints that disagree with my own and confute them—invalidate or discredit them. Thus, "Some say that holding to judicial tradition is more important than reform. I say, the legal system never in the past had such complexities to deal with as it does now, and it must change to keep up with present realities." At this point I would, as the speaker, follow the performance directions of seventeenth-century manuals on rhetoric by showing excitement and using broader and more expressive gestures than before. Musically, confutation can involve, for example, modulations through various tonalities and the rejection of them by reaffirming the tonic key, as at a recapitulation. Among many possibilities, it can also take the form of a contrasting section, as a B section may differ in mode, key, and themes from an A section in an aria or pair of dances.

7. *Peroratio.* Finally, at the crest of my emotive speech, I could try to spur the audience to complete acceptance of my argument, or even to action, by using the device ("figure") of a rhetorical question (not expecting direct reply): "Are we to live in a legal museum?" (This question includes another technical device: the metaphor "legal museum.") Both of these figures of speech are used to intensify my presentation. Figures can be used at any point in the presentation to intensify the speaker's argument. In my speech, the intensification coordinates with the point where my voice and gestures would reach their peak of intensity. Musically, if there is a peroration, it can take the form of a coda, a final affirmation of the tonic and perhaps of the primary theme. We are all familiar with this from sonata-form movements. However, the peroration can consist of anything that lends intensity and finality, from a summary of the thematic material to, for instance, the four-part stretto (direct and inverted simultaneously) that concludes Fugue No. 22 from *WTC* 2.

This, then, was for millennia the model for shaping or analyzing any verbal construct; and for centuries it stood also for musical structures, large or small. Not all the elements need be included in a given work; rather, the point is that this basis directs logical development of a "topic" (musical or otherwise), but is not especially prescriptive as to compositional form or procedure, except that it assumes one should state a theme or idea before developing it.

(One criticism on this ground could be that the model takes somewhat for granted an increase in intensity through the course of the work; but this, like the peroration, can be sidestepped.) Indeed, one of the strengths of this approach is its immense flexibility. Rhetorical principles can inform anything, from a statement made in one or two sentences to a full book.

It is easy to see a relationship between how the dispositio relates to a speech and how it relates to such forms as the concerto grosso and sonata. (The term *sonata principle* is more apt than *sonata form*, since the form of sonata movements is not so constricted as some analyses and textbooks suggest.) Indeed, these genres may well have developed from the rhetorical model. This is true of fugue, also, although the newcomer might feel that fugue is too discursive to work in these terms. However, a good fugue, like most good contrapuntal development, operates on the principle of "working out," that is, demonstrating every possibility that is inherent in the material; and the elements of the rhetorical model are usually in evidence. (Chopin liked to talk about the logic of fugal development, and Bach was one of his favorite composers.)

The analogy of the dispositio to a sonata-allegro movement is so direct that I will not offer more than a bare outline. An introduction, if present, would be the exordium; the exposition is the propositio and/or partitio; and development corresponds to the activities of the confirmatio and confutatio. Haydn and Beethoven particularly liked to include further development in the recapitulation by various means ("continuing the argument"); the recapitulation otherwise corresponds to the reaffirmation (of tonic or subject matter) inherent in the confirmatio; and a coda is in the nature of a peroration.

A more challenging musical example would be a movement without so many well-defined external features as a sonata-form movement. I offer in Example 12-1 an analysis of Bach's Prelude No. 7, *WTC* 2, that I arrived at in conference with a group of graduate students while teaching a seminar on baroque music. The students showed complete unanimity in their reasoning out of the elements of the dispositio as reflected in the Prelude. The analysis divides the movement:

Mm. 1–4, partitio: statement of subject matter, the primary motivic elements.

Mm. 4–11, propositio: initial development of the opening material in a particular way (like an orator putting a certain slant on his subject).

Mm. 11–12, epistrophe: repetition of a closing statement. Here, the repetition uses an inversion of material from the end of m. 1.

Mm. 12–19, confirmatio: development of motivic material.

Mm. 19–20, digressio (digression): motion toward the relative minor (C minor).

Mm. 20–32, epistrophe material (cf. m. 11) extended and fragmented.

Mm. 32–46, confutatio: adducing and rejecting various tonal areas.

Mm. 46–55, digressio: another development of epistrophe material.

Mm. 55, beginning of peroratio, with the tonic confirmed.

Mm. 57, beginning of climactic motion. Note use of both gradatio (ascending motion by step) in the soprano and of commoratio ("dwelling on the strongest point of the argument") in the use of the repeated dominant B-flat pedal tone in the bass, which reinforces the sense of the tonic E-flat.

I should mention that the model can apply to a composition in both large- and small-scale ways. In a work of several movements, each one can usually be analyzed independently: finding, within each, at least the fundamental elements of propositio, confirmatio, and so on. When two movements are linked, a larger-scale structure might be found. On a yet grander scale, various movements might contribute to one large utterance of the model. Certainly a prelude can act as an exordium, although within itself it will follow its own sequence of events, with its own small-scale propositio, confirmatio, and so on.

How does a multimovement work relate to the dispositio of the rhetorical model? Let us look at the large-scale aspects of the Toccata in D Major (BWV 912). This dramatic and outgoing piece has many clear parallels to rhetoric geared to public oratory, from the attention-getting opening flourish to the brilliant, highly intense peroration. A briefly outlined overall analysis on the basis of the dispositio would include the following points:

1. Exordium: the preliminary "warm-up" gesture establishes the tonic key of D, with an interruption (interruptio) by G-sharp (m. 8, with a downward broken chord and tremolo), as if challenging the key.

2. Propositio: allegro (from m. 10). Establishment of D major in the first main segment of the work.

3. Antithesis: adagio (recitative) from m. 68. In this and the following fugato, an antithesis (one of the many devices under decoratio) to the subject matter of the first movement is introduced, in complete contrast of mood, themes, and tonality to the preceding material.

4. Establishment of a foreign tonality: fugato in F-sharp minor (from m. 80).

5. Confutatio: "con discrezione" from m. 111. Modulatory transition away from F-sharp minor and rejection of certain themes as well as

Example 12-1. Bach, Prelude No. 7, *WTC* 2, BWV 876i, with suggested rhetorical analysis.

other tonal possibilities ("rejecting other arguments"), finally moving toward D major again (from m. 122). Changes of direction are made first by redeployment of the descending-fourths motive which ushered in the fugato in F-sharp minor (compare mm. 78–79 with mm. 111–114) and next by interruption: the tremolo before the crucial G-sharp (see No. 1 above, and also No. 6) at m. 114; new use of the recitative's descending-sixth motive, now in a "hopeful" context (compare mm. 71–74 with mm. 117–118); and the dismissal of C major as

(Example 12-1 continued)

a possible new tonal center in a rapid downward figuration (presto, at mm. 118–119). Further tonal exploration and dismissal ensues: a harmonically tentative figure (m. 119) descends to A-sharp, quickly harmonized in a gesture toward B major, which is also negated by an unexpected F-major chord. The latter, acting as a Neapolitan chord, turns the tonal direction toward E minor, which in turn begins a circle-of-fifths progression that reestablishes D major as the tonic.

6. Reconfirmation of D major with the final fugue (gigue-derived, in 6/16); increasing tension (as toward the end of an effective speech);

241

(Example 12-1 continued)

and a highly energized peroratio (from m. 261) with a long swirl of thirty-second-note figuration before the final cadence. The latter begins (m. 276) with another interruption by the same bass G-sharp as at the opening, now preparing a cadence on the tonic.

Gestures recur with outcomes different from what was heard in sections 3 and 4. The rhetorical term for this device is repetitio, or, in Greek, anaphora—the repetition of the same word or group of words at the start of each of a series of lines or clauses:

(Example 12-1 continued)

1. The bass G-sharp, used as a springboard to a half cadence at the opening, is also touched on in the tenor at an important juncture in the "con discrezione" section (at m. 115) and used to introduce the final cadence at the conclusion.
2. The "exploratory" phrase using descending fourths, which ushers in the F-sharp minor fugato, also begins the modulatory section before the final fugue.

(Example 12-1 continued)

3. The figure of the descending sixth from the first recitative briefly reappears, in a more "hopeful" context, in the confutatio.
4. The tremolo in thirty-second notes from the opening page is reused at m. 114 and again at m. 276, transformed into a highly energized passage for the peroration. The G-sharp that expressed disruption and doubt at the opening now presses confidently toward a conclusion.

I have based much of my analysis on tonal rather than thematic relationships. Tonal considerations obviously inform the overall structure: the opening flourish that centers on a half-cadence, the first full movement in the tonic, a departure to F-sharp minor that is surrounded on both sides by tonal uncertainty, and a conclusion that reaffirms the tonic. (Similarly, eighteenth-century analyses of sonata form are founded on tonal, not thematic, elements; the emphasis on themes per se originated in the nineteenth century, when the sonata principle was already dying.)

DECORATIO (FIGURES OF SPEECH)

Let us now look more closely at decoratio—the choice and use of images, motives, and techniques. The general term for them, which has persisted in musical usage, is "figures," as in "figures of speech."

As mentioned, various theorists produced long lists of common types of musical motives and techniques. They were attempting to create an encyclopedic reference for music to match the elaborate codification of literary devices that had evolved over the centuries. Naturally, the musical field is too open-ended for such an endeavor to be completely successful, but the significant amount of common ground that emerges from the different theorists arises readily from the parallels of style found in most baroque music. Composers quite consciously drew on a common repertory of materials ranging from specific motivic types to aspects of phrasing, from specific compositional devices to programmatic usages. For example, hypotyposis, a term that refers, in rhetoric, to using illustrative examples, has the musical meaning of tone painting—suggesting funeral bells, birdsong, and so forth. Epistrophe, the repetition of a closing statement, has the same meaning in oratory and in music. Congeries, the accumulation of repetitions of an idea, refers to stretto in musical terms: overlapping thematic entries. This device is a means of building intensity in both oratory and music.

Another aspect of motivic structuring is the building of an entire composition from one or more figures (small motivic units). The energy of the various motives may be entirely abstract or inspired by pictorial elements. J. G. Ziegler's comment, as one of Bach's pupils, that one should play chorales according to the meaning of the text has a programmatic basis. As is well known, some of Bach's motives in the chorale settings are specifically programmatic, for instance the bass line (a falling diminished seventh, relating to the fall of humanity), in *Durch Adams Fall ist ganz verderbt* (BWV 637), from the *Orgelbüchlein* (see Example 12-2).

In his cantatas and other church music, Bach frequently used musical material with reference to programmatic elements in the text. But because the nineteenth century had developed some aspects of programmatic musical

Example 12-2. Bach, *Durch Adams Fall ist ganz verderbt*, BWV 637, mm. 1–2.

thinking to an embarrassing extent, the twentieth century rather strongly rejected the notion of programmatic ideas in Bach's music. (Harold Schonberg, in *The Great Pianists*, quotes some of Hans von Bülow's programmatic "analyses" of the Chopin Preludes. As Schonberg remarks, "That this inanity could have come from what was conceded to be the sharpest musical mind of the time passes belief" [Schonberg, 136–138].) However, the balance has since been righted, and the added color that comes with the recognition of baroque program elements hardly detracts from the purely musical (rather than the storytelling or programmatic) development that Bach finds for his themes.

RHETORIC AND PERFORMANCE

The rhetorical aspects of performance are most often discussed by modern scholars and players in terms of decoratio, particularly regarding programmatic aspects; the cataloging of motivic types; and the articulation in performance of the figural aspects of compositions. However, those features that the performer can clarify—from knowledge of the topical genres to phrase shapes, larger-scale forms, dramatic gestures, and so on—are all parts of the rhetorical framework. Large- and small-scale structures alike are aspects of the rhetorical model, not to mention performance itself, wherein the performer tries to clarify the musical structures and impart their emotional content to the audience (of course, becoming more agitated toward the peroration).

Let us begin with the foreground level. Figural writing has been touched on a number of times in this book, for instance regarding the construction of the famous Prelude No. 1, *WTC* 1, from a single arpeggiation figure. Bach, like Haydn in a quite different style, is fond of generating an entire movement from one or a few ideas contrasted and/or combined. How the player projects the many statements of a figure in performance depends entirely on the musical context. In the case of works built from one or two constantly iterated figures, strong articulation of each statement is akin to shouting single syllables in a speech or concentrating, one at a time, on the single stones of a mosaic: with extreme concentration on this foreground aspect of the material, its larger-scale use goes out of focus. Musically, the single iterations of a figure are grouped into subphrases, phrases, periods, and larger units; but as Kirnberger and Mattheson said, a proper rhetorical approach takes all these levels into balanced account. Apart from the image of shouting that I just used rhetorically, what effective public speaker stresses every word equally? Good communication takes account of a work's overall form as well as its blow-by-blow detail.

It is possible to overstress a building-block figure that is motivic and yet designed to blend into the fabric. See, for instance, Example 12-3, from Fugue No. 5, *WTC* 2. Dynamic or agogic stress on the motive of repeated tones in this fugue subject immediately becomes excessive; the figure's effect is essentially additive, not soloistic, and it is repeated continually. A performer's understanding and projection of musical figures is not limited to pedantic enunciation of individual events, but extends to understanding the large-scale use and peculiar energy of each figure: how they droop or propel forward, how they combine, how the linear juxtapostion of iterations of one or more figures can shape the larger phrase—above all, how they group and how they form contrasts.

Example 12-3. Bach, Fugue No. 5, *WTC* 2, BWV 874ii, mm. 1–4.

Treatment of motives must also take into account the interplay between the harmonic background and surface or linear events. Often, very fast tempos will bring out background elements—the harmonic framework and large-scale phrasing—but are insensitive to foreground issues such as motivic play, delicate adjustments of the voicing, and subphrase relations. Extremely rapid tempos thrust the large-scale background upon the listener, partly by blurring the foreground elements, rather as in some impressionist paintings. The change in perspective can be interesting and the tempo exhilarating, but the player is better advised to find the optimum tempo to balance background, middleground, and foreground events. Often the background or middleground must be allowed to function as such, without being projected so as to blur smaller-scale events (see chapter 7).

Much ink can be spilled concerning how a performer can convey large-scale musical structure. Theorists and composers have told me that it cannot be done; performers often do not want to talk about it, and I do not blame them. My own feeling, as a pragmatist, is that it all depends. Making the dispositio (to speak of it in baroque terms again) clear in performance is usually more a matter of the performer's comprehension than something that can be directly expressed. Indirectly, of course, it is expressed by the player's understanding of how the different elements interrelate and contrast; this knowledge then informs the way continuities and disruptions, thematic and harmonic contrasts, and so on are handled and projected. When the various features are given proper proportion, the performer has accomplished most of what can be done to allow the perceptive listener to absorb the structure of the music. (Short of caricature. I once heard a performance of the *Goldberg Variations* in which the player added a long, multirepercussion mordent to the end of every half of every variation—and all repeats were taken. Even the most casual listener must gradually have become aware of the binary form repeated thirty-two times in the course of the work, if only by means of approximately 120 long mordents.)

What makes a speaker expressive? A dull, inexpressive speaker often presents everything in a monotone, failing to convey conviction or passion. What is missing is contrast: a good speaker highlights differences and stresses important points; so does a good musical performance. One should not play in a monotone, as if talking to one's self. In addition to understanding the musical structure, one has to delineate its variety, to bring its main features and pertinent details to the listener's attention. Even a nominally unvaried movement by a good composer will usually turn out to be full of contrasts, and Bach provides them constantly—not always overt contrasts, but a variety of effects that evolve naturally out of the musical material. A look at the Allemande of the Partita in B-flat Major (see chapter 7) shows that nearly every phrase does something in contrast to the phrase that precedes or follows it.

A watchword, then, for thinking rhetorically as a performer of baroque music is "contrast." Always be on the lookout for any sort of change: of rhythm, of harmony, of phrase length, of any pattern. Once you have found them, take note of how the changes work in terms of logical development of the material. Thinking in a nineteenth-century way, in terms of the long line only, will tend to smooth out meaningful contrasts. The alert player will seek out the variations in the time line, particularly the rhythmic contrasts, and characterize each as much as possible. (Rhythm and dynamics are the most malleable elements for the performer.) Again, this point applies to contrasts within phrases as well as between phrases and sections. Of course, looking only at the close foreground will lose the larger line, which is also readily apparent in Bach's multilayered structures. Bach's music owes part of its richness to his way of combining foreground variety with longer groupings.

This same principle of characterizing all contrasts relates as well to the finding and characterization of whatever topics are discovered. Suddenly recognizing in a movement the elements of a flute solo, a sarabande, a trio sonata, or a programmatic element, can cause a host of colorful associations to spring up in the player's imagination.

There is yet a further aspect of the analogy between music and rhetoric that concerns the nature of characterization. When highlighting the contrasts and logical developments that emerge from careful consideration of a composition, their divergent energies can be thought of almost in programmatic terms. I do not mean to suggest assigning superficial story lines or similar notions. I refer only to the abstract roles (such as high-energy figures, in opposition to those of low energy) that emerge from the contrasts and developments that one looks for in terms of the rhetorical model. This way of thinking can be a most stimulating springboard to expressive playing.

Note that the elements exposed by this sort of analysis can indeed be seen as almost essentially programmatic. They form, so to speak, the relationships of a story line without hanging extramusical specifics upon those relationships. The dispositio serves as an abstract framework, taking the place of the story line. Thinking rhetorically will dramatize the progress, development, and conflict of musical entities, without the cumbersome personification and often silly particulars that plague the programmatic concept. The baroque era was generally content to leave it at that. In the nineteenth century, romantic performers (and often composers) were inclined to analyze by applying specific storylines to the same contrasts and developments that might be more clearly and objectively sorted out by use of the rhetorical model. Thus, a nineteenth-century view of Bach's D Major Toccata might produce a typical story about joyful lovers who are happy together, become separated for some reason, and are eventually reunited (*pace* Beethoven's "Les Adieux" Sonata). Such stories are sometimes useful as emotional props, but they do not, to say the least, usually account for as many structural details as other kinds of analysis. The advantage of the rhetorical model is that it can combine technical detail with a sense of dramatic development.

SUGGESTIONS FOR FURTHER READING

Butler, Gregory. "Fugue and Rhetoric." *Journal of Music Theory* 21 (1977): 49–110.

Harrison, Daniel. "Rhetoric and Fugue: An Analytical Application." *Music Theory Spectrum* 12 (1990): 1–42.

Kloppers, Jacobus. "Musical Rhetoric and Other Symbols of Communication in Bach's Organ Music." *Man and Nature/L'homme et la nature* 3 (1984): 131–162.

Mattheson, Johann. *Der vollkommene Capellmeister.* Hamburg: Christian Herold, 1739; facs. ed., Kassel: Barenreiter, 1954. Translated into English by

Ernest C. Harriss under the title *Johann Mattheson's Der vollkommene Capellmeister: A Revised Translation with Critical Commentary.* Chapter 6, "On the Length and Shortness of Sound, or the Construction of Tone-Feet"; chapter 9, "On the Sections and Caesuras of Musical Rhetoric." Studies in Musicology 21. Ann Arbor, Michigan: UMI, 1981.

Schulenberg, David. "Musical Expression and Musical Rhetoric in the Keyboard Works of J. S. Bach." In *Johann Sebastian Bach, A Tercentenary Celebration,* edited by Seymour L. Benstock. Westport, Connecticut: Greenwood Press, 1992.

Williams, Peter. "J. S. Bach's Well-Tempered Clavier: A New Approach." *Early Music* 11 (1983): 46–52 (Part 1) and 332–339 (Part 2).

Chapter 13

TEMPERAMENT

What did Bach mean by "well-tempered"? The subject has been dealt with exhaustively in an extensive literature. This chapter will provide some facts and background on tuning generally and on the meaning of "well-tempered" specifically. Here, I will merely sum up some basic points.

Keyboard instruments are tuned by establishing the pitch relationships (the bearing) in the middle of the range, then tuning pure (beatless) octaves from these established pitches, up through the treble range and down through the bass. (Some tuners minutely spread the extremes of the range, tuning the octaves a little larger than pure to give an effect of heightened consonance. This practice compensates for some dissonances that otherwise appear in the overtones. It is commonplace in the tuning of modern pianos and was described in the eighteenth century for tuning harpsichords.)

The pitch level selected for the starting point has, of course, no relationship to the relative pitch relationships established in the bearing. Prior to the development of a standard pitch (a very long process drawn out over the course of the nineteenth and twentieth centuries), instruments could be pitched over a wide range of possibilities. Usually, chamber pitch (used in secular venues) was lower than choir pitch (used in churches), and musicians often had to transpose parts for different situations—as when the organ was pitched a tone above the tuning of other instruments, for instance. In early-music performance today, a' is typically pitched anywhere from 392 (often the pitch of baroque wind instruments), 409, 415 (a semitone below today's standard of 440), and 420–430 (often found on fortepianos and other classical-period instruments), to 440. Use of these different pitches today is necessary in order to avoid compromising the design of instruments built as replicas of particular historical models.

Alteration of the string scaling sets into motion a sequence of other alterations that can easily change the character of the very instrument the builder is trying to replicate. Pitch, by the way, continued to rise in the nineteenth century, in some areas reaching something like a' = 470 by the 1870s. Orchestras today often tune to anything from a' = 442 to a' = 448.

When setting the bearing there are many ways to relate the pitches; any system of relating them is called a temperament. The bearing is normally established by tuning through part or all of the circle of fifths. The variety of temperaments and the need to temper (compromise) the purity of any interval arise from a natural acoustical imbalance in that circle. Let us say that the tuner tunes pure (beatless) fifths through the complete circle of fifths, starting on and returning to C. The C on which the tuner ends will be quite significantly sharp relative to the C from which he or she began. This difference is called the Pythagorean comma, and it can be distributed among some or all of the 12 fifths of the circle in any of a myriad of ways. Equal temperament puts one-twelfth of the comma on each fifth of the circle, so every fifth is slightly (but not disturbingly) flat; this is the standard way to tune pianos today. Most (but not all) keyboard temperaments are based on tuning through the complete circle of fifths, distributing the comma one way or another.

If you tune 4 fifths up from one note, you arrive at a pitch a major third above the first note. Thus, when starting from C, one would tune G, D, A, and E, E being a major third above C. If the fifths are tuned pure (that is, absolutely beatless), the E will be pitched very high, and the major third it makes with C will be almost intolerably wide (sharp). In fact, the fifths of equal temperament are tempered (in this case, flattened) so slightly that the major thirds (all tuned equally wide) are very near to being unacceptable to the ear. Temperaments that temper the fifths unevenly through the circle do so in order to favor some major thirds over others. Usually, the fifths on the naturals (the "white" keys) are tempered more (tuned flatter; that is, the fifths beat faster and more noticeably) so that the major thirds of those "natural" tonalities (C, D, F, G, and others) will be correspondingly sweeter and more consonant in quality. That sweetness is achieved at the expense of the major thirds in the more distant tonalities—for instance, F-sharp to A-sharp—which will sound harsher than those in the natural tonalities. Any temperament that follows a course through the complete circle of fifths, tempering them so that all the fifths are acceptable and all keys usable (however different from or similar to one another), is called a circular temperament. Each of the many circular temperaments juggles the tempering of the fifths one way or another and thus produces different shadings of consonance in different keys. Endless juggling for different subtleties of effect is possible. Equal temperament is a circular temperament, and the only one in which all of the fifths are tempered by exactly the same amount. Any other circular temperament that tempers the fifths (and hence the major thirds) more here and less there, but in such a way that they are all acceptable or at least tolerable, is by modern consensus said to be well tempered.

A temperament that breaks the circle of fifths with 1 or more fifths that are so out of tune as to be unacceptable (called a howling "wolf" interval) is a noncircular temperament. Noncircular temperaments favor some tonalities very greatly over others. Pythagorean tuning (it is not technically a temperament) is a simple example: pure fifths are tuned throughout, up and down from C, the entire Pythagorean comma being situated on one wolf interval, often E-flat–G-sharp, as also in meantone, described further on. Most of the resulting major thirds are very harsh. This way of tuning seems to have been used mainly in medieval times, when the open fifth was the predominant consonance.

Meantone is a noncircular temperament that was very generally used from the sixteenth century through the eighteenth. (Meantone is often confused with Pythagorean temperament, even among some early-music aficionados who have no hands-on experience with tuning. Yet the two are almost diametrically opposite in effect.) There are several types of meantone. The most common, and the one normally meant by the term today, is quarter-comma meantone. This temperament features pure (beatless) major thirds and very flat fifths. Meantone divides not the Pythagorean comma, but rather the syntonic comma, which is the difference between a pure major third and the very sharp one that results from tuning 4 consecutive fifths in the cycle so that they are beatless. (See Example 13-1. The E that forms a pure major third with C is noticeably lower in pitch than the E that results from a sequence of beatless thirds. To relate this to what one usually hears on an equal-tempered piano: the pure major third of meantone sounds much sweeter and more consonant, the wide major third of Pythagorean even harsher than the fast-beating third characteristic of equal temperament.) To produce the pure major third, the four intervening fifths are each tempered by one-quarter of the syntonic comma—hence the term quarter-comma meantone.

To give some background to the discussion below concerning Bach and temperament, I will describe meantone, first technically and then aesthetically—that is, how it is tuned and what it sounds like. Most of this temperament is very easy to tune: the only tempering is the juggling of G, D, and A between the preset poles of C and E. The tuner sets C to the fork; tunes E as a pure third to C; and tempers the intervening G, D, and A so that each of the 4 fifths (C–G, G–D, D–A, and A–E) is equally flat. ("As flat as the ear can bear" was the old rule of thumb.) The remaining notes are then tuned as pure major

Example 13-1. Tuning pattern over the syntonic comma

thirds to the notes already established: F-sharp pure to D, F pure to A, and so on. The main disadvantage to this temperament is that no enharmonic usages are available: for instance, a note tuned as F-sharp will not work as G-flat. Therefore, the tuner has to choose which accidentals to tune. The usual choice is C-sharp, E-flat, F-sharp, G-sharp, and B-flat, but any of their enharmonic relatives could be chosen—for instance, A-flat instead of G-sharp. The choice depends upon the requirements of a specific composition. Eight of the twelve major thirds are pure, but the other four are wildly sharp. Because of the lack of enharmonics, there is also a break in the temperament, usually placed between E-flat and G-sharp, which is again a wolf interval. The colors of meantone are often startling to an ear accustomed only to equal temperament. The more rapidly beating fifths contribute to the effect, but in my experience the listener is most often surprised by the great sweetness and the sense of almost complete repose (not to say inertia) that characterizes the perfectly in-tune major thirds. Meantone is very effective for diatonic music, making the contrasts between dissonance and consonance more intense than they are in equal temperament, especially because the consonances have a strong sense of repose. Its use for chromatic music is limited because of the lack of enharmonic relationships. Meantone provides a wonderful sweetness that seems to enhance the resonance of harpsichords, clavichords, and organs. Changing a harpsichord's tuning from equal temperament to meantone can give the effect of moving to an entirely different, and more resonant, instrument. Of course, listening will tell the reader much more than any number of words. This temperament can readily be heard in many performances and recordings of early music. Organs built to replicate Renaissance and early baroque instruments are sometimes tuned this way.

Meantone, one of the most common temperaments of Bach's day and before, contrasts with the circular temperaments Bach preferred. Meantone was widely used for several generations because most music did not require enharmonic relationships, did not modulate into distant, out-of-tune regions, and did not utilize distant tonalities such as D-flat major.

J. S. Bach is sometimes (incorrectly) credited with inventing equal temperament. In fact, equal temperament was known, at least theoretically, as early as the sixteenth century. From that time onward, many experiments in temperament and even multiple-division keyboards (with different keys for F-sharp and G-flat, for instance) were made—partly because equal temperament was considered to be too unpleasant-sounding as a compromise. In the later seventeenth century and in the eighteenth there were many "well-tempered" systems that approximated equal temperament. (One that is much used today was described by Francesco Antonio Vallotti, an organist and composer at Padua [1697–1780]. The Pythagorean comma is divided over half of the circle of fifths—the fifths covering the natural keys, F–C–G–D–A–E–B—rather than all 12 fifths of the circle. The remainder, B–F-sharp–C-sharp–G-sharp–D-sharp–A-sharp/B-flat–F, are pure, that is, beatless. This system gives a slightly purer, warmer effect to the natural tonalities but allows unrestricted modulation and use of any key as a tonic. It is popular with some ensembles and is frequently used by soloists, as it is colorful and versatile. I found it to be exactly what I was looking for when preparing to record Bach's toccatas.)

With the full spectrum of tonics in the *WTC* and the widely ranging modulation in some of Bach's works, it is clear that Bach was making extensive practical use of the newer temperaments, although he did not necessarily invent any. We simply do not know what temperament or temperaments Bach preferred (although some modern commentaries attribute one or another system to him). However, his music demonstrates that he expected a circular temperament: we find frequent enharmonic use of notes, many movements written in distant tonics such as F-sharp, and often far-ranging modulation. He probably expected unequal temperaments in his earlier career and may have come somewhat later to the use of equal temperament (see below). However, even his early compositions often require a circular temperament. He is said to have disliked Gottfried Silbermann's unequal way of tempering an organ, deliberately improvising in the harsher-sounding tonalities and thereby reportedly driving Silbermann out of the church (*New Bach Reader*, 410–411). When C. P. E. Bach mentioned tuning in his treatise, he casually remarked that one should "take away from most of the fifths a barely noticeable amount of their absolute purity. All twenty-four tonalities will thus become usable" (*Essay*, 37.) Tempering "most of the fifths" means a well-tempered system; tempering "all of the fifths" would signify equal temperament. F. W. Marpurg was told by Kirnberger that Bach "expressly required of him that he tune all the [major] thirds sharp" (*New Bach Reader*, 368). A temperament in which "most of the fifths" are tempered would cause all the major thirds to be sharp to varying degrees. It is possible that in practice, J. S. Bach and his son tuned circular but unequal temperaments favoring whatever keys they expected to utilize at the time and relishing the contrasts in key color from one tonality to another. (Many present-day early-keyboard performers follow this practice.) Kirnberger specifically inveighed against equal temperament, claiming that it eliminated the distinct flavors of different keys and reduced them all to the same qualities, and it is conceivable that this reflects some aspect of his teacher's attitude. On the other hand, Rudolph Rasch has demonstrated convincingly that equal temperament was probably expected for collections that spanned most or all of the tonalities. His evidence includes the views expressed by important early-eighteenth-century musicians, including Johann Georg Neidhardt (1706 and 1724), Johann Mattheson (who published figured bass examples in all keys), Georg Andreas Sorge (1746), and Friedrich Wilhelm Marpurg.

In further response to Kirnberger's view, I should point out that some of the preludes and fugues of the *WTC* are transposed from their original keys to fit the scheme of twenty-four tonalities: thus, Prelude No. 3 of *WTC* 2 originated in C Major. So much, perhaps, for individual key colors. As the reader may already have gathered, temperament was the subject of much controversy in the eighteenth century.

Many performers and writers have noted that Bach occasionally concludes a movement with a surprisingly brief chord. For instance, why does Prelude No. 23, *WTC* 2, end with a chord whose duration is an eighth-note value? Does this mean that the work, nominally lyrical, in fact is aggressive enough to end so abruptly? Or is there another reason? Possibly Bach expected the major third on B to be harsh sounding, as it is in many well-tempered tuning systems, and so he wanted the player to hold the chord no longer than necessary. Either reason might also apply to the concluding chord (also an eighth-note value) of the Toccata in F-sharp Minor.

Organs obviously require a temperament that can remain fixed for long periods. It would be interesting to make a study of what limitations, if any, on the choice of tonic keys and modulations are to be found in Bach's organ works. Stringed keyboard instruments of the eighteenth century are of course tuned more frequently than an organ, and the temperament is readily subject to modifications for this or that occasion. (Contrary to popular myth, by the way, a good harpsichord holds its tuning quite well under stable conditions. Clavichords, properly tuned, have extremely durable tuning.) For Bach's larger-scale works (such as a complete suite or partita, or the *Goldberg Variations*) I often tune a mildly unequal temperament that favors the tonic and its related keys, to produce a warmer resonance from the instrument than equal temperament would allow. However, equal temperament or something close to it is often preferable for a more varied program, or for a performance of a complete book of the *WTC*, which Bach is said to have played in its entirety on three separate occasions for his pupil Gerber. Bach's tuning habits could easily have embraced this kind of flexibility around a basis of circular temperament.

SUGGESTIONS FOR FURTHER READING

Lindley, Mark. "Instructions for the Clavier Diversely Tempered." *Early Music* 5 (1977): 18–23.

Rasch, Rudolf. "Does 'Well-Tempered' Mean 'Equal-Tempered'?" In *Bach, Handel, Scarlatti: Tercentenary Essays*, edited by Peter Williams. Cambridge: Cambridge University Press, 1985.

Troeger, Richard. "Flexibility in Well-Tempered Tuning." *Diapason* 73, no. 6 (June 1982): 6–7.

———. *Technique and Interpretation on the Harpsichord and Clavichord.* Chapter 9, "Temperament." Bloomington: Indiana University Press, 1987.

Chapter 14

MUSICOLOGY AND
THE PERFORMER

I hope readers of this book will not think I am advocating a change of career by recommending consideration of scholarly matters. I am well aware that anything other than an almost fully instinctive approach (apart from matters of technique) is scorned in some musical quarters. However, the practical aspects of research should be reasonably apparent from this and similar books. Indeed, for any serious player, some knowledge of style and early performance practice provides many shortcuts to solving musical and even technical problems. There is also a romantic aspect to this kind of study. We have all had the thrill of witnessing some remote historical event on "ancient" film—some event so remote in time (or at least in technology, that now almost ruling factor) that it is startling to see a moving picture of it. The footage of Queen Victoria's funeral procession is perhaps an apt example (certainly it represents the end of an era quite different from our own), although more dramatic occasions have been preserved. Think of the interest that would be generated if, by some miracle, a recording could surface of the playing of Bach, Mozart, or Chopin. The eighteenth-century treatises are the nearest we have to such an experience: statements by one or another important observer (one of them, C. P. E. Bach, the most articulate son of the great Sebastian) about how artists of that period approached musical performance. Such documents are not sound recordings, but they are, nonetheless, vital human documents—often full of very specific particulars—that give us concrete information, sometimes enough to make a really imaginative leap into a bygone era.

Notice that I say "imaginative." The performance conventions described in this book are no more limiting to interpretive individuality than are the conventions and notation of, for example, Liszt's music. The main difference, as I have mentioned, is that Bach's conventions are no longer part of common practice. They need special consideration from a player who has been trained in a different norm of notation and performance. But there is as much latitude for interpretive variation in earlier music as in music of the nineteenth and twentieth centuries—in fact, there is often more.

Without question, it can be a bit daunting to be confronted with so many unfamiliar factors, notational and otherwise. However, those to whom these issues are new should examine them one at a time and try to absorb them over time into performance responses. Unless it is felt as a musical function, any performance inflection will tend to sound unconvincing. Use of performance practices, from French *notes inégales* to a simple crescendo, has to emanate finally from the player's inner responses—from the guts.

There was for a long time a great gulf between scholars and performing musicians. It is often still found in the mainstream. For years, harpsichordists particularly were in the unenviable position of being "in the know" and citing information that fellow ensemble players often did not want to hear. "I don't care if it's a gavotte; I just care about the *music*," was the response of one cellist to a colleague of mine when he briefly explained, during rehearsal, the nature of an unlabeled cantata movement (at the conductor's deferential request). The fact that the nature of a gavotte might be relevant to the music meant nothing to this very gut-level player. On the other hand, the "authenticity" movement is filled with performing scholars and scholarly performers, sometimes citing chapter and verse of various treatises at one another through half the rehearsal. Although readily caricatured (and it sometimes caricatures itself), this sincerity of purpose in recreating music of bygone times has been essential. Equally essential, of course, is the avoidance of half-baked ideas. Application of chapter and verse requires a firm grasp of the context of a treatise's meaning and intent, and of the musical context being addressed. Somewhere between the two extremes lies a useful middle ground.

When trying to interpret the performance indications preserved in period documents, one's conclusions must fit all the facts. For instance, applying inequality, extra embellishment, or a mannered articulation without regard to the musical context will produce a questionable musical effect. As regards authenticity, to say nothing of sheer musicality, a performance is a hypothesis that either accommodates all the facts (both musical and historical), or accommodates only some, to leave other important considerations dangling. A performance of the latter type is as questionable as any postmodern interpretation.

Historical information should be used from a positive point of view. Although it shows a sincere attitude, the frame of mind that leads a performer to ask, "Am I safe in playing this way?" or, "Is this allowed, am I within the rules?"

is unproductive in the long run. A good grounding in historical information both answers questions and provokes new ones while allowing one to play with a greater sense of context. The historical approach should be a stimulus to creative musical feeling and music making.

There is more to this endeavor than mere points of performance practice. The performer has to achieve a holistic view that encompasses the compositional structure; the medium (clavichord, harpsichord, or piano, and the interplay among these media); relationships to other media (such as ensemble imitation); and relevant notational habits and performance practices. To try to assimilate all of this into your player's gut produces the nearest thing, short of a time machine, to real authenticity.

In the course of this book I have surveyed a wide range of genre features and notational signals that are not in present-day use. However, they employ signs that have remained in use even as their meaning changed in the nineteenth century: slurs, dots, dashes, and so forth, even down to time signatures. (Note, for example, how differently Max Reger uses 18/16 time, as opposed to what it meant to Bach: for Reger, it can be allied to a very slow tempo.) We have to learn what the signs that we today read one way meant to someone in the seventeenth or eighteenth century. Often, a twenty-first-century rendering makes little or no sense for the eighteenth-century context. Even postmodern performers should take these issues into account, so as to know, at least, where they are departing from the original intent. (I will concede that, to the postmodern outlook, the last point may be irrelevant.)

For those just beginning to wade into the formidable secondary literature (modern-day articles, books, and monographs), the best advice I have to offer is: keep an open mind, proceed with caution, and make sure that the arguments are well founded. Also, be wary of older publications, for they are often superseded as new information becomes available, and some ideas presented early in the revival were decidedly off-base. (Doubtless the same will be said of the present generation, and of this book.) Any viewpoint can be biased; critical reading is essential. Differentiate between the real facts that are presented and their interpretation by the author.

In dealing with the complex realm of early performance practices, there is a great danger of applying a few basic considerations as if from a rulebook. This makes for playing that may be anything from dull to bizarre—or, worse, highly mannered. I once heard a harpsichord student in a competition play with a very, very strong agogic accent at the start of every odd-numbered measure. (Thus, in common time, "*one* . . . two three four, one two three four, *one* . . . two three four.") The degree of accent was literally the same every time and not graded at all in relation to the different meters of the various movements, the shapes of the phrases, the point in the phrase or movement, the tempo, the harmonies, or anything else. This style, as regular and insistent as an off-level metronome, persisted through forty-five minutes of repertoire. I had never heard anything like it and, to make it worse, the performance was delivered with immense conviction and technical security. This student had been taught agogic accent and the concept of strong beats, but apparently the host of modifying factors related to time accents had not made any impression. I would prefer to hear someone play entirely from instinct rather than from such rigid and limited theory.

When learning about a new musical style or genre, or about a host of new details relevant to a style, it is essential that one be exposed to at least several examples of the phenomenon. Thus, if you are studying a sarabande, do not keep working over a single specimen, but read through, examine, work with, and make comparisons among a good many sarabandes, both by Bach and by his contemporaries.

The issues of performance practice as described by early authors are only attempts to describe a living practice. It is revealing to try, yourself, to describe in really concrete terms a performance trait such as some kind of rhythmic finesse or dynamic treatment. These are matters of delicate adjustment and require flexibility in application, both within a movement and when moving from one piece to another. Inequality, the flexible dot, bar-line inflection, and all other such matters must be realized in terms of the immediate musical context. Trying to find the approach that feels right may lead to new perceptions of both the particular composition and the performance convention. Again, the perspective and experience gained through working with several examples of a given genre is crucial. Only when the musical needs of the composition and the application(s) of the convention "click" has anything valid been achieved. Then one often realizes what was missing, in terms of musical shape or expression, before one was able to integrate the once-foreign performance practice.

In adopting practices from treatises, a sense of perspective is needed; otherwise, one may apply a few basic notions without reference to their musical function. (Imagine trying to reproduce, two hundred years from now, a modern-day performance of Wagner or Stravinsky according to miscellaneous written descriptions and without reference to recordings.) If a performance practice idea does not ring true, continue to experiment with it, and use it only after its musical meaning has become clear. That clarity will emerge solely by considering musical contexts in a number of pieces for which the practice in question is relevant or potentially relevant. Thus, some performers take a while to assimilate French inequality, and some conservatively trained student musicians have trouble with the idea of agogic accents (a development that would be very surprising to the composers and performers of the nineteenth-century standard repertory). Opening oneself up to new musical treatments is similar to responding to an instrument on its own terms, rather than forcing it to do something it is not suited to doing.

Naturally, one's ingrained habits will sometimes conflict with the absorption of new ideas or even experimentation with them. From the realm of researching the manufacture of ancient cloth, Elizabeth Barber gives an apt parallel:

> Finding one's own unwarranted assumptions is one of the most difficult things to wrestle with, precisely because they are so hard to recognize. Trying simply to *state all one's assumptions explicitly* is the first major step. . . . I had been working for years with the Egyptian material on spinning before I realized that nowhere was there a picture of a distaff in use, and nowhere among the thousands of textile artifacts a surviving distaff. So how were they draft-spinning a fiber that is typically longer than one's arm? (A distaff . . . acts basically as an arm extender when the fibers are very long.) . . . The answer, I gradually discovered, was that they were not draft-spinning (unwarranted assumption discovered). Instead of *pulling* the fibers past each other, the Egyptians were separating them entirely and splicing them end to end. All the phases of the work were represented in the tomb paintings, but I was not ready to understand the details of what I saw until I had been forced to discard my wrong assumptions. This occurred when I noticed that a crucial element for my theory was *missing*, as the result of careful comparison to well-known examples of how people spin in most other parts of the world. . . . Finally, none of these [research] methods will be of use unless the researcher is willing to learn what the subject has to say about itself instead of trying to make the topic come out in some predetermined way. (Barber, 298–299)

The constant interaction of research, sensitive musical response, and thoughtful experimentation can contribute to understanding, to vibrant performance, and above all to the knowledge that there are no once-and-for-all conclusions to be reached for a living art.

Appendix A

EDITIONS AND FACSIMILES

The mere fact that something appears in print does not mean that it is correct. This thought applies to this book, to most others, to newspapers, and to the deceptively decisive appearance of many a musical edition.

Editorial decisions and performance markings must be recognized as being just that. The editor's authority does not rank with Bach's. Editions by famous musicians such as Ferruccio Busoni or Bela Bartók are fascinating accounts of how these musicians viewed Bach and other composers, but they cannot be used as a starting point for realizing the composer's intentions. They are for consultation only, and it is unlikely that their editors would disagree with this statement.

The so-called Urtext ("original text") editions rarely provide final solutions to the tangle of original sources. If there are only one or two surviving sources for a work, an edition that presents the music accurately and accounts for any and all differences between the sources can probably claim to be final. However, Urtext editions often represent only the editor's personal choice among a myriad of divergent source readings, whose relative validity cannot always be decisively argued. Even this situation is acceptable if a complete account of the source divergencies is presented. (A "critical report" is usually provided in an appendix, or, as in the *Neue Bach-Ausgabe*, in separate volumes.) However, the editor's preferences and choices can be arbitrary and editorial reports sometimes quite incomplete: different readings among the original sources are not always accounted for, or necessarily mentioned. Therefore, and worst of all, the appearance of finality can be entirely deceptive. Let the buyer beware. Read the fine print; make comparisons.

To some very pragmatic performers, the use of facsimile copies of original printed editions and, "worse," of only semilegible photoreproductions of centuries-old manuscripts, often seems like an unmusical side excursion into anti-quarianism and irrelevant bibliophilia. It is not. What was just said concerning printed editions should convince the skeptic of the need to deal with textual matters at least in part from the sources themselves. Seeing is believing. You can only believe the source itself, not someone's translated conception of it. Details of slurrings (sometimes quite debatable), ornament signs, corrections, even the notes themselves—all sorts of details can often be confirmed only by looking for yourself at the original. Then you can join the throng of people, each of whom has his or her own idea about it. But at least the idea is your own.

Appendix B

TEMPO RELATIONSHIPS

In the seventeenth century, proportional tempos were sometimes applicable to the successive dances within a suite. Indeed, the suite has its origin in the proportional relationship between paired dances (the first in duple meter, the second in triple), such as the pavane and galliard. This relationship was often explicit in the Renaissance: the second dance was sometimes entitled merely "Proportz," indicating the proportional relationship. There is no evidence known to me that specifically links proportional tempos with Bach's suites or other keyboard music, and the following is presented solely as speculation. However, the principle is of interest. Striving for a relationship between or among movements, even if it is eventually abandoned, can reveal interesting details of accent, of the relationship of large underlying values to surface activity, and of the essentials of enunciation in both or all movements. For example, one of the advantages of working out a tempo proportion between a prelude and a fugue is that puzzling cases require precise consideration of the groupings and accents one is trying, however subconsciously, to bring out in one movement or another. If the fugue, let us say, seems at first to require a brisk pace that does not accommodate any proportion with the prelude, deeper consideration of the accentual characteristics of the fugue might suggest a way to present them just as acutely at a slightly slower pace, and in addition to bring out more detail generally.

An important candidate for tempo relationships is the *Goldberg Variations*. This is one of the most highly integrated keyboard works that Bach composed. Unifying elements include the chaconne basis, the series of canons (every third variation) at ascending intervals with interspersed duets and character pieces, and the structured climaxes at middle and end. These factors suggest a scheme

265

to the tempo relationships as well. The resulting approach could also be applied to suites.

The work is notable for the rarity with which the same time signature is used in successive variations. When this does happen, a change of tempo or character is strongly marked. One hears 3/4 time in Variations XXVIII–XXIX (of differing character), and it underlies Variation XXVI (with parallel 18/16), which follows Variation XXV (also in 3/4 marked adagio). The 3/4 signature persists in Variations XII–XIV, but Variation XIII is of a slow or andante character.

A valid constant pulse must allow tempos that are consistent with known style features (such as dances or the French overture style of Variation XVI) and with the tempos implied by time words and signatures. Thus, the 18/16 signature of Variation XXVI signifies (as Kirnberger tells us specifically about this movement) that it be played rapidly and without stresses. The same kind of speed and lightness is appropriate to Variation XI, in 12/16. Variation II, in 2/4, and Variations IV, VI, XVI (second section), and XIX in 3/8, are brisk, albeit of vastly differing characters. (Variations VI and XIX are often rendered more slowly than their notation suggests.) Movements in 3/4, C, and even alla breve are intrinsically open to a wider latitude of tempo.

Dance-related movements in the set include the theme (3/4), which is a sarabande; Variation VII, which is marked Giga (6/8); and Variation XXIV in 9/8, a siciliano. Variation XXI (C) may relate to allemande style; Variation XIX, in 3/8, possibly derives from the passepied.

Most of the duet movements (Variations V, VIII, XIV, XVII, XX, XXIII, and XXVI) are in 3/4 time. Variation XI, in 12/16, is an exception. They are all of an obviously extrovert character; however, their brilliance need not be overstressed at the expense of reducing the variety among them.

Finding a single pulse rate to accommodate the tempo and other characteristics of the entire set hardly seems at first to be a promising venture. The most viable solution is probably to find two related tempos: one for the quarter-note pulse in C, alla breve, and 3/4 time, and one for the dotted quarter in compound signatures (such as 6/8 and 3/8). A confirmation of this approach can be found in the work itself. Variation VIII, although provided only with a 3/4 signature, is in fact largely bimetric, opposing 6/8 against 3/4 (see Example 6-1). The two concurrent meters yield two related tempos: the quarter pulse of 3/4 and the dotted-quarter pulse of 6/8. Using these as bases for the triple- and quadruple-pulse tempos on the one hand, and for the compound-signature movements on the other, results in proportioned tempos that fulfill the requirements of each individual variation as outlined above. The speed of m.m. = 88 is a reasonable basis for the pulse rate of most of the triple- and quadruple-meter movements, which produces M.M. = 60 for the compound meters. (For example, the theme would use M.M. = 88 for the eighth notes; Variation I would use M.M. = 88 for the quarter value.) Again, the relationship can be heard in the opening of Variation VIII: the 3/4 upper line in ♩ = 88 coincides with a tempo of ♩· = 60 for the 6/8 lower line. A few triple- and quadruple-meter variations are most successful in tempos based on M.M. = 60 rather than M.M. = 88.

This formula for relating tempos in the *Goldberg Variations* fits the requirements enumerated above, but it remains speculative. It is not presented as the definitive solution, but as a logical approach that can also be used to interrelate the movements of suites and other works. Even a performance using tempo proportions might flex the tempo once the basic relationships have been worked out; but this and like matters depend upon individual taste.

Appendix C

STYLES IN THE
KEYBOARD WORKS

The following tabulation lists works that can be typed by certain primary style elements, for instance using lute or orchestral style, being based in a dance type, and so forth.

From the Twelve Little Preludes
Preludes No. 1 and No. 2 in C Major, No. 3 in C Minor (in lute style; originally written for the lute), and No. 5 in D Minor: figural chords.
Prelude No. 7 in E Minor: menuet
Preludes No. 8 and No. 9 in F Major: orchestral style
Prelude No. 10 in G Minor: menuet (added by Bach as a trio to a menuet in G minor by G. H. Stölzel)
Prelude No. 12 in A Minor: gigue

From the Six Little Preludes
Prelude No. 2 in C Minor: menuet
Prelude No. 4 in D Major: trio sonata with continuo bass

From the Inventions and Sinfonias
Invention No. 4 in D Minor: gigue
Invention No. 6 in E Major: corrente (compare to the Corrente of Partita No. 6)
Invention No. 10 in G Major: gigue (considered to be corrente by Jenne and Little)
Sinfonia No. 2 in C Minor: gigue? (compare to the gigue-like Fugue No. 19, WTC 1)

Sinfonias No. 4 in D Minor, No. 5 in E-flat Major: trio sonata with continuo bass

Sinfonia No. 6 in E Major: gigue elements? Considered to be a corrente by Jenne & Little

Sinfonia No. 13 in A Minor: corrente

Sinfonia No. 15 in B Minor: gigue

From the Seven Toccatas

Toccata in G Minor, 3/2 section following opening flourish: sarabande; final fugue: gigue

Toccata in G Major, final fugue: gigue

Toccata in D Major, final fugue: gigue

Toccata in F sharp minor, final fugue: chaconne, disguised in 6/8 rhythm, according to Schulenberg, who cites the similarity to the first chorus from the cantata *Weinen, Klagen, Sorgen, Zagen* (BWV 12) (Schulenberg, *The Keyboard Music of J. S. Bach*, 79).

From The Art of Fugue

Canon alla Decima: gigue.

Canon in Hypodiapason: gigue (compare to the Gigue of English Suite No. 6).

Contrapuncti 13a and 13b: gigue.

From The Well-Tempered Clavier, Book 1

No.	Key	Prelude	Fugue
1	C	chordal figure (simple arpeggios)	a4; stretto
2	C Minor	chordal figure; recitative passage	a3; *galant*
3	C-sharp	chordal figure	a3; *galant*; sonata-like recapitulation
4	C-sharp Minor	loure	a5; *stile antico* (ricercar)
5	D	chordal figure	a4; "stile Francese" (cf. *The Art of Fugue*, No. 6)
6	D Minor	chordal figure	a3; many stretti and inversions
7	E-flat	toccata (free opening; chorale; fugue)	a3; clavieristic polyphony
8	E-flat/	sarabande	a3; *stile antico* stretto fugue D-sharp Minor

No. Key	Prelude	Fugue
9 E	pastorale-like sinfonia	a3; motoric
10 E Minor	continuo aria–presto	a2; orchestral style
11 F	chordal figure	a3; passepied
12 F Minor	allemande	a4; cross symbolism?
13 F-sharp	invention	a3; *galant*
14 F-sharp Minor	invention-like	a4; loure-derived?
15 G	duple gigue? Chordal figure	a3; gigue
16 G Minor	allemande-derived?	a4; cross symbolism? "textbook fugue"
17 A-flat	orchestrally derived	a4; combination of old and new elements
18 G-sharp Minor	sinfonia	a4; fugue based on a cadential gesture!
19 A	sinfonia (the only prelude in triple counterpoint)	a3; gigue
20 A Minor	invention (with clavieristic elements)	a4; related to organ style
21 B-flat	toccata	a3; *galant*
22 B-flat minor	orchestral style (strings and continuo)	a5; related to choral style
23 B	organ-derived	a4; *galant*
24 B Minor	trio sonata texture	a4; cross symbolism?

From *The Well-Tempered Clavier*, Book 2

No. Key	Prelude	Fugue
1 C	allemande-derived; organ style?	a3; motoric
2 C Minor	invention; allemande-derived?	a4; organ-derived
3 C-sharp	chordal figure (orchestral style)	a3; clavieristic passages
4 C-sharp Minor	trio plus fugue sonata texture	a3; gigue
5 D	orchestral style (trumpets and timpani)	a4; stretto fugue

No.	Key	Prelude	Fugue
6	D Minor	orchestrally derived?	a3; loosely structured clavieristic fugue
7	E-flat	lute style	a4; choral style stretto fugue
8	D-sharp Minor	invention; quasi-allemande	a4; *stile antico*; choral style
9	E	sinfonia	a4; *stile antico* (ricercar); choral style
10	E Minor	invention	a3; gigue
11	F	dense figural writing; organ style*	a3; gigue
12	F Minor	gavotte? suggests trio sonata texture	a3; bourrée
13	F-sharp	chordal figures; suggests tutti/soli	a3; gavotte
14	F-sharp Minor	aria-style	a3; *stile antico* triple fugue
15	G	binary form	a3; clavieristic; corrente
16	G Minor	allemande grave	a4; stretto fugue
17	A-flat	orchestral style (tutti/soli)	a4; almost orchestral, with a5 conclusion
18	G-sharp Minor	invention (allemande-derived?)	a3; gigue
19	A	sinfonia	a3; motoric
20	A Minor	invention; allemande-derived	a3; clavieristic passages
21	B-flat	sinfonia; lutenistic elements	a3; menuet
22	B-flat Minor	sinfonia	a4; stretto fugue
23	B	suggestions of tutti/soli; lute elements	a4; *stile antico*
24	B Minor	invention, with orchestral suggestions	a3; passepied

*This prelude is often compared to the French unmeasured preludes. These, however, never develop a single motive to this extent, and they appear to be based in common time rather than 3/2 meter.

Appendix D

PERFORMANCE PRACTICE
MYTHS

A great multitude of completely unsupported notions about early music and its performance practices developed in the twentieth century and some of them still linger. Many of these are just plain silly; some are serious misunderstandings. This appendix includes a sampling of these misconceptions.

Expression

"Early music is more limited in emotional depth than later music."
"Each piece of music expresses only a single mood."

Fingering

"Thumb crossings are limited by short keys."
(Yet, sixteenth-century Spanish sources for the clavichord advocate this very fingering, and the clavichords of the period had very short keys. We know from Bach's pupil Agricola that Bach himself liked short keys.)

"The thumb was never used before Bach."
(How did the virginalists manage to play those four-note chords assigned to a single hand? The thumb often appears in fingerings prior to Bach's time.)

"Before Bach, the hand was held flat and the thumbs hung down in front of the keyboard."
(The supreme example of misunderstanding.)

"Finger crossing necessarily produces rhythmic unevenness or articulatory interruptions."
(C. P. E. Bach advocates finger crossings for "unbroken continuity.")

"Every change from left hand to right makes an articulation."

Articulation

"Legato was invented by François Couperin in 1716."
(That was the year Couperin first published his little treatise on harpsichord playing; he discusses legato, but not as a new invention.)

Dynamics

"Bach is always loud."
(Certainly a rule of thumb that gets around the effort of a thought-out performance.)

"Only terrace dynamics apply to baroque music."

Tempo and timing

"Music before Beethoven is always to be played metronomically."
(Note that the metronome came into general use only around Beethoven's time.)

"Slow movements in the eighteenth century were not as slow as they were later; fast movements were not as fast."
(This notion has been repeated from at least the mid-nineteenth century through to the late twentieth, and probably since.)

Technique

"Really fast playing was not possible before Carl Czerny's exercises were invented."

"There is a 'toccata touch' appropriate to toccatas."
"'Fugue touch' is appropriate to fugues."
(I suppose there should be a "sonata touch" for sonatas.)

"Hand position at the keyboard is shown in many old paintings and other images."
(In some, doubtless, but the person posing for the picture was just as likely to sit with the hands in a position completely unrelated to actual playing. The same thing can be seen in many posed photographs of keyboard players today.)

Ornaments

"Mordents are upside-down trills."

"The speed of a trill is twice that of the fastest written note values."

Scansion

"Bach is always iambic."
Try this concept with the opening of the Italian Concerto.

Instruments

"Four octaves, C–c''', is the extreme limit of keyboard range in Bach's time."
(Why, then, did Bach occasionally write as low as GG, often as high as d'''?)

"Bach, on the piano, should be played without dynamic inflection because this is how the harpsichord sounds."

"The pedal should never be used in Bach because the harpsichord does not have one."

"The clavichord cannot handle homophony, or polyphony, or project a bass line."
(How astonishing, then, that Kirnberger and C. P. E. Bach liked it so much—in common with most of northern Europe.)

"The harpsichord is without any nuance."

"The harpsichord's action is always very light, it is easy to play."

"Bach did not like to play polyphony on the harpsichord."
(Probably a simplification of Forkel's statement that Bach's favorite instrument was the clavichord.)

"Bach [or any composer before 1850] wrote with the modern piano in mind, or at least would regard it as an improvement over the instruments he actually used and for which he wrote so splendidly."
(The same is often asserted about Bach and the modern violin and other instruments. Would you write a sonata for the violin and piano as you know them, or for what you imagine them to be like in 250 years? Anton Rubinstein saw through this idea back in the nineteenth century [see chapter 1].)

The ultimate example of invention applied to misinterpretation is the "Vega Bach Bow," a bow with pronounced outward curve and the capacity for the bow hair to be loosened so that it can contact all four strings of the violin for a literal performance of the multistop writing in Bach's violin solos. The fact that the baroque violin's bridge (which features a gentler slope than the modern standard) is already designed to facilitate an arpeggiated rendition of these passages was overlooked or ignored by Vega and his followers.

Tuning and temperament

"Temperament in Bach's time and just before was based on pure, beatless perfect fifths."
(This would, in fact, result in extremely harsh-sounding tuning.)

"Bach wrote for a well-tempered, not equal-tempered, tuning system."
(The truth is, we simply do not know.)

"Werckmeister invented equal temperament and this inspired Bach to write the WTC."
(Equal temperament had been known, certainly in theory and probably in some practical use, long before the time of Andreas Werckmeister [1645–1706]. Again, we do not know whether Bach preferred equal temperament to a well-tempered system.)

"Eighteenth-century orchestras were always out of tune."
(In fact, with the correct knowledge of the techniques of the early instruments, period-style ensembles can be better in tune than the standard modern orchestra.)

"Baroque flutes were built out of tune."
(The intonation is subject to the player's control through wind pressure and embouchure.)

On performance practices generally

"We cannot be sure, so historical performance issues do not matter."
(A frequently encountered mainstream viewpoint.)

"If it is written one way, there is no reason to play it another way."
(There are many treatises explaining what is intended to be played another way. "We write differently from the way we play" [François Couperin, 1716–1717].)

GLOSSARY

accent 1. A stressed point in a musical phrase; 2. J. S. Bach's term for appoggiatura.

acciaccatura A keyboard ornament featuring a dissonant note "crushed" against its neighbor or played briefly and released between arpeggiated members of a chord.

adagio 1. The slowest usual tempo notation; 2. a generic indication for a slower pace.

affect Emotional state that is portrayed musically; for example, joy, sorrow.

agogics A term referring to flexibility of time in music.

air Movement in which an accompanied melody is the main feature.

allemande 1. A rapid court dance. 2. An instrumental movement in duple/quadruple meter, of a grave or solemn character.

andante Tempo indication for a moderate pace with equality of rhythm and accent.

anticipation Nonharmonic note in a rhythmically weak (often upbeat) position that iterates a note (usually in a soprano-line melody) in anticipation of an immediate restatement of that note with its consonant harmony.

appoggiatura Rhythmically accented dissonant note that resolves by step.

articulation A word that generally concerns the clear utterance of music in performance: attack, connection and separation of notes, phrasing generally. More narrowly, it addresses the treatment of detached notes.

assimilation, rhythmic Making the difference between different note values less apparent, either generally or in respect to "assimilating" one specific value to another, for example, making dotted rhythmic figures match long-short triplet values.

augmentation Lengthening of the notes of a theme, as in halves rather than quarters.

Bach-Gesellschaft Edition of the complete works of J. S. Bach, published between 1850 and 1900 by the German Bach Society (Bach-Gesellschaft).

basso continuo *See* continuo.

Bebung Vibrato on the clavichord, effected by moving the depressed key up and down, thus increasing and decreasing the string tension. The effect is really a half-vibrato, because the pitch can only be raised above its basic level, not lowered.

bicinium (pl. *bicinia*) A composition in strict two-part writing.

bourrée A brisk dance in duple meter with an upbeat.

BWV abbreviation for *Bach-Werke Verzeichnis* (Catalogue of Bach's Works) prepared by Wolfgang Schmieder (1950). The works are grouped by medium.

cadence 1. Generally, any point of repose in the course of a composition, or the chordal or melodic formula that leads to that point. 2. Bach's term for the turn.

cadenza Anything from a short flourish to a lengthy development in free style, to highlight an important cadence area in a composition.

canari A rapid dance in 3/8 or 6/8 time, using dotted figures on the strong beats throughout.

canon A contrapuntal movement in which one part is strictly imitated by the other(s) throughout.

cantabile In a singing manner.

cantata A work, sacred or secular, in several movements, based on a narrative text, for voice(s) and ensemble, usually alternating recitatives, arias, and choruses.

capriccio 1. Light hearted movement; 2. strict contrapuntal composition.

chaconne 1. An intense, rather grave triple-meter dance; 2. a type of variation, related in style and meter to the dance, using a continuously repeated harmonic pattern.

clavecin French for harpsichord; often used in a generic way to refer to stringed keyboard instruments, especially in Germany.

clavichord Keyboard instrument in which the strings are struck by brass tangents, of soft, clear, and flexible tone. One of the major keyboard instruments of J. S. Bach's time.

clavier Lit., keyboard; any stringed keyboard instrument in the baroque era. After ca. 1750, it tends to signify the clavichord specifically.

comes The imitating line in a canon. The *comes* (companion) imitates the *dux* (leader).

concerto A work in several (most often three) movements in which a full ensemble and a small group of soloists (concerto grosso) or single soloist (solo concerto) play together on equal terms, the work alternating among various combinations of full ensemble (tutti) and soloists playing together themselves or accompanied by the tutti group.

continuo The bass line of an ensemble or solo work, performed by a keyboard or other chordal instrument (realizing the figured harmonies notated with the bass line) together with a stringed or other melodic instrument (viol, cello, bassoon, and the like).

continuo fugue A fugue without strict part-writing.

contrapunctus A strict contrapuntal movement; term used by J. S. Bach for the individual movements of his composition *The Art of Fugue.*

corrente A rapid, light triple-meter dance of Italian origin.

coulé A melodic one-note grace.

Couperin, François (1668–1733) French composer, known as "le Grand," considered one of the preeminent composers of his time.

Couperin, Louis (ca. 1626–1661) French composer and keyboard player, noted for the powerful harmonies of his works and his composition of unmeasured preludes.

courante A slow-to-moderate French dance in triple meter, often featuring hemiola.

diminution 1. Presenting a theme in shortened (usually halved) note values; 2. embellishing a work or melody with figurations in rapid, usually rhythmic note values.

discretion A direction for free timing in performance, notably used by J. J. Froberger.

double A variation on a movement characterized by elaborate expansion of ornamentation and embellishment. One characteristic form of *double* is to recast the original movement into a continuous surface rhythm, usually half of the beat value.

double counterpoint Invertible counterpoint in two parts.

double dotting *See* overdotting.

double fugue Fugue with two subjects, either heard together thoughout or presented one at a time and then in combination.

dux The first line heard in a canon. The *dux* (leader) is imitated by the *comes* (companion).

dynamics Variations in loudness, or variations in intensity that are more or less perceived by the listener as inflections of the volume level.

echo Repetition of a phrase or short unit at a softer level than the prevailing dynamic.

eight-foot A term referring to pitch level in an instrument (mainly organ or harpsichord) with several stops. The term 8-foot refers to the "normal" pitch level, as opposed to stops an octave below or above the norm, or stops at other intervals (as commonly on the organ).

embellishment Decoration of the basic musical line with notes of smaller value. *Ornamentation* has the same basic meaning, but is often used to refer to the stereotypical formulas, often shown by sign rather than written out. *Embellishment* is often used (as in this book) to refer to nonstereotypical decoration, either written out or improvised, or both. It can be free and rubato in nature or rhythmically strict (as with many diminutions; *see* diminution).

episode *See* fugue.

exposition Opening statement of thematic material. In a fugue, the successive entries of the several voices stating the theme (subject).

fantasia 1. A strictly contrapuntal work; 2. a work in very free style.

figural composition Musical composition based on intensive use of one or a few brief motives.

figure In rhetoric, a verbal device, as a "figure of speech." In musical rhetoric, a motive or technique.

figured bass A bass line annotated with numbers that indicate harmonies. Used in continuo playing (*see* Continuo; Thoroughbass).

fortepiano A term used in modern times to specify any early form of piano-forte, usually from Beethoven's era and before.

four-foot On a harpsichord or organ, a stop sounding an octave above the written pitch, used mainly as a reinforcement of the octave overtone.

fugato An area in fugal style, forming a section within a nonfugal work.

fugue Imitative, contrapuntal work that usually alternates expository areas (presenting alternations of subject and answer) and episodes that develop related material.

galant A term denoting the new, light, homophonic style that succeeded the baroque.

gavotte A light dance in duple meter, beginning on the half-measure.

gigue A dance that appears in a variety of meters and styles, usually fugal in the works of J. S. Bach.

harpsichord A keyboard instrument with one, two, or (very rarely) three manuals and one or more registers of strings. The strings are plucked, and the instrument is not dynamically touch-sensitive.

hemiola A duple metric grouping that occurs (without explicit notation) in triple or compound meter. Often used at cadences.

homophony Accompanied melody.

imitation Counterpoint in which a theme or any melodic unit is heard in common among the various parts.

invention A term, rarely used otherwise, employed by Bach for his fifteen two-part contrapuntal studies and adopted since to mean, generally, contrapuntal works of brief duration but intense and concentrated development.

inversion 1. Melodic inversion refers to turning a line upside down by changing each interval to the reverse of its original direction, so that a descending third becomes an ascending third, and so forth; 2. contrapuntal inversion: *see* Invertible counterpoint.

invertible counterpoint Counterpoint in which one part can function with correct voice-leading against another line when the two lines exchange position—the upper voice becomes the lower, and vice versa.

largo A tempo designation meaning very slow.

Lautenwerck Lit., lute machine; a harpsichord built with gut strings and lute proportions.

legato Lit., linked; a playing style in which the notes are linked one to another.

loure A stately dance in compound meter.

lute A plucked stringed instrument with a half-pear-shaped body, gut strings and gut frets. Made in a variety of sizes, including bass instruments (theorbo and chitarrone).

manual Another word for keyboard, as in "two-manual harpsichord."

manualiter Indication used for organ music meaning "for manuals only."

menuet A moderate-to-brisk dance in triple meter, phrased in two-measure groups, the dance steps moving in two-beat units.

mordent An ornament in which the main (written) note rapidly oscillates once (or several times) with the note a step or half step lower.

Neue Bach-Ausgabe New Bach Edition, usually abbreviated *NBA*. A new edition of Bach's complete works, based on more thorough examination of the sources than the nineteenth-century Bach-Gesellschaft edition and intended to replace it.

notes inégales Lit., unequal notes. The term used by the French for their practice of playing equally notated notes in certain contexts with slight inequality (long-short). The practice applies to the prevailing note value, usually half the beat value.

ornamentation Term that refers to the formulaic figurations applied to the basic notes of a composition. Ornaments are sometimes written out fully, sometimes indicated by sign, and sometimes improvised. A combination of all three of the preceding is common in baroque music.

overdotting Rendering of dotted passages (normally a 4:1 proportion of time values) with sharper rhythm, lengthening the dotted note and proportionally shortening the short note.

overlegato Heavy legato, characterized by sustaining one note past the time when another is sounded.

overture A movement, usually festive in nature, that opens a sequence of movements.

partita (pl. **partite**) 1. A term used in the later baroque to signify a suite; 2. a section of a musical work, usually one of several variations (plural: partite).

passepied A brisk, triple-meter dance, usually in 3/8 time, with an upbeat.

pedal tone A pitch that is sustained through several changes of harmony. Usually a bass note.

period A musical grouping that consists of two or more phrases.

phrasing A term that refers to the linear musical groupings of a composition.

plein jeu 1. Regarding organ registration, use of a full chorus of principal stops. Sometimes designates use of all the stops on a harpsichord; 2. In French baroque terminology, a title often given to movements calling for the *plein jeu* registration.

polonaise A dance of Polish origin, in moderate triple time, characterized by a short rhythmic figure involving one long and two short notes.

polyphony Music in which several independent musical lines sound in harmony together.

port de voix A suspension or appoggiatura that resolves upward, often ornamented with a mordent on the tone of resolution.

Pralltriller A short, usually accentual trill beginning on the upper or main note.

prelude A movement that establishes a tonality and precedes one or more further movements in the same key.

presto Tempo indication meaning very fast.

recitative Musical imitation of speech, with free timing, the voice accompanied by a continuo group or full ensemble. This style is sometimes imitated in purely instrumental music.

registration The use of different combinations of stops on the organ, harpsichord, and other instruments.

resolution Movement of a dissonance into a consonance.

rhetoric The art of oratory, particularly toward development and organization of materials and persuasive delivery. Used as a model for musical analysis prior to the early nineteenth century.

ribatutta Italian style of trill, beginning with a dotted formula on the first two repercussions.

ricercar Imitative movement, of a grave to moderate character, the theme(s) usually of long notes. Derived from the Renaissance motet.

ritardando A slowing of the overall pace of a movement, as toward a final cadence.

ritornello The opening tutti material of a concerto grosso, repeated (in various keys) in the course of the movement.

rubato Freedom in time, usually against a strict time basis on the local or large level.

sarabande A moderate-to-slow dance in triple meter, of a proud character.

Schleifer *See* slide.

short octave A term to describe a keyboard abbreviated at the bass end, a practice deriving from economy in organ building to save making pipes for bass notes that were never called for. Typically, a four-octave keyboard from great C would place C on what appeared to be E (the first note of the keyboard), D on apparent F-sharp, and E on apparent G-sharp. Thus the only accidental in the lowest octave was B-flat. On keyboards beginning at apparent BB, the lowest key would be tuned to GG, apparent C-sharp to AA, and apparent D-sharp to BB.

siciliano A lyrical, dance-derived movement in compound time, featuring a dotted rhythm.

sixteen-foot On a harpsichord or organ, a stop sounding an octave below the written pitch.

slide An ornament that modifies the written note by two notes ascending stepwise to it.

stile antico Lit., antique style. The baroque term for the earlier Renaissance style of strict polyphony, often quasi-imitated in the baroque era with use of many more "modern" elements.

stretto A contrapuntal technique whereby successive entries of a theme come "one on top of another," one beginning before the preceding has completed the thematic statement. Often used as an intensifying device, for example, at the conclusion of Fugue No. 22, *WTC* 2.

stretto fugue A fugue characterized by extensive use of stretto technique.

style brisé Lit., broken style; refers to arpeggiated rather than block-chord textures, usually quasi-polyphonic. This (very useful) term is of twentieth-century invention.

stylus phantasticus The free style of the baroque, characterized by (usually) duple or quadruple meter, freedom of timing, variety of figuration, contrasts, and extreme fantasy.

subphrase A smaller unit that contributes to a phrase.

suite A sequence of movements intended to be played consecutively. In the baroque era, normally a sequence of dance movements, often preceded by a prelude.

surface rhythm The aggregate rhythmic movement of a composition; the combined rhythmical effect to which all the parts contribute.

suspension 1. In harmony, a dissonance prepared as a consonance that becomes dissonant as other parts shift, after which the suspension resolves to a consonance; 2. in keyboard playing, a slight arpeggiation of a two-part texture, usually playing the upper part very slightly later than the bass.

syncopation Placement of the main melodic notes, that would normally be heard on the main beats, on offbeats.

temperament A term that refers to the relationship of pitches in the tuning of an instrument. There are many possibilities. Different temperaments can favor various tonalities, and in various shadings. Equal temperament favors no one tonality over any other: all tonalities are in (or out of) tune to the same degree.

tempo The pacing of a musical composition or section thereof. Designated by style, descriptive words (usually in Italian, e.g., Allegro), choice of time signature and other style features.

terrace dynamics Alternation between very distinct dynamic levels.

theorbo A large type of lute, used primarily for accompaniment.

thoroughbass Accompaniment (for ensemble or soloist) notated with a figured bass line. The term also refers to the practice of realizing the harmonies of the figured bass to provide an accompaniment.

toccata Usually a multisection work, often alternating free, rhapsodic sections with fugal sections.

tombeau A musical lament for a deceased person, usually in the form of an allemande or pavane.

trill An ornament characterized by rapid alternation between the main (written) note and the upper auxiliary (a step or half step above the main note).

trill prefix A figuration (usually a turn from above or below) played as the beginning of a trill.

trill suffix A figuration included in the conclusion of a trill that carries the trill into the ensuing note.

triple counterpoint Invertible counterpoint in three voices.

triple fugue A fugue using three subjects, usually presented individually and then in combination.

tuning The setting of pitch on an instrument; distinct from temperament.

turn A four-note ornament that circles the written pitch. It can accent a single note or connect two notes.

tutti Lit., all; the full ensemble of an orchestra, as opposed to solo instruments.

upbeat The note(s) before the first bar line of a piece or phrase.

Urtext Lit., original text; often used (and often inaccurately) of editions.

SELECTED BIBLIOGRAPHY

Primary and secondary sources

The citations for all non-English-language primary sources include English translations when available.

Adlung, Jacob. *Anleitung zur musikalischen Gelahrheit*. Erfurt: J. D. Jungnicol, 1758; facsimile ed., Kassel: Bärenreiter, 1953.

Ahlgrimm, Isolde. "Current Trends in Performance of Baroque Music." Translated by Howard Schott. *Diapason* 73, no. 4 (April 1982): 1–10. [A bombshell article that elegantly put into perspective numerous misconceptions underlying the reconstruction of baroque performance practice.]

Aldrich, Putnam. "Classics of Music Literature: Wanda Landowska's *Musique ancienne*." *Music Library Notes* 27, no. 3 (March 1971): 461–468.

———. "'Rhythmic Harmony' as Taught by Johann Philipp Kirnberger." In *Studies in Eighteenth-Century Music*, edited by H. C. Robbins Landon. London: Allen and Unwin, 1970.

Apel, Willi. *The History of Keyboard Music to 1700*. Translated and revised by Hans Tischler. Bloomington: Indiana University Press, 1972. [An invaluable general reference work for the pre-1700 repertory.]

Bach, Carl Philipp Emanuel. *Versuch über die wahre Art das Clavier zu spielen*. Berlin: C. F. Henning, 1753 (Part 1) and G. L. Winter, 1762 (Part 2). Translated by William Mitchell under the title *Essay on the True Art of Playing Keyboard Instruments*. New York: Norton, 1949.

Bach Dokumente I. Edited by Werner Neumann and Hans-Joachim Schulze. Kassel: Bärenreiter; Leipzig: Deutscher Verlag für Musik, 1963.

Bach Dokumente II. Edited by Werner Neumann and Hans-Joachim Schulze. Kassel: Bärenreiter; Leipzig: Deutscher Verlag für Musik, 1969.

Bach Dokumente III. Edited by Hans-Joachim Schulze. Kassel: Bärenreiter; Leipzig: Deutscher Verlag für Musik, 1972.

Bach, Johann Sebastian. *Neue Ausgabe Sämtlicher Werke*. Edited by the Johann-Sebastian-Bach-Institut, Göttingen, and the Bach-Archiv, Leipzig. Kassel: Bärenreiter, 1954–. [Abbreviated *NBA*.]

Badura-Skoda, Paul. *Interpreting Bach at the Keyboard*. Translated by Alfred Clayton. Oxford: Clarendon Press, 1993. Originally published as *Bach-Interpretation*, Laaber: Laaber Verlag, 1990.

Barber, Elizabeth Wayland. *Women's Work: The First Twenty Thousand Years*. New York: Norton, 1994. [I highly recommend this fascinating book.]

Bartel, Dietrich. *Musica poetica: Musical-Rhetorical Figures in German Baroque Music*. Lincoln: University of Nebraska Press, 1997.

Bodky, Erwin. *The Interpretation of Bach's Keyboard Works*. Cambridge: Harvard University Press, 1960. [This work is entirely out of date, being full of observations that are misleading for the unwary. It is included here merely for the sake of this warning.]

Benjamin, Thomas. *Counterpoint in the Style of J. S. Bach*. New York: Schirmer, 1996. [A clear, beautifully written and illustrated textbook study of Bach's counterpoint, which takes due account of the interdependence of line and harmony.]

Bonds, Mark Evan. *Wordless Rhetoric: Musical Form and the Metaphor of the Oration*. Cambridge: Harvard University Press, 1991.

Brauchli, Bernard. *The Clavichord*. Cambridge: Cambridge University Press, 1998. [The first survey of the history of the clavichord, although the technical history to complement Hubbard's work on the harpsichord has yet to be written.]

Brossard, Sebastien de. *Dictionnaire de la musique*. Amsterdam: Roger, 1708; facsimile ed., Geneva: Minkoff, 1992.

Buelow, George. "The 'Loci Topici' and Affect in Late Baroque Music: Heinichen's Practical Demonstration." *Music Review* 28 (1966): 161–176.

Butler, Gregory. "Fugue and Rhetoric." *Journal of Music Theory* 21 (1977): 49–110.

Butt, John. *Bach Interpretation: Articulation Marks in Primary Sources of J. S. Bach*. Cambridge: Cambridge University Press, 1990.

Caswell, Judith. "Rhythmic Inequality and Tempo in French Music between 1650 and 1740." Ph.D. diss., University of Minnesota, 1973. [Contains translations of all the texts relating to French inequality.]

Chasins, Abram. *Speaking of Pianists*. New York: Knopf, 1957.

Chiapusso, Jan. *Bach's World*. Indianapolis: Indiana University Press, 1968. [Chapters 1–4 offer an interesting account of Bach's education, cultural heritage, and the worldview with which he grew up.]

Cooper, Kenneth, and Julius Zasko. "Georg Muffat's Observations on the Lully Style of Performance." *Musical Quarterly* 53 (1967): 220–245. [A clear translation of the composer's preface to a 1698 collection of French-style orchestral music and an eyewitness account of performance practices of the French court orchestra under Lully.]

Couperin, François. *L'art de toucher le clavecin*. Paris: By the author. Translated into English by Mevanwy Roberts; translated into German by Anna Linde. Wiesbaden: Breitkopf und Härtel, 1933.

David, Hans T., and Arthur Mendel. *The Bach Reader: A Life of Johann Sebastian Bach in Letters and Documents*. Revised edition, with a supplement. New York: Norton, 1966.

———. *The New Bach Reader: A Life of Johann Sebastian Bach in Letters and Documents*. Revised and enlarged by Christoph Wolff. New York: W. W. Norton, 1998.

Donington, Robert. *The Interpretation of Early Music, New Version*. New York: St. Martin's Press, 1974.

Dreyfus, Lawrence. *Bach and the Patterns of Invention*. Cambridge: Harvard University Press, 1996.

———. *Bach's Continuo Group: Players and Practices in His Vocal Works*. Cambridge: Harvard University Press, 1987.

Emery, Walter. *Bach's Ornaments*. London: Novello, 1953.

Faulkner, Quentin. *J. S. Bach's Keyboard Technique: A Historical Introduction*. St. Louis, Missouri: Concordia, 1984.

Ferguson, Howard. *Keyboard Interpretation from the Fourteenth to the Nineteenth Century: An Introduction*. Oxford and New York: Oxford University Press, 1975.

Forkel, Johann Nikolaus. *Über Johann Sebastian Bachs Leben, Kunst, und Kunstwerk*, Leipzig: 1802. Translated into English by A. C. F. Kollmann under the title *On Johann Sebastian Bach's Life, Genius, and Works*. London: 1820, reproduced in *New Bach Reader*, 417–482.

Franklin, Don O. "Articulation in the Cembalo Works of J. S. Bach: A Notational Study." In Dietrich Berke and Dorothee Hanemann, *Alte Musik als ästhetische Gegenwart: Kongressbericht Stuttgart 1985*. 2 vols. Kassel: Bärenreiter, 1987.

Frescobaldi, Girolamo. *Toccate d'intavolatura di cimbalo et organo . . . Libro Primo*. Rome: Borboni, 1615, 1637; facs. edition, Florence: Studio per edizioni Scelte, 1980.

Fuller, David. "Dotting, the 'French Style,' and Frederick Neumann's Counter-Reformation." *Early Music* 5 (1977): 517–543.

Gerber, Ernst Ludwig. *Historisch-biographisches Lexicon der Tonkünstler*. 2 volumes. Leipzig, 1790–1792.

Harrison, Daniel. "Rhetoric and Fugue: An Analytical Application." *Music Theory Spectrum* 12 (1990): 1–42.

Haskell, Harry. *The Early Music Revival: A History*. London: Thames and Hudson, 1988.

Heinichen, Johann David. *Der Generalbass in der Composition*. Dresden: By the author, 1728; facsimile edition, Hildesheim: Georg Olms, 1969.

Heinrich, Adel. *Bach's "Kunst der Fuge": A Living Compendium of Fugal Procedures, with a Motivic Analysis of All the Fugues*. Washington, D.C.: Catholic University of America Press.

Henkel, Hubert, "Remarks on the Use of the Sixteen-Foot." In *The Harpsichord and its Repertoire: Proceedings of the International Harpsichord Symposium, Utrecht, 1990*. Edited by Pieter Kirksen. Utrecht: Foundation for Historical Performance Practice, 1992.

Hilton, Wendy. "A Dance for Kings: The Seventeenth-Century French Courante." *Early Music* 5 (1977):160–172.

———. *Dance of Court and Theatre: The French Noble Style, 1690–1725*. Princeton, New Jersey: Princeton Books, 1981.

Hubbard, Frank. *Three Centuries of Harpsichord Making*. [Cambridge]: Cambridge University Press, 1965. [The first and to date only survey of the major historical schools of harpsichord building. Perhaps the most beautifully written technical book in the English language.]

Kirkpatrick, Ralph. *Domenico Scarlatti*. New York: Apollo, 1968.

———. *Interpreting Bach's Well-Tempered Clavier: A Performer's Discourse of Method*. New Haven: Yale University Press, 1984.

———. "On Playing the Clavichord." *Early Music* 9 (1981): 293–305.

Kirnberger, Johann Philipp. *Die Kunst des reinen Satzes in der Musik*. Berlin: Decker und Hartung, 1776–1779. Translated into English by David Beach and Jurgen Thym under the title *The Art of Strict Musical Composition*. New Haven, Connecticut: Yale University Press, 1982. [Most of this work is a treatise on counterpoint. However, it includes a very specific and important explanation of performance practices relating to meter, tempo, and time signatures.]

———. *Recueil d'airs de danse caracteristiques, pour servir de modèle aux jeunes compositeurs et d'exercice à ceux qui touchent du clavecin* [Collection of Characteristic Dance Melodies, to Serve as Models for young composers and as Repertory and Exercises for Keyboard Players.] Berlin: Hummel, 1777.

Preface translated in Newman W. Powell, "Kirnberger On Dance Rhythms, Fugues, and Characterization," in *Festschrift Theodore Hoelty-Nickel*, edited by Newman W. Powell (Valparaiso, Indiana: Valparaiso University, 1967). [This brief preface includes important comments on the subjects of dance and musical rhetoric.]

Kloppers, Jacobus. "Musical Rhetoric and Other Symbols of Communication in Bach's Organ Music." *Man and Nature/L'homme et la nature* 3 (1984): 131–162. [A clear and concise explanation of the rhetorical model, including a representative list of basic grammatical and pictorial figures.]

Krummacher, Friedrich. "Bach's Free Organ Works and the Stylus Phantasticus." In *J. S. Bach as Organist: His Instruments, Music, and Performance Practices*, ed. George Stauffer and Ernest May. Bloomington: Indiana University Press, 1986.

Landowska, Wanda. *Musique ancienne*. Paris: 1909. Translated by William Aspenwall Bradley under the title *Music of the Past*. New York: Knopf, 1924. Revised translation by Denise Restout as part 1 of *Landowska on Music*. New York: Stein & Day, 1964. [This was a pioneer work in the revival of early music, challenging the then all-prevalent notions of progress in the arts.]

Lebègue, Nicolas. *Pièces de clavecin*. Paris: 1677.

Ledbetter, David. *Continuo Playing According to Handel*. Oxford: Oxford University Press, 1990.

Leonhardt, Gustav. *The Art of Fugue: Bach's Last Harpsichord Work*. The Hague: Martinus Nijhoff, 1952.

Lindley, Mark. "Early Fingering: Some Editing Problems and Some New Readings for J. S. Bach and John Bull." *Early Music* 17 (1989): 60–69.

———. "Instructions for the Clavier Diversely Tempered." *Early Music* 5 (1977): 18–23.

Little, Meredith, and Natalie Jenne. *Dance and the Music of J. S. Bach*. Bloomington: Indiana University Press, 1991.

Lowinsky, Edward. "On Mozart's Rhythm." *Musical Quarterly* 42 (1956): 162–186. [Classic study of symmetry and asymmetry in Mozart's music. The principles expounded here are relevant to Bach's music as well.]

Lunde, Nanette. *The Continuo Companion*. 2d edition. Eau Claire, Wisconsin: Skyline, 2001.

Marpurg, Friedrich Wilhelm. *Anleitung zum Clavierspielen*. Berlin: 1755; facsimile of 1765 edition, New York: Broude, 1969. English translation by Elizabeth Hays. Ph.D. diss., Stanford University, 1976.

———. *Die Kunst das Clavier zu Spielen*. Berlin, 1750; facsimile of Part 1 (1762 ed.) and Part 2 (1761 ed.), Hildesheim: Georg Olms, 1969.

Marshall, Robert L. "Tempo and Dynamic Indications in the Bach Sources: A Review of the Terminology." In *Bach, Handel, Scarlatti: Tercentenary Essays*, edited by Peter Williams. Cambridge: Cambridge University Press, 1985.

Masson, Charles. *Nouveau traité des regles pour la composition de la musique*. 2d ed. Paris: 1699.

Mattheson, Johann. *Der vollkommene Capellmeister*. Hamburg: Christian Herold, 1739; facs. edition, Kassel: Barenreiter, 1954. Translated into English by Ernest C. Harriss under the title *Johann Mattheson's Der vollkommene Capellmeister: A Revised Translation with Critical Commentary*. Studies in Musicology 21. Ann Arbor, Michigan: UMI, 1981.

Mozart, Leopold. *A Treatise on the Fundamental Principles of Violin Playing*. Translated by Edith Knocker. 2d ed. London: Oxford, 1951.

Muffat, Georg. *An Essay on Thoroughbass*. Edited by Hellmut Federhofer. Rome: American Institute of Musicology, 1961.

————. *Floregium Secundum*. Edited by H. Rietsch. Denkmäler der Tonkunst in Osterreich 4. Graz: Akademische Druck- und Verlagsanstalt, 1895. Originally published, Passau: Höller, 1698.

Niedt, Friedrich Erhard. *The Musical Guide*. Parts I (1700–1710), II (1721), and III (1717). Translated by Pamela L. Poulin and Irmgard C. Taylor. Oxford: Clarendon Press, 1989.

Neumann, Frederick. *Ornamentation in Baroque and Post-Baroque Music, with Special Emphasis on J. S. Bach*. Princeton, New Jersey: Princeton University Press, 1978. [The most exhaustive survey of the subject. A magnificent accomplishment, but the reader must carefully distinguish the facts unearthed by Neumann from the interpretation he gives of them.]

————. *Essays in Performance Practice*. Ann Arbor, Michigan: UMI Research Press, 1982.

————. *New Essays on Performance Practice*. Ann Arbor, Michigan: UMI Research Press, 1989.

Neumann, Frederick, and Jane Stevens. *Performance Practices of the Seventeenth and Eighteenth Centuries*. New York: Schirmer Books, 1993.

Newman, Anthony. *Bach and the Baroque*. 2d ed., East Norwalk, Connecticut: T. D. Ellis, 1994.

Pont, Graham. "French Overtures at the Keyboard: 'How Handel Rendered the Playing of Them.'" *Musicology* 6 (1980): 29–50.

————. "Handel and Regularization: A Third Alternative." *Early Music* 13 (1985): 500–505.

————. "Handel's Overtures for Harpsichord or Organ: An Unrecognized Genre." *Early Music* 11 (1983): 309–322.

————. "Rhythmic Alteration and the Majestic." *Studies in Music* 12 (1978): 68–100.

Pollens, Stewart. *The Early Pianoforte*. Cambridge: Cambridge University Press, 1995.

Poulin, Pamela L., ed. *J. S. Bach's Precepts and Principles for Playing the Thorough-Bass or Accompanying in Four Parts*. Early Music Series 16. Oxford: Oxford University Press, 1994.

Powell, Newman. "Kirnberger on Dance Rhythms, Fugues, and Characterization." In *Festschrift for Theodore Hoelty-Nickel*. Valparaiso, Indiana: Valparaiso University, 1967.

Printz, Wolfgang. *Compendium musicae signatoriae*. Dresden, 1689; facs. ed., Hildesheim: Georg Olms, 1974.

Quantz, Johann Joachim. *On Playing the Flute*. Translated by Edward R. Reilly. London: Faber, 1966.

Raison, André. *Livre d'orgue*. Paris: 1688.

Rasch, Rudolf. "Does 'Well-Tempered' Mean 'Equal-Tempered'?" In *Bach, Handel, Scarlatti: Tercentenary Essays*, edited by Peter Williams. Cambridge: Cambridge University Press, 1985.

Ratner, Leonard. *Classic Music: Expression, Form, and Style*. New York: Schirmer Books, 1980.

Rothschild, Fritz. *The Lost Tradition in Music: Rhythm and Tempo in J. S. Bach's Time*. London: Adam and Charles Black, 1953. [An important early study of the subject, but too rigid in its theorizing.]

Rubinstein, Anton. *A Conversation on Music*. Translated by Mrs. John P. Morgan. London: Augener [ca. 1892].

Sachs, Barbara, and Barry Ife. *Anthology of Early Keyboard Methods*. Cambridge, England: Gamut, 1981. [An invaluable compilation and translation of seven early keyboard treatises.]

Saint Lambert, Michel de. Principles of the harpsichord. Translated by Rebecca Harris-Warwick. Cambridge: Cambridge University Press, 1984. Originally published as *Les principes du clavecin* (Paris: Ballard, 1707).

Schonberg, Harold. *The Great Pianists*. Rev. ed. New York: Simon and Schuster, 1987.

Schott, Howard. *Playing the Harpsichord*. London: Faber, 1970.

————. "The Harpsichord Revival." *Early Music* 2 (1974): 85–96.

Schulenberg, David. *The Keyboard Music of J. S. Bach*. New York: Schirmer Books, 1992. [The most complete survey of the repertory and issues surrounding it.]

————. "Musical Expression and Musical Rhetoric in the Keyboard Works of J. S. Bach." In *Johann Sebastian Bach, A Tercentenary Celebration*, edited by

Seymour L. Benstock. Westport, Connecticut: Greenwood Press, 1992.

Schulenberg, David, ed. *Bach Perspectives*. Vol. 4, *The Music of J. S. Bach: Analysis and Interpretation*. Lincoln: University of Nebraska Press, 1999.

Spanyi, Miklos. "Johann Sebastian Bach's Clavichord Technique Described by Griepenkerl." *Clavichord International* 4, no. 2 (November 2000): 47–52.

Spitta, Philipp. *Johann Sebastian Bach*. 3 vols. Leipzig: Breitkopf & Hartel, 1873–1880. Translation by Clara Bell and J. A. Fuller Maitland. London: Novello, 1889; reprint, New York: Dover, 1952.

Staatsbibliothek Preussischer Kulturbesitz, Mus. Ms. P. 804.

Stauffer, George. "Bach's Organ Registration Reconsidered." In *J. S. Bach as Organist: His Instruments, Music, and Performance Practices*, edited by George Stauffer and Ernest May. Bloomington: Indiana University Press, 1986.

———. "Fugue Types in Bach's Free Organ Works." In *J. S. Bach as Organist: His Instruments, Music, and Performance Practices*, edited by George Stauffer and Ernest May. Bloomington: Indiana University Press, 1986.

Stauffer, George, and Ernest May, eds. *J. S. Bach as Organist: His Instruments, Music, and Performance Practices*. Bloomington: Indiana University Press, 1986.

Tagliavini, Luigi Ferdinando. "The Art of 'Not Leaving the Instrument Empty'." *Early Music* 11 (1983): 299–308.

Terry, Charles Sanford. *Bach's Orchestra*. London: Oxford University Press, 1932.

Tilney, Colin. *The Art of the Unmeasured Prelude for Harpsichord: France, 1660–1720*. Mainz and New York: Schott, 1991.

Troeger, Richard. "The Clavichord and Keyboard Technique." *American Organist* 30, no. 3 (March 1996): 58–63.

———. "Flexibility in Well-Tempered Tuning." *Diapason* 73, no. 6 (June 1982): 6–7.

———. "The French Unmeasured Harpsichord Prelude: Notation and Performance." *Early Keyboard Journal* 10 (1992): 89–119.

———. "Metre in Unmeasured Preludes." *Early Music* 11 (1983): 340–345.

———. "Speculations on Bach's Clavichord Technique." *Diapason* 73, no. 12 (December 1982): 12–13.

———. *Technique and Interpretation on the Harpsichord and Clavichord*. Bloomington: Indiana University Press, 1987.

Türk, Daniel Gottlob. *Clavierschüle*. Leipzig: 1789. Translated into English by Raymond Haggh under the title *School of Clavier Playing*. Lincoln: University of Nebraska Press, 1982.

Walther, Johann Gottfried. *Musicalisches Lexicon*. Leipzig: 1732; facs. ed., Kassel: Bärenreiter, 1953.

———. *Praecepta der musicalischen Composition*. Edited by Peter Bendry. Leipzig: VEB Breitkopf und Härtel, 1955.

Williams, Peter. *Figured Bass Accompaniment*. 2 vols. Edinburgh: Edinburgh University Press, 1970.

———. "J. S. Bach's Well-Tempered Clavier: A New Approach." *Early Music* 11 (1983): 46–52 (Part 1) and 332–339 (Part 2).

———. *The Organ Music of J. S. Bach*. 3 vols. Cambridge: Cambridge University Press, 1980–1984.

———. *Playing the Organ Works of Bach: Some Case Studies*. New York: American Guild of Organists, 1987.

Williams, Peter, ed. *Bach, Handel, Scarlatti: Tercentenary Essays*. Cambridge: Cambridge University Press, 1985.

Wolf, Ernst Wilhelm. Preface to *Eine Sonatine . . . .* Translation with commentary by Christopher Hogwood, "A Supplement to C. P. E. Bach's *Versuch*: E. W. Wolf's *Anleitung* of 1785." In *C. P. E. Bach Studies*, edited by S. L. Clark. Oxford: Clarendon Press, 1988.

Wolff, Christoph. *Bach: Essays on His Life and Music*. Cambridge: Harvard University Press, 1991.

———. *Johann Sebastian Bach: The Learned Musician*. New York: W. W. Norton, 2000. [By far the most complete and up-to-date biography of the composer.]

Facsimile editions of Bach's works

The following list is only representative and includes some of the more readily available facsimile editions of Bach sources. Not all of the keyboard works have appeared in facsimile. These publications tend to stress the important "fair copies" (such as the autograph manuscript of *WTC* 1) and the original prints (such as the *Clavierübung* volumes; those listed below are facsimiles of special copies corrected by Bach). A number of works, including the Toccatas and the French and English Suites, which pose complex editorial problems, do not usually offer a single "main-focus" source. Hence, and most unfortunately, they have appeared rarely, if at all, in facsimile editions.

Bach, Johann Sebastian. *Clavier-Büchlein vor Wilhelm Friedemann Bach*. Edited by Ralph Kirkpatrick. New Haven: Yale University Press, 1959; reprint, New York: Da Capo Press, 1979.

———. *Clavier Übung, 1er Partie (1731) et Chorales Schübler (1746)*. Edited by Philippe Lescat. Courlay, France: Jean-Marc Fuzeau, 1991. [Facsimile of the most important surviving copy of the partitas, with Bach's most extensive corrections.]

————. *Clavier Übung, 3e Partie* (1739). Edited by Philippe Lescat. Courlay: Jean-Marc Fuzeau, 1990.

————. *Clavier Übung, 4e Partie (Variations Goldberg), 1741*. Edited by Philippe Lescat. Courlay: Jean-Marc Fuzeau, 1990. [The composer's personal copy, with handwritten corrections.]

————. *Klavierbüchlein für Anna Magdalena Bach 1725*. Facsimile with afterword by Georg von Dadelsen. Kassel: Bärenreiter, 1988.

————. *Part Two of the Clavier Übung, 1735*. Facsimile with introduction by David Kinsela. Godstone, Surrey, and Brookfield, Vermont: Gregg International, 1985. [A facsimile of the British Library copy, with Bach's handwritten corrections, and a superb account of the original publication's history. Includes three alternate pages re-engraved for the second edition.]

————. *Preludes and Fugues, Book One: The Well-Tempered Clavier 1*. With analytical notes by Warren Thomson. Melbourne, Australia: Allans Music Australia, 1985. [A facsimile of the autograph manuscript, together with a clean modern printing of the text—and with the added benefit of no editorial fingering having been added, a trait that one could wish for in other "urtexts." The analytical notes provide a good synopsis of the structure of each movement. Other facsimiles of Book 1 have appeared, notably by the VEB Deutscher Verlag für Musik (1962), but the Allans edition is perhaps the most readily available.]

————. *Preludes and Fugues, Book Two: The Well-Tempered Clavier II*. With analytical notes by Warren Thomson. Melbourne, Australia: Allans Music Australia, 1986. [See preceding entry for comments.]

————. *Sechs Sonaten für Orgel*. Edited by Wolfgang Goldhan. Leipzig: Zentralantiquariat der DDR, 1987. [A beautiful facsimile of the composer's fair copy of the six Trio Sonatas, BWV 525–530. As has been noted for generations, the titles of the pieces designate them not as "for organ" but as "a 2 Clav: et Pedal"—that is, "for two keyboards and pedal." They are equally suited to organ, pedal harpsichord, and pedal clavichord.]

————. *Two- and Three-Part Inventions: Facsimile of the Autograph Manuscript together with a Reprint of the Bach-Gesellschaft Edition*. Introduction by Eric Simon. New York: Dover, 1968.

GENERAL INDEX

INDEX OF WORKS CITED